DOUGHERTY STATION

D0045677

THE ILLUSTRATED
GUIDE *to*
WORLD RELIGIONS

Dedicated to the team members and co-laborers
of International Students, Inc.,
who exemplify what it means to live tirelessly, sacrificially, and joyfully
in the service of the Lord as they share their lives
and the love of Jesus Christ with their friends—international students.

THE ILLUSTRATED
GUIDE *to*
WORLD RELIGIONS

DEAN C. HALVERSON
GENERAL EDITOR

CONTRA COSTA COUNTY LIBRARY

- ISLAM
- BUDDHISM
- HINDUISM
- TAOISM
- JUDAISM
- SECULARISM
- THE NEW AGE
- OTHER WORLD FAITHS

3 1901 03703 1046

The Compact Guide to World Religions
Copyright © 1996
International Students, Inc.

This edition © 2003 Angus Hudson Ltd/
Tim Dowley & Peter Wyart trading as
Three's Company

All scripture quotations, unless indicated, are
taken from the HOLY BIBLE, NEW
INTERNATIONAL VERSION ® Copyright ©
1973, 1978, 1984 by International Bible Society.
Used by permission of Zondervan Publishing
House. All rights reserved. The "NIV" and "New
International Version" trademarks are registered
in the United States Patent and Trademark Office
by International Bible Society. Use of either
trademark requires the permission of International
Bible Society.

All rights reserved. No part of this publication
may be reproduced, stored in a retrieval system,
or transmitted in any form or by any means—
electronic, mechanical, photocopying, recording,
or otherwise—without the prior written
permission of the publisher and copyright
owners.

Published by Bethany House Publishers
11400 Hampshire Avenue South
Bloomington, Minnesota 55438
www.bethanyhouse.com

Bethany House Publishers is a Division of
 Baker Book House Company,
Grand Rapids, Michigan.

Library of Congress Cataloging-in-Publication Data

The illustrated guide to world religions / Dean C.
Halverson, general editor.
      p. cm.
Rev. ed. of: The compact guide to world religions.
c1996. Includes bibliographical references and
index.
  ISBN 0-7642-2838-2 (alk. paper)
  1. Religions. I. Halverson, Dean C. II. Compact
guide to world religions.

  BL80.3.I45 2003
  200--dc22

2003013903

Printed in Singapore

Worldwide co-edition organized and produced by
Angus Hudson Ltd.,
Concorde House, Grenville Place,
Mill Hill,
London NW7 3SA, England
Tel: +44 20 8959 3668
Fax: +44 20 8959 3678
e-mail: coed@angushudson.com

PICTURE ACKNOWLEDGMENTS
Tim Dowley: pp. 11, 15, 21, 38, 103, 106, 112,
118, 125, 135, 141, 147, 150, 225, 239, 259,
260, 263, 269, 275, 278
Illustrated London News: pp. 154, 156, 157, 158,
159, 161, 163, 217
Israel Government Press Office: p. 136
Getty Images: pp. 17, 19, 25, 27, 29, 35, 36, 41,
49, 52, 53, 56, 57, 58, 60, 61, 63, 85, 86, 88,
90, 92, 93, 94, 95, 97, 98, 99, 100, 105, 109,
110, 111, 114, 121, 133 top, 137, 139, 140,
142, 143, 144, 145, 146, 151, 173, 174, 185,
186, 188, 191, 200, 211, 213, 214, 215, 233,
237, 247, 252, 253, 257, 262, 267
Trip/T. Bognar: p. 66
Trip/H. Rogers: pp. 67, 68, 74, 79, 81
Trip/J. Stanley: pp. 120/171
Trip/Trip: p. 75
Peter Wyart: pp. 3, 18, 23, 31, 39, 43, 46, 54,
108, 113, 115, 119, 128, 133 bottom, 134, 138,
155, 165, 169, 172, 175, 176, 177, 178, 179,
180, 182, 183, 184, 187, 189, 190, 192, 207,
229, 241, 250, 254, 261, 273, 277

About the Contributors

Dr. David Clark grew up in Japan. He received his Ph.D. in the Philosophy of Religion from Northwestern University and is Professor of Theology at Bethel Theological Seminary in St. Paul, Minnesota. He wrote *The Pantheism of Alan Watts* (InterVarsity, 1978) and coauthored with Norman Geisler *Apologetics in the New Age* (Baker, 1990).

Dr. Norman Geisler is one of the best-known Christian apologists of our time. He has written some forty books, including *A General Introduction to the Bible* (Moody, 1986) and *When Skeptics Ask* (Victor, 1990). He is Dean of the Southern Evangelical Seminary in Charlotte, North Carolina

Mr. Dean C. Halverson works for International Students, Inc., as their World Religions Specialist and Ministry Resource Development Team Leader. Before joining ISI in 1988 he worked for the Spiritual Counterfeits Project, researching and writing on the new religions. He has written a book on the New Age movement, entitled *Crystal Clear: Understanding and Reaching New Agers* (NavPress, 1990).

Rev. William Honsberger is working with Mission to the Americas (formerly Conservative Baptist Home Missions Society) as their missionary to the New Agers. He earned his M.A. in the Philosophy of Religion from Denver Seminary, and he is taking classes at the University of Colorado, Boulder, with the hope that he will be accepted into their Ph.D. program in History.

Mr. Kent Kedl is earning his Ph.D. in Mass Communications with an emphasis on China from the University of Minnesota. He is studying how the mass media bring about change in China. Mr. Kedl earned his Master's degree in the history and philosophy of China. He has made several trips to China and speaks Mandarin fluently.

Dr. Thomas I. S. Leung received his Master's degree from the New Asian College in Hong Kong, which is a key center for promoting neo-Confucianistic thought. Dr. Leung then studied under two Confucian masters, but later became a Christian. He went on to earn his Ph.D. in Philosophy from the University of Hawaii, writing his dissertation on the methodology of Confucian philosophy. He now works as president of the Culture Regeneration Research Society in Burnaby, British Columbia, and he edits a journal called *Cultural China*.

Dr. Richard Robinson is a senior staff member at Jews for Jesus in San Francisco, where he directs the Research Library and is in charge of developing the organization's World Wide Web site. He received his Ph.D. from Westminster Theological Seminary and is an adjunct professor for Fuller Theological Seminary.

Mr. Rick Rood works as Director of Publications for Probe Ministries. He is also a member of Probe's speaking team for Mind Games conferences (a college survival conference for students). Plus, he occasionally writes and produces programs for Probe's daily radio program, which is aired on approximately 300 stations. Mr. Rood developed his approach to pluralism while working on a Ph.D. degree at Dallas Seminary.

Contents

Introduction

You will see periodical references in this book to "international students." These chapters were written originally as Religion Profiles to equip the staff and volunteers of International Students, Inc, (ISI) as they seek to share the love of Christ with the hundreds of thousands of international students. ISI is a nationwide Christian organization, founded in, 1953, whose mission is to work with the church to reach the goal of offering every International student the opportunity to hear the good news of Jesus Christ.

These students have come from virtually every nation in the world to study in the U.S. at the undergraduate and graduate levels. They are the best and brightest of their nations, and many of them will return to become leaders in their nations. The Lord has given us Christians in the U.S. an exciting opportunity to impact the world for Christ by reaching these international students whom He has sent to our neighborhoods. Through them, the mission field has come to us!

These chapters, however, are relevant not just to those who work with international students, but to any Christian who wants to understand where his or her non-Christian friend—whether American or international—is coming from spiritually and to consider some ideas as to how to share the love of Christ with him or her.

This book was written primarily with the Christian in mind but not exclusively for the Christian. If you are not a Christian, I invite you to consider the arguments for Christianity that are presented here.

I hope that as a result of reading this book, whether or not you are a Christian, you will have a better appreciation for the uniqueness of Christianity. In our tolerant and relativistic age it is not in vogue to talk about a particular religion as being unique. But such attitudes cloud the claims to exclusivity that Christianity and other religions make, not allowing a person to actually grapple with those claims.

If you would like to know more about ISI, please contact us at:

ISI
P.O. Box C
Colorado Springs, CO 80901
Phone: (719) 576-2700
Fax: (719) 576-5363

World Religions Overview

Dean C. Halverson

What is a religion? The definition that we will be working from in this book is that a religion is a set of beliefs that answers the ultimate questions: What is ultimate reality? What is the nature of the world? What is the nature of humanity? What is humanity's primary problem? What happens after death?

Such a definition means that a religion does not necessarily include a belief in God, a set of rituals or a class of clergy or priests. Secularism and Marxism are examples of what could be called religions in that they answer the ultimate questions, but they do not teach the existence of a supernatural realm, nor say anything about God.

To many people, the world religions are a confusing array of beliefs, practices, and histories. Unless a person is willing to devote a fair amount of time to studying the various religions, it is difficult to keep the distinctives of each straight, such as who founded which religion when, and what each believes.

What I hope to accomplish in this chapter is to help you make sense of the world religions. We will step back and look at each from a wider perspective, so as to get the big picture.

First, we will place the religions on a spectrum of beliefs and look at the trends contained in that spectrum.

Second, we will look at the nature of humanity's religious urge and how it has affected world religions.

Third, we will see what is unique about Christianity.

Finally, we will discuss some general principles for evangelism.

THE SPECTRUM OF RELIGIONS AND RELIGIOUS BELIEFS

The spectrum of religions and religious beliefs (see pages 12–13) can be viewed as being a continuum where the extremes and the middle exhibit certain patterns and trends, as seen in the following examples.

Concept of God

On the far left side of the spectrum are the monotheistic (one God) religions that say God is the transcendent Creator of the world, and as such He is distinct and separate from His creation.

On the right side of the spectrum are the monistic (God is a oneness) religions that emphasize God's immanence; they believe that God's essence and the world's essence are one and the same.

On the far right side, beyond the monistic religions, are those atheistic (no God) worldviews that deny God's existence. Yet atheism is similar to monism in that both say ultimate reality is a oneness of substance— with monism, the substance is *spirit;*

with atheism, it's *matter* (or energy).

In between the two extremes of the spectrum are the dualistic (two forces) and polytheistic (many gods) religions. There are two kinds of dualistic religions: competing and balancing. The competing dualistic religions share affinities with the monotheistic religions, and the balancing dualistic religions are similar in some ways to monism.

The gods of the dualistic and polytheistic religions serve as intermediaries to the ultimate reality, or Supreme Being; they are not the ultimate reality itself. The ultimate reality is usually either monotheistic or monistic in nature. As such, the middle of the spectrum has relationships with the two opposing extremes (monotheism and monism/atheism).

Conversely, though, the "folk" forms of the monotheistic, monistic and, to some extent, the atheistic religions resemble polytheism. Thus, the two extremes of the spectrum have a relationship with the middle (polytheism).

View of Humanity

Other patterns are also present in the spectrum. To the left, for example, where God is separate from His creation (monotheism), there is more of an appreciation for the unique value of humanity as compared to the rest of creation.

To the right (monism/atheism) there is less of a sense that humanity is unique and of special value, because humanity is different from the rest of nature only in degree, not in kind.

Humanity's Primary Problem

With respect to humanity's primary problem—sin—to the left of the spectrum there is the sense that humanity fails to live up to the moral precepts of a holy God.

To the right, on the other hand, the issue of "sin" has to do with ignorance, whether of one's true divinity (Hinduism) or of a rational solution to humanity's problems (Secular Humanism).

Ruins of Mayan Temple, Palenque, Mexico.

THE SPECTRUM OF RELIGIONS AND RELIGIOUS BELIEFS

	MONOTHEISM	COMPETING DUALISM	POLYTHEISM
CONCEPT OF GOD	One transcendent God	Two opposing gods	Many gods
PRIMARY EXAMPLES	Judaism, Christianity, Islam	Zoroastrianism	So called "Tribal" religions, Santeria, voodoo, Shinto, any form of a "folk" religion
VIEW OF HUMANITY	Part of creation, but different in kind from the animals	Made to join in the battle against evil	Can be influenced and even possessed by the spirits
HUMANITY'S PRIMARY PROBLEM	Breaking God's law (Judaism); rebellion against God (Christianity); failing to seek God's guidance (Islam)	Choosing to do evil	Angering the gods
THE SOLUTION	Living according to God's law (Judaism); being justified by faith based on God's saving work (Christianity); seeking God's guidance (Islam)	Choosing to do right	Appeasing the gods
THE AFTERLIFE	The person continues in existence in either heaven or hell.	The person continues in existence in either heaven or hell.	Sometimes the person advances to the spirit world.

The Afterlife

With respect to the afterlife, to the left of the spectrum, the person continues to exist as a conscious individual after death, either in a heaven-like or a hell-like place.

To the right of the spectrum (monism) the goal is for the individual to lose his or her individuality by merging into the impersonal oneness of ultimate reality.

At the extreme right (atheism), because the person consists only of matter, he or she ceases to exist at the point of death as a conscious entity altogether.

RELIGIONS AND THE RELIGIOUS URGE

The religious urge within humanity is what sets us apart from the rest of the created order. While the animal kingdom is like humanity in that animals exhibit varying degrees of creativity, emotions, intelligence, communication, and even humor, they are unlike humanity in that only humans have the need to relate to that which is ultimate, the need to have a foundation for meaning and hope that goes beyond our everyday existence. We can deny that such things are important, but to do so

BALANCING DUALISM	MONISM	ATHEISM
Two opposing but interacting and balancing forces	An impersonal oneness	No god
Taoism, the *yin/yang* concept	Hinduism, Buddhism, Sikhism, Sufisrn, the New Age movement	Secular Humanism, Marxism, Confucianism
A microcosm of the two interacting forces	Caught in the illusion of separateness, but identical in essence to the oneness	A complex form of matter
Living out of alignment with the ways of nature	Ignorance of one's innate divinity	Superstition and irrational thinking
Living in harmony with the ways of nature	Realizing that our essence is the same as the oneness (enlightenment)	Applying rational thinking to our problems.
Usually the person advances to some form of the spirit world.	Either the person is reincarnated or merges into the impersonal oneness.	The person ceases to exist.

leads to meaninglessness and despair (see Jaki). Even atheists have the need to give themselves over to a cause that is greater than themselves.

At the same time, though, while we have this religious urge, each person is spiritually torn; within us are two conflicting kinds of reactions to God. On the one hand, we are drawn to Him, but, on the other hand, we want to run away from Him. One person has labeled such a malady as "spiritual schizophrenia."

This sense of being spiritually torn is illustrated through one of Jesus' parables—the prodigal son (Luke 15:11–24). Jesus tells about a son who couldn't wait to get away from his father but was then drawn back to him. As we look at this parable and consider the motivations behind why the son acted in the way he did, we will learn several things about our religious urge and the impetus behind the religions of the world.

1. The Rejection (vv. 12–16)

The son demanded his "share of the estate" from his father. After receiving it he took off for a "distant country." Not only did the son want to get away from his father as soon as possible but he wanted to make the break as complete as possible. He rejected everything about his father. He rejected his financial advice (the son spent everything, v. 14), his moral advice ("wild living," v. 13), his religious customs (the son ended up feeding the pigs, v. 15), and even his physical presence (the son "set off for a distant country," v. 13).

But why did the son want to get away so badly? Because he felt constrained by his father; he felt trapped. His actions reveal several reasons why he felt constrained.

First, he felt constrained with respect to his enjoyment, his sense of living life to its fullest. He wanted *immediate gratification.* He didn't want to wait for his inheritance; he wanted it now!

Second, he felt constrained with respect to his independence. He felt that he could make it on his own. He wanted to be *self-sufficient.*

Third, he felt constrained with respect to his ability to choose the rules by which to live his life. While he was "under his father's roof," he had to live by his father's rules. But he wanted to be the one to make those kinds of decisions. In essence, he wanted *moral relativity,* in which there are no absolutes, only personal preferences.

What does this have to do with the world religions and our religious urge? It is relevant because we are like the son. Just as the son pushed the father away, we push God away. This is the rebellion side of our "spiritual schizophrenia."

As sinful human beings, we have an urge to escape that which we believe constrains us, and we see God as the Source of that constraint. Give us a law and we rebel against it. Paul wrote about this urge:

Indeed I would not have known what sin was except through the law. For I would not have known what coveting really was if the law had not said, "Do not covet." But sin, seizing the opportunity afforded by the commandment, produced in me every kind of covetous desire (Romans 7:7-8).

We rebel against moral authority because it restricts us. It infringes on our independence and pride.

We also push away what threatens us, and we see God as being a threat. That is because His absolute holiness challenges our moral independence, His sovereignty challenges our self-sufficiency, and His omniscience (infinite knowledge) exposes our duplicitous thoughts (Sproul, 73).

Paul's words in Romans 1 indicate that there is a three-step process to our pushing God away: awareness, suppression, and replacement (Sproul, 72–78).

Step 1: Awareness. Paul wrote about our awareness of God in this way: "For since the creation of the world God's invisible qualities—his eternal power and divine nature—have been clearly seen, being understood from what has been made, so that men are without excuse" (Romans 1:20).

How are we aware of God's existence? What is the evidence that Paul says is so clear? Consider the following:

■ The presence of an intelligent design, not just a repetitive pattern, on every level of the universe—from the micro to the macro levels—points to an intelligent and almighty Designer. People used to think that the smaller something was the less complex. But now, with more advanced equipment, we can see the amazing complexity that even a single cell has. Microbiologist Michael Denton writes that if we were to magnify a cell a thousand million times, "What we would then see would be an object of unparalleled complexity and adaptive design" (Denton, 328). Such complexity could not come about through mere chance.

■ The fact that the energy of the universe is finite and is decreasing in accessibility indicates that the universe is contingent with respect to its existence, that is, it needed a Creator who had existence within himself to give it existence. In other words, the

existence of the universe is not necessary but derived from something else. Without this "something else" having existence within itself (a necessary existence), there would be no First Cause—only an infinite regression of effects, which is an impossibility.

■ The fact that we have a conscience indicates that a holy and personal God is the source of our sense of right and wrong (Romans 2:14–15). Holiness indicates God is personal, rather than an impersonal oneness or an impersonal energy, because only persons are able to make moral distinctions. Our conscience also indicates that we have failed to live up to the standard of this personal, holy Being because we aren't able to live up even to our own standards.

■ The provision that we receive through nature indicates that God is good and that He cares for those whom He created (Acts 14:17). We also have the sense, however hidden, that we ought to have an attitude of thankfulness and gratitude toward this Source of goodness.

■ As we look at the grandeur and the beauty of creation, we ought to be struck with wonder and awe. We should also be humbled. Psychologist and theologian Dan Allender writes, "One ought to look at a sunrise and be aware that an infinite and merciful Being has painted our existence with order, wonder, beauty . . . it ought to further dawn on us that we are His art, created for His glory. Such an awareness ought simultaneously to humble us and to enlarge our sense of gratitude" (Allender, 14).

Step 2: Suppression. Although God has made His existence abundantly evident, we have nevertheless suppressed that truth. Paul writes,

The wrath of God is being revealed from heaven against all the godlessness and wickedness of men who suppress the truth by their wickedness, since what may be known about God is plain to them. . . . For although they knew God, they neither glorified him as God nor gave thanks to him, but their thinking became futile and their foolish hearts were darkened (Romans 1:18–19, 21).

One ought to look at a sunrise and be aware that an infinite and merciful Being has painted our existence with order, wonder, beauty.

15

Humanity has suppressed the truth of who God is in two ways in particular: His *knowableness* and His *holiness*.

The Suppression of God's Knowableness: In our rebellion against God, humanity has pushed Him away. We make God out to be distant, abstract, unknowable, even inconceivable.

Such suppression is seen repeatedly as one looks at the concepts of ultimate reality in the world religions. In Hinduism, for example, the most ultimate reality—*Brahman*—is described as *nirguna*, which means "without attributes." In Buddhism, ultimate reality is described as a Void or emptiness. The following is written in one of the Sanskrit scriptures for Buddhism:

> Why is there no obtaining of nirvana? Because nirvana is the realm of no "thingness".... If he is to realize nirvana, he must pass beyond consciousness (Goddard, 86).

Obviously, to say that God is "without attributes" or that we must pass beyond consciousness in order to "know" God is to make God out to be distant, abstract, unknowable, and inconceivable.

Other examples of suppressing God's knowableness: Margot Adler, who is a Wiccan priestess (a witch) and a leading spokesperson for the Pagan movement, said, "We need rituals because we're humans and we can't understand *the unknowable*" (Rabey, F3, emphasis added), thus denying that the ultimate is knowable. The first words of the *Tao Te Ching*, Taoism's scripture, are: "The way that can be spoken of is not the constant way; the name that can be named is not the constant name" (Ellwood, 181). Therefore, we're in a theological "Catch-22." If we talk about "the way," we make it clear that we don't know it.

In Islam, the *Qur'an* says of Allah that "Nothing is like Him" (*Surah* 42:11). Now, while a Christian would concur with such a statement (see Isaiah 40:18, 25; 55:8–9), Islam takes such a statement to an extreme. For example, one Muslim commentator writes, "So transcendent is the Divine Being [that He is] even above the limitation of metaphor" (Ali, 918). If God is unlike all metaphors, then it becomes impossible for humanity to conceive of what He is like. In essence, then, nothing can be known about God, which is to push Him away.

A distinction must be made between God being *incomprehensible* or *inconceivable*. While the Christian would agree that God is *incomprehensible*, he or she would not say He is *inconceivable*, which is what the non-Christian religions are making God to be. Because God is infinite, says Christianity, He is indeed incomprehensible to our finite minds. Because God is personal, though, we can know Him and make statements of truth about Him. Because God is personal, He is knowable at the core of who He is, even though He is incomprehensible to us in the infinity of His Being.

The Suppression of God's Holiness: The God of the Bible is absolute in His holiness.

> You are not a God who takes pleasure in evil; with you the wicked cannot dwell (Psalm 5:4).
> Holy, holy, holy is the LORD Almighty (Isaiah 6:3).
> God is light; in him there is no darkness at all (1 John 1:5).

Such a concept of God's absolute holiness is unique among the world religions, however, in that, while they call God great, they have either denied, diminished, or disregarded His holiness.

Holiness Denied: In the monistic religions, God is an impersonal oneness that is beyond all distinctions, including those distinctions between good and evil. Thus, God's moral holiness is denied.

Holiness Diminished: One indicator concerning the extent to which a religion upholds God's holiness is found in its means by which salvation is attained. In Islam, for example, each person's deeds will be weighed in the balance on the Day of Judgment in order to determine his or her fate. Theoretically, then, a person who is 51% righteous would be sufficiently righteous to attain Paradise.

The Bible, on the other hand, says that God's holiness requires that we be 100% righteous before we can be accepted by Him (Matthew 5:48; 1 Peter 1:15-16). Islam, then, does not uphold God's absolute holiness in that the God of the *Qur'an* allows into His presence those who are less than righteous.

Holiness Disregarded: Others disregard God's holiness altogether. Diane Dreher, for example, in her book *The Tao of Peace*, writes,

> In ancient China, to lead wisely meant to live wisely, to *seek personal balance and integration with the cycles of nature....* Peace, Lao Tzu realized, is an *inside job.* Only when we find peace *within ourselves* can we see more clearly, act more effectively, cooperating with the energies within and around us to build a more peaceful world (Dreher, xiii, emphasis added).

Dreher's search for peace never rises above the horizontal, or natural, realm—the "cycles of nature" and the "inside job." This indicates that reconciliation with a holy God never becomes a consideration for her as a way by which to gain peace. God's holiness, then, is disregarded.

We have just discussed the first two steps by which humanity pushes God away—"awareness" and "suppression." We will cover the third step of "replacement" shortly.

But, now, back to the story. Like the prodigal son who wanted to get away from his father, humanity has an urge to push God away. Where, though, does such rejection take us?

Richly tiled dome of an Islamic mosque.

2. The Realization

It is significant that, upon his arrival in the distant country, a famine hit the land, and the son found himself close to starvation (vv. 14, 17).

In the same way, many people experience a sense of spiritual hunger. We long for something more to life, but we don't know what we're looking for. For example, Simone Weil, a Jewish philosopher during World War II, wrote,

> In the period of preparation the soul loves in emptiness. It does not know whether anything real answers its love. It may believe that it knows, but to believe is not to know. Such a belief does not help. The soul knows for certain only that it is hungry. The important thing is that it announces its

Young Muslim men carry a coffin to the ancient El Aksa Mosque, Jerusalem, Israel.

hunger by crying. A child does not stop crying if we suggest to it that perhaps there is no bread. It goes on crying just the same. The danger is not lest the soul should doubt whether there is any bread, but lest, by a lie, it should persuade itself that it is not hungry. It can only persuade itself of this by lying, for the reality of its hunger is not a belief, it is a certainty (Coles, 29).

Our secularistic culture has tried to deny the spiritual hunger, but the need to search for the sacred persists (see *Newsweek*, November 28, 1994).

When René Descartes said, "I think, therefore I am," he was looking for that point of certainty that could not be questioned and from which he could build his belief system. In Weil's statement above we have another point of certainty—our spiritual hunger, our yearning for something to fill the spiritual emptiness within.

The following principle could be drawn from Weil's statement of certainty: "I yearn, therefore God is." Just as the baby yearns for milk, and there is milk, so we yearn for that which is beyond us, and there must be a God. Just as people yearn for love, and there is intimacy, so we yearn for meaning and hope and forgiveness, and there must be the transcendent foundation for such things.

3. The Return

Having experienced the starvation that resulted from his leaving his father, the son decides to return to his father.

This is the other side of our "spiritual schizophrenia." While, on the one hand, we reject God by pushing Him away, we, on the other hand, are drawn to Him.

Consider, though, on what basis the son chooses to return.

I will set out and go back to my father and say to him: Father, I have sinned against heaven and against you. I am no longer worthy to be called your son; make me like one of your hired men (Luke 15:18–19).

The son's words sound so penitent, so humble—"I am no longer worthy to be called your son." But there's something going on here that is not readily apparent. Since when was being a son an issue of worthiness? You either are a son, or you aren't. It's true that you can be a bad son and break your parents' hearts, but you are still a son.

The status of being a son can only be accepted, not earned. If the son wasn't a son already, there was nothing he could have done to earn his way into such a relationship. Since he was already a son, however, all he needed to do was to receive his father's forgiveness and love and to accept the relationship of being a son. But there is humility involved in receiving a gift, and the son wasn't willing to humble himself to such an extent. The experience of starvation had not changed him internally. The pride was still there. This is seen in two ways.

First, he based his relationship to his father on his own worthiness or merit. As such, he maintained his sense of independence and self-sufficiency. It is humbling to be the recipient of unmerited favor and to say thank you. The son was unwilling to humble himself that far. Instead, he wanted to be a hired hand, and to thereby maintain a relationship of merit between him and his father.

Consider the irony here. The son, on the one hand, rejected his father because of the constraints, but now chooses to return on the basis of his own merit. He has, in effect, replaced the Law of God with his own law, which is legalism. He thereby invented his own constraints. He did this because he wanted to return to the father on his own terms, not those of his father.

Second, the son's pride is seen in that even as he returns to his father he maintains a distance from him. By offering to become a hired hand, the son reveals that he is willing to *return to the place of his father* but not to become *reconciled with his father*. He persists in his rejection of his father, while at the same time enjoys the benefits of his father's realm.

This is where the third step of "replacement" comes in.

Step 3: Replacement. We are like the son. Initially, we push God away because of the constraints we feel He is placing on us, or because we view Him as a threat to our secure world.

We fill that void with various things, such as

- living a good life so as to earn God's favor,
- filling our lives with material goods, worldly successes, or exhilarating experiences,
- techniques for manipulating spiritual energy,
- rituals by which to evoke the gods,
- getting in touch with spiritual beings who are less threatening than an absolutely holy and sovereign God (see Romans 1:22-23).

In Hinduism, for example, we must strive over the course of innumerable lifetimes to release ourselves from attachment to the individual ego and to thereby escape the wheel of life, death, and rebirth. In Buddhism, we must desire to cease desiring. In the New Age movement, we must, through many lifetimes, learn the lessons of love. In Islam, we must live a life so that our good deeds will outweigh our bad deeds on the Day of Judgment.

A Burmese Buddhist monk at prayer.

Like the prodigal son, we too have replaced the language of grace with the language of merit.

By way of an example, one student objected to Christianity by saying, "It's unfair that Christians can be forgiven when others, whose lives may have been very exemplary, receive judgment."

What this student has done is mix the language of grace (forgiveness) with the language of merit (exemplary lives). The student, by pointing to the exemplary lives of those in other religions, is coming from the mistaken idea that forgiveness can be earned. He is in effect saying, "Those in other religions who live exemplary lives *deserve to be forgiven* just like Christians." "Deserved forgiveness," however, is a contradiction in terms. The language of grace cannot be mixed with the language of merit, for a gift can only be received, not earned.

We have not, however, only replaced grace with merit but we have also replaced the true God with false gods, and then forgotten that we replaced Him. Allender explains:

> Idolatry is not the by-product of forgetting God; it is the means by which we forget him.... All existential forgetfulness [i.e., forgetting God] begins with suppression, builds on the energy of idolatry, and binds us to an illusion that both numbs the heart to what is missing and blinds us even to our forgetfulness (Allender, 14–15).

In essence, then, humanity is so spiritually blinded that we have forgotten that we have replaced God with something less than who He is.

4. The Relationship of Love

The father, however, would have nothing to do with his son trying to earn his way back into his favor. All he wanted was to be in full relationship with his son as his father, not as the employer of a hired hand.

> But while he was still a long way off, his father saw him and was filled with

compassion for him; he ran to his son, threw his arms around him and kissed him (v. 20).

It is clear that the father in Jesus' parable represents God. What does this kind of love do to us? Does it move us to know that God longs to be in a relationship of love with us who have rejected Him?

The idea that God is One who longs to be in relationship with us who have rebelled against Him sets the Christian Gospel apart from all other ways to salvation offered in the world religions. After all, are the gods of the other religions able to sustain such love? Is the *Brahman* who is without attributes able to love? Is the Void of Buddhism able to long to be in a relationship with us? Has the God of the *Qur'an*, who is beyond all metaphors, demonstrated the kind of love illustrated by the father?

5. The Restoration of the Relationship

Jesus continued with the story and told how the father declared that it was time to celebrate,

> Bring the fattened calf and kill it. Let's have a feast and celebrate. For this son of mine was dead and is alive again; he was lost and is found (vv. 23–24).

The analogies that the father used—death and life, lost and found—reveal the seriousness of sin. We are dead in our sins and lost to, or separated from, God. As these analogies indicate, and as we will see in "The Distinctives of the Gospel," Christianity is unique among religions in that it depicts humanity as being as bad off spiritually as we could possibly be. After all, we could not be worse off than being spiritually dead! But that makes the good news—being given new life and being found—all that much sweeter.

What have we learned about the world religions and our own religious urge by looking at the parable of the prodigal son? Humanity is spiritually torn. We are drawn to God, but at

the same time we feel constrained and threatened by God. So we push Him away, making Him out to be distant, abstract, unknowable, and inconceivable.

We are uncomfortable with a spiritual void, though, so we attempt to fill that void with replacements for God and then base our relationship with Him on our own effort and merit.

We have also seen that God longs to be in relationship with us, even while we are in the midst of our rebellion against Him. There is no greater love.

Finally, we saw that forgiveness, like being a son, is a gift to be received, not earned.

Statue of Jesus healing, beside the Sea of Galilee, near Capernaum, Israel.

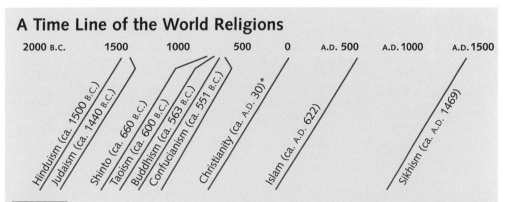

A Time Line of the World Religions

| 2000 B.C. | 1500 | 1000 | 500 | 0 | A.D. 500 | A.D. 1000 | A.D. 1500 |

Hinduism (ca. 1500 B.C.)
Judaism (ca. 1440 B.C.)
Shinto (ca. 660 B.C.)
Taoism (ca. 600 B.C.)
Buddhism (ca. 563 B.C.)
Confucianism (ca. 551 B.C.)
Christianity (ca. A.D. 30)*
Islam (ca. A.D. 622)
Sikhism (ca. A.D. 1469)

* On the one hand, this date is technically correct, but, on the other hand, a case could be made that Christianity, which is based on the good news of Jesus Christ, was in the mind of God from before "the creation of the world" (Ephesians 1:4; see also, 2 Timothy 1:9) and also in particular, soon after the Fall of humanity (Genesis 3:15).

IS THERE TRUTH IN NON-CHRISTIAN RELIGIONS?

All religions contain some truth, and Christians should be encouraged to recognize and appreciate that truth.

Islam, for example, is strong in its appreciation for the greatness of God.

Zoroastrianism emphasizes the purity of God, which demands that we too are called to be pure.

Animism helps us appreciate the truth that our battle is not just against flesh and blood (Ephesians 6:12).

Taoism encourages us to be sensitive to the underlying ways of nature and to deal with people with gentleness and understanding, not imposing our wills on them.

Paul's words that God "is not far from each one of us" (Acts 17:27) can help us appreciate Hinduism's emphasis on the immanence of God.

And even atheism's hope of finding solutions through rational thinking can encourage us as Christians to be clear in our thinking and consistent in our living.

While we can acknowledge, appreciate, and respect the truth that can be found in other religions, that does not mean that such religions contain saving truth, or a truth that leads to salvation.

THE DISTINCTIVES OF THE GOSPEL

What sets Christianity apart from the other world religions? Simply, the Person of Jesus Christ. But what precisely is it about Jesus Christ that makes Christianity unique? Much of what is unique about Jesus Christ and His Gospel is given in 1 John 4:9–10:

> This is how God showed his love among us: He sent his one and only Son into the world that we might live through him. This is love: not that we loved God, but that he loved us and sent his Son as an atoning sacrifice for our sins.

The following six points, based on

John's words, above, set Christianity apart from the other world religions.

1. Jesus Lived in History.
John emphasizes the historical nature of Jesus' life through the words "among us" and "into the world." The events of Jesus' life, death, and resurrection are historical, not mythical (see France). While this uniqueness does not deny that the founders of other religions lived in history or that specific events in those religions are historical, it is to say that their being rooted in history is not as essential to the truthfulness of their claims as it is to Christianity (with the possible exception of Judaism).

This is because the other religions are oriented primarily toward teachings and practices, whereas Christianity is oriented toward the actual saving work of a particular Person—Jesus Christ. If Jesus did not live, die on the cross, and rise from the dead *in history*, then Christianity is without foundation (1 Corinthians 15:17). Whether or not Buddha or Muhammad lived, however, is not essential to the truth-claims they made, for the same truth-claims could have been made by someone else. (For ways to address questions concerning the historicity of Christianity and other objections, see Geisler and Brooks.)

2. God Himself Became Flesh.
John writes that God sent "his one and only Son." Through the words "one and only" it is clear that John is not saying that Jesus is the Son of God in some mystical sense where, being part of the divine oneness, we are all sons of God. Instead, Jesus is the Son of God in an entirely unique way.

The word "son" implies one who is of the same nature. So, Jesus is unique because He is of the same nature as God. This means that Jesus is not a mere appearance or manifestation or representative of God, but an *incarnation* of God. Through Jesus, God became man in the flesh (John 1:1, 14).

The Garden Tomb, Jerusalem, Israel. Jesus' story ends in victory, with Jesus rising physically from the dead.

3. Humanity Is Spiritually Dead.

The words "that we might live" and "atoning sacrifice for our sins" indicate that Christianity considers humanity in its sinful condition to be spiritually dead. Otherwise, there would be no need for us to be made alive.

Humanity's spiritual condition is far worse off in Christianity than in any other religion (Romans 6:23; Ephesians 2:1; Colossians 2:13). While non-Christian religions acknowledge that humanity has problems, they also teach that we have the innate ability to fix them. It might not be easy, but we're still fixable.

Only Christianity says that humanity is spiritually dead and that,

apart from God's transforming power to give us new life, we have absolutely no hope (Romans 8:6–8).

4. God Is Absolutely Holy.

The implication behind God's requiring the severest of all penalties—death—as the payment for sin is that God is absolute with respect to His moral holiness. God has zero tolerance for sin. Habakkuk wrote, "Your eyes are too pure to look on evil; you cannot tolerate wrong" (Habakkuk 1:13). It is also written, "Without holiness no one will see the Lord" (Hebrews 12:14b).

Our tendency as humans is to rebel against such an absolute standard. We want to diminish it in some way,

The Relationship Between God's Holiness and Our Assurance

	THE CHRISTIAN GOSPEL	THE WAY TO SALVATION IN OTHER RELIGIONS
GOD'S HOLINESS	Upheld as being absolute	Denied, diminished, or disregarded
BASIS FOR SALVATION	God has completed the work of salvation on our behalf through Jesus Christ	Human effort
LEVEL OF ASSURANCE	Complete assurance	No assurance

make it attainable and less of a threat.

Many are of the opinion that God's love cannot be reconciled with God's justice (moral holiness). John indicates, though, that God demonstrated His love for us by sending His Son, while at the same time He demonstrated His justice by giving His Son "as an atoning sacrifice for our sins" (1 John 4:10; see also Romans 3:25–26; 5:8). Through Christ's sacrificial death, both God's love and justice are fully satisfied, without diminishing either.

5. Jesus Conquered Death.

Thankfully, Jesus' story does not end in defeat, with death having the final word. Instead, it ends in victory, with Jesus rising physically from the dead (John 20—21; 1 Corinthians 15:3–8). No other founder of a religion has even considered making such a claim.

Jesus' victory over death means victory for us as well, for Jesus' resurrection is why John could write, "that we might live through him." As Paul similarly wrote, just as "we have been united with him ... in his death, we will certainly also be united with him in his resurrection" (Romans 6:5).

6. Salvation Is a Free Gift.

John writes that it's "not that we loved God, but that he loved us." Notice that the direction of love is *from God to us*, not from us to God.

Salvation is not based in the least on the individual's merit, but entirely on the free grace of God (see also Romans 1:17; Ephesians 2:8–9).

What is interesting is that as we diminish God's holiness to make salvation more attainable, we lose assurance. The more that salvation is dependent upon our own effort, the less assurance we will have that we have attained it.

On the other hand, as God's absolute holiness is maintained, and as it becomes clear to us that we can in no way live up to such a standard, then, somewhat surprisingly, we gain assurance. That is because when we choose to depend upon God alone to provide the way of salvation through Jesus Christ, we can have complete assurance that we have received salvation—because it depends on Him who is true and faithful, and not on us.

Is the concept of grace present in the non-Christian world religions? Grace is mentioned, but it is redefined to include human effort. In Islam, for example, the phrase "those who believe" appears frequently in the *Qur'an* Such a phrase sounds similar to the Christian phrase "salvation by faith." But the phrase "those who believe" is usually accompanied with "and do good deeds." The emphasis, then, is placed on salvation being earned through human merit.

SUGGESTIONS FOR EVANGELISM

The following are some general principles to keep in mind when sharing the Gospel of Jesus Christ with a friend who has little understanding of Christianity.

Our approach should be gradual. We should not try to move our friend from, say, his or her denial of God's existence to signing his or her name at the end of the *Four Spiritual Laws* booklet in one evening. Take it a step at a time.

The primary issue should be, Who is God? All other issues are, at this point, secondary. As we have seen, humanity has a tendency to push God away. We are trying to move our friend's thinking toward the truth that God is personal, and because He is personal He can make himself known, which He has done through Jesus Christ.

We must be holistic in our approach rather than reductionistic. By that I mean that we must resist reducing a person to a single level of their being, the intellect being the level that is usually singled out. Instead, we should see each individual as a whole person, as someone who is motivated not just by rational arguments but also by needs and emotions.

The following suggestions show how to approach a person on each level of his or her being.

1. The Intellectual Level

The many variations of world religions can be summarized into three basic worldviews:

■ Naturalism (atheism):
• Ultimate reality is physical matter.
• The physical universe is eternal in some form or another, closed (no supernatural influence), and operates according to natural laws.
• Humanity is a physical being that is the result of only evolutionary forces.

■ Monism:
• Ultimate reality is spiritual, or immaterial, and usually characterized as

Mysterious statues from Easter Island.

being impersonal and undifferentiated.
• The universe is an emanation from the spiritual and in some sense less real (illusory).
• Humanity is identical in its nature to that of ultimate reality.

■ Theism:
• Ultimate reality is an eternal, infinite, and personal God.
• The universe was created by God out of nothing and is both material and immaterial.
• Humanity was created by God in His image and is both material and immaterial.

How can a person tell which worldview is true? By testing them against three criteria for truth:
1. *Logical Consistency:* A true worldview will not contradict itself.
2. *Factuality:* A true worldview will fit the facts.

3. *Viability:* One can live consistently with a worldview that is true.

How do the three worldviews measure up to the above tests?

Naturalism

Logical Consistency: It is inconsistent for a naturalist to argue that the evidence for Naturalism is convincing and that one ought to choose it. Why? Because a naturalist says that only matter exists. If that is true, then our thoughts are determined by biological stimuli, not by the evidence or by principles of reason. In addition, there is no "enduring 'I'" that is doing the reasoning or the arguing (Moreland, 96).

Factuality: If matter (or energy) is all there is, which is the assumption of Naturalism, then the implication that follows from the fact that something exists is that the universe has existed in some form or another forever. Astronomers, however, have found evidence that indicates the universe had a beginning. The second law of thermodynamics, for example, which says that energy becomes increasingly inaccessible, indicates that the universe began at a certain finite point in time, otherwise all the available energy would have dissipated long ago. In other words, an infinite amount of time would already have outlasted a finite amount of energy.

Viability: Most people attach unique value to human life—at least to their own human life. But such a sense of value is inconsistent with Naturalism because in Naturalism there is no foundation for considering human life to be uniquely valuable compared to animal life. That is because Naturalism says humanity is nothing more than an advanced form of animal.

Also, as witnessed by the fact that people judge the immoral actions of other people and of various cultures, they live as though morality is based on some standard that is external to themselves and to culture. But Naturalism cannot provide such an objective moral standard.

Monism

Logical Consistency: Monism—the belief that ultimate reality is beyond all differentiation—leads one to say that there is no absolute truth. Why? Because truth implies a distinction between truth and non-truth. Monism, however, being undifferentiated, does not allow for such distinctions. It, therefore, includes and absorbs all concepts of truth.

But the statement that there is no absolute truth is itself an absolute truth, and thereby self-refuting, which is a logical inconsistency.

Factuality: Monism, again, says that ultimate reality is without differentiation or separation. It is thus not a form of intelligence, because intelligence makes distinctions between things. Such an undifferentiated source is inadequate as a First Cause for a reality that manifests distinctions and for a humanity that exhibits intelligence.

Viability: Most monistic worldviews say that one should act non-violently toward all life. But one cannot do so and also eat food, for even vegetarians kill plants, which is a form of life.

Theism

Logical Consistency: Humanity lives with the sense that we have value as persons, that life has a purpose, and that morality has meaning. Such things are sufficiently founded only on the Creator-God who is personal (therefore we have value), who created us to be in fellowship with Him (therefore life has an ultimate meaning), and who is holy (therefore morality has a sufficient foundation).

Factuality: The theory that the universe was created by an intelligent Cause is consistent with the principle of causality, which says that every effect requires a sufficient cause.

Viability: Since we are made in the image of a personal God, it is natural for us to live consistently with the understanding that persons have value and that morality has meaning.

2. The Needs Level

As we have seen, the non-Christian world religions make God out to be distant, abstract, unknowable, and inconceivable. On the other hand, the God of Christianity is unique in that He is inherently personal, and therefore knowable at the core of His Being.

Take a moment and imagine what it would be like to live in a world where we could not be in a relationship with God. What kinds of spiritual needs would be left unfulfilled in our lives?

1. Life would lack significance, knowing that it is so fleeting.

2. There would be a feeling of being unfulfilled, sensing that the beauty around us must mean there is something out there to relate to, but not being able to connect with it.

3. We might also experience a sense of frustration at the failure to improve ourselves morally, not only as individuals but as the human race in general. After all, wars have been a constant in human history.

4. We would be anxious about death, not knowing what happens after we die.

The following is a discussion of those spiritual needs as they are met through the God of the Bible. Note how each Person of the Trinity—Father, Son, and Holy Spirit—is involved in a specific way in meeting these common needs.

A. The Need for Significance. Significance, or meaning, in life is best founded in that which is eternal. We can strive for wealth or accolades or political change, but such things are temporary and fleeting. We can leave a legacy for others, but there is no guarantee that it will last. The writer of Ecclesiastes bemoaned this fact:

> I hated all the things I had toiled for under the sun, because I must leave them to the one who comes after me. And who knows whether he will be a wise man or a fool? Yet he will have control over all the work into which I have poured my effort and skill under the sun. This too is meaningless (Ecclesiastes 2:18–19).

The phrase "under the sun" (used twice above and twenty-nine times altogether in Ecclesiastes) refers to the idea of being earthbound, confined to the limitations of what this world has to offer apart from God (Wright, 1152).

Only as our lives are grounded in the eternal God will we have a sense that this life has significance and that it is not mired in futility.

B. The Need for Emotional and Relational Fulfillment. We are by nature social creatures, which means we are most fulfilled when in loving relationships with other people. You can take away the accolades, the riches, and the education, and life will go on. Without loving relationships, though, life becomes empty, void of meaning.

In a world where we could not be in a relationship with God, we would be anxious about death, ignorant of what happens after we die.

27

What we as Christians are saying is that just as we find fulfillment in relationships on a human level, so we can find even greater fulfillment as we relate to a personal and loving God on the spiritual level.

The truth that God is personal—possesses the characteristics of a person—is something that we as Christians often take for granted, but it is significant nevertheless. Consider, for example, the implications that flow from the fact that God, by His very nature, is personal.

Only if God is personal . . .

■ can we have a relationship with Him.
■ can He communicate with us.
■ can He hear our prayers.
■ can He love us.
■ can He forgive us.
■ can He empathize with our suffering.
■ can there be a sufficient foundation for our value as persons.
■ can there be a sufficient foundation for our moral sensitivities.
■ can there be a sufficient foundation for meaning in life.
■ can there be a sufficient foundation for hope.

Love, empathy, value, meaning, and hope are essential to life. They are what fulfill us. We could not experience them, however, if God were anything less than a personal Being.

Speaking of love in particular, we are fulfilled in love, and we can be especially fulfilled knowing that God loves us. And we know that He loves us because He has demonstrated His love in history through His Son (Romans 5:8; 1 John 4:8–10).

In addition, we can go beyond knowing about God's love to having fellowship with Him through the Holy Spirit, who gives us "access to the Father" (Ephesians 2:18; Galatians 4:4–6).

C. *The Need for the Power to Change.* We fail morally because we

know the good that we want to do but are often unable to do it (Romans 7:18).

Humankind has made myriads of attempts to transform itself. But the real problem goes much deeper than anything humankind can come up with, because it goes to the nature of the human heart itself.

Only a holy God can change the human heart, and He has done so through the indwelling and transforming Holy Spirit (Ezekiel 36:26–27; Romans 8:5–17; 2 Corinthians 5:17).

D. *The Need for Hope and Assurance.* That which lies beyond death is both unknown and fearful, causing anxiety and despair.

As Christians, we are assured of what will happen after death, because Jesus Christ demonstrated in history His victory over death. The historical fact of Jesus' resurrection gives us hope in this life and the assurance of being accepted with God in the life to come.

The Holy Spirit has a role in this too, because God has "set his seal of ownership on us, and put his Spirit in our hearts as a deposit, *guaranteeing what is to come*" (2 Corinthians 1:22, emphasis added).

3. The Emotional Level

"People need facts to know what decision to make," wrote one evangelist, "but emotion to get them to make the decision" (Innes, 125). The way to touch a person deeply is by touching him or her on the emotional level. And the way to do that is through an image or word picture, such as a testimony, a story, or an illustration.

The following story illustrates how much God cares for us and how He demonstrated that care by suffering on our behalf through Jesus Christ.

Author Bob Stromberg tells of the time he broke his arm as a young boy. As his dad drove him to the hospital, the numbness wore off and the pain suddenly shot through his newly injured arm. Bob pleaded, "Oh,

please, Dad, can't you do something?" His dad responded, "Son, I wish I could take the pain of that broken arm right out of your body and into my own."

Bob questioned that his dad would really want to do that, but his dad responded, "Someday, Bob, you'll understand."

Years later, on a fall day, Bob watched helplessly as his son, distracted by his effort to launch a kite, tripped into a pile of burning leaves and sticks, severely burning his hands. As Bob drove him to the hospital, his son said, "Oh, Dad, it hurts so bad." At that moment Bob remembered and understood what his dad had told him years before, and he responded, "Son, if I could, I would take the pain in your hands and put it right into my own."

Then it occurred to Bob that that is precisely what God had done through Jesus when Jesus took our sins upon himself and paid the penalty of that sin on our behalf (Stromberg, ch. 4).

Such a story will stick in the mind of a student and stimulate his or her thinking.

CONCLUSION

We've covered a lot of ground! We've gone all the way from discussing the patterns within the spectrum of world religions, to talking about the motivations behind our religious urge, to articulating the six distinctives of the Gospel of Jesus Christ, and finally to suggesting some principles to keep in mind for sharing the good news of Christ with a friend. I hope that as a result you have gained a greater appreciation for the uniqueness of the Gospel of Jesus Christ.

Gigantic statue of Christ with outstretched arms, Rio de Janeiro, Brazil.

BIBLIOGRAPHY AND RESOURCES

Ali, Maulana Muhammad. *The Holy Qur'an*. Chicago: Specialty Promotions Co., Inc., 1985.

Allender, Dan. "Remembering That We Forget." *Mars Hill Review*. Littleton, Colo.: Kim Hutchins, May 1995, no. 2.

Anderson, J. N. D. *Christianity and Comparative Religion*. Downers Grove, Ill.: InterVarsity Press, 1977.

Coles, Robert. *Simone Weil: A Modern Pilgrimage*. Reading, Mass.: Addison-Wesley Publishing Co., Inc., 1987.

Crockett, William and James Sigountos, eds. *Through No Fault of Their Own: The Fate of Those Who Have Never Heard*. Grand Rapids, Mich.: Baker Book House, 1991.

Denton, Michael. *Evolution: A Theory in Crisis*. Bethesda, Md.: Adler & Adler, 1986.

Ellwood, Robert, Jr. *Words of the World Religions*. Englewood Cliffs, N.J.: Prentice-Hall, Inc., 1977.

Fernando, Ajith. *The Christian's Attitude Toward World Religions*. Wheaton, Ill.: Tyndale House Publishers, Inc., 1987.

France, R. T. *The Evidence for Jesus*. Downers Grove, Ill.: InterVarsity Press, 1986.

Geisler, Norman and Ron Brooks. *When Skeptics Ask: A Handbook on Christian Evidences*. Wheaton, Ill.: Victor Books, 1990.

Goddard, Dwight, ed. *A Buddhist Bible*. Boston: Beacon Press, 1966.

Hexham, Irving. *Concise Dictionary of Religion*. Downers Grove, Ill.: InterVarsity Press, 1993.

Hinnells, John. *The Facts on File Dictionary of Religions*. New York: Facts on File, 1984.

Innes, Dick. "The Art of Using Appropriate Vocabulary." *The Art of Sharing Your Faith*. Joel Heck, ed. Tarrytown, N.Y.: Fleming H. Revell Co., 1991.

Jaki, Stanley. *The Purpose of It All*. Washington, D.C.: Regnery Gateway, 1990.

Kreeft, Peter and Ronald Tacelli. *Handbook of Christian Apologetics*. Downers Grove, Ill.: InterVarsity Press, 1994.

Lewis, James and William Travis. *Religious Traditions of the World*. Grand Rapids, Mich.: Zondervan Publishing House, 1991.

Moreland, J. P. *Scaling the Secular City: A Defense of Christianity*. Grand Rapids, Mich.: Baker Book House, 1987.

Muck, Terry. *Alien Gods on American Turf*. Wheaton, Ill.: Victor Books, 1990.

—— *World Religions in Your Neighborhood*. Grand Rapids, Mich.: Zondervan Publishing House, 1992.

Nash, Ronald. *Worldviews in Conflict*. Grand Rapids, Mich.: Zondervan Publishing House, 1992.

Netland, Harold. *Dissonant Voices: Religious Pluralism and the Question of Truth*. Grand Rapids, Mich.: William B. Eerdmans Publishing Co., 1991.

Noss, John. *Man's Religions*, 5th ed. New York: Macmillan Publishing Co., Inc., 1974.

Parrinder, Geoffrey. *World Religions: From Ancient History to the Present*. New York: Facts on File Publications, 1984.

Rabey, Steve. "The Pagan Nature." *Gazette-Telegraph*. Colorado Springs, Colo.: Freedom Communications Inc., July 24, 1993.

Raguin, Yves. "Themes of Classical Taoism." *Areopagus*. Brant Pelphrey, ed. Hong Kong: Tao Fong Shan Christian Centre; Trinity 1990, Vol. 3, no. 4.

Seamands, John T. *Tell It Well: Communicating the Gospel Across Cultures*. Kansas City, Mo.: Beacon Hill Press, 1981.

Sproul, R. C. *If There's a God, Why Are There Atheists?* Wheaton, Ill.: Tyndale House Publishers, Inc., 1988.

Stromberg, Bob. *Why Geese Fly Farther Than Eagles*. Colorado Springs, Colo.: Focus on the Family, 1992.

Wright, J. Stafford. "Ecclesiastes." *The Expositor's Bible Commentary*. Frank Gaebelein, gen. ed. Grand Rapids, Mich.: Zondervan Publishing House, 1991.

Animism

Dean C. Halverson

DEFINITION OF ANIMISM

The term "animism" comes from the Latin word *anima*, which means "soul" or "breath." As such, it refers to that which empowers or gives life to something. It follows, then, that animism is the religion that sees the physical world as interpenetrated by spiritual forces—both personal and impersonal—to the extent that objects carry spiritual significance and events have spiritual causes.

Thus, if there is an accident, or if someone is sick, there are spiritual reasons behind such things that must be taken into consideration. Otherwise, the cause behind the accident or the sickness cannot be fully understood or remedied.

The animistic form of a religion is called "folk religion," such as "folk Hinduism" or "folk Islam." The tendency for people to gravitate toward a folk form of their religion explains why many people who come from a country with a Hindu or a Buddhist heritage do not believe the way the "textbook" description of their religion says they should believe.

Buddhist worshipers, Thailand. Many people from a country with a Hindu or a Buddhist heritage do not believe the way the "textbook" description of their religion says they should.

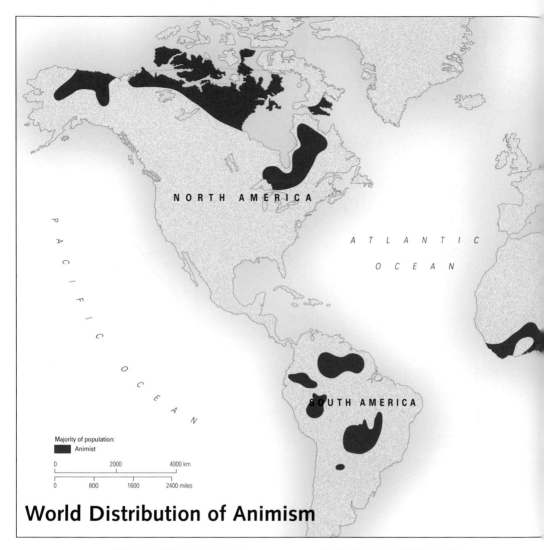

Majority of population:
Animist

| 0 | 2000 | 4000 km |
| 0 | 800 | 1600 | 2400 miles |

World Distribution of Animism

WHY UNDERSTAND ANIMISM?

Why should we seek to understand animistic religions? After all, aren't those the kinds of religions that are practiced by primitive tribal groups wearing weird masks and dancing around a fire? How relevant can such a primitive religious system be to the people with whom we "rub shoulders" who are both modernized and well-educated?

It is important for us to understand animism because it is both pervasive and attractive to people.

THE PERVASIVENESS OF ANIMISM

Most world religions have a concept of God that makes Him out to be distant, abstract, and unknowable (see the World Religions Overview). For example, Hindus say that *Brahman*—their term for ultimate reality, or God—is *nirguna*, which means "without attributes." A God without attributes is obviously abstract to the extreme. The result of *Brahman's* being so distant and abstract is that people are left with a spiritual void that calls out to be filled. Hindus have

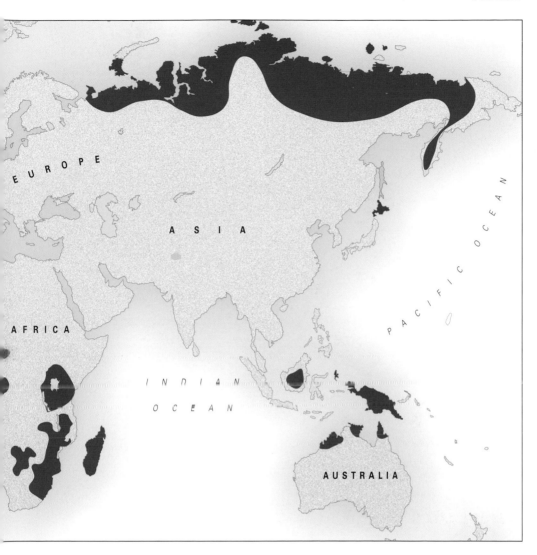

filled that void with 330 million intermediate gods.

We in the U.S. have witnessed this tendency to move toward animism in the phenomenon of the New Age movement. When that movement began 20–30 years ago, meditation, in which the meditator sought to experience unity with the divine oneness, was central to the movement. But now channeling—contacting one's personal spirit–guide—rivals meditation as being at the center of the movement. Again, this is an example of humanity's tendency to move from an abstract concept of God—the divine oneness—to filling the void with personal spirit-beings.

This tendency also explains why many in our secularized culture, in which God has been replaced by the theory of evolution, have become so enamored with angels and with SETI (the Search for Extraterrestrial Intelligence) during the past few years.

So, animism needs to be understood because it is the form of religion to which people gravitate.

Additionally, although precise figures are hard to come by, the estimates concerning the percentages of animists in the world are significantly large. For example, Gailyn Van Rheenen, an expert on animistic religions, estimates that "at least 40 percent of the world's population" is animistic (Van Rheenen, 30). Also, an article entitled "What's going on" points to the growth of animism as being a trend of the future:

> Religious pluralism reigns; any god will do. Neo-paganism is emerging with disturbing force. There are more registered witches in France than there are Catholic priests (Myers, 4).

The *International Bulletin of Missionary Research* lists "Tribal Religionists" as making up around 17% of the world's population (Barrett, 25). This percentage is lower than Van Rheenen's probably because it counts only those who are strictly tribal religionists and does not take into consideration those who are numbered as, say, Buddhists, but who adhere to more of a folk form of Buddhism than to the original teachings of Buddha.

THE ATTRACTION OF ANIMISM

Another reason animism should be studied is because it holds a tremendous attraction for people.

First, it is popular for some because it infuses the sacred into a reality that has been emptied of anything spiritual by the scientific/evolutionary perspective. Animism puts the mystery back into the secularized, matter-only world.

Second, animism holds an attraction because it offers people a way to cope with one's everyday needs and problems, such as the need

■ to be healed of an illness,
■ to be successful in a business endeavor,
■ to find a job,
■ to excel in school,
■ to restore a soured relationship,
■ to find a mate,
■ to gain guidance for the future.

Religion Watch reported, for example,

> The new religions making the most impact in Japan today are those stressing individual spiritual powers and techniques. . . . Today's young recruits are little interested in religious doctrine. The focus on the current wave has turned from belief to techniques (Cimino, 6–7).

We have all experienced those times when God seems silent and distant and when His apparent lack of action leaves us feeling helpless. The feelings that God is distant and that He doesn't care might overtake us after hearing the news that one has cancer, or after experiencing the death of a child, or being laid off from a job. At such times we become desperate, and we are tempted to grab for something that works—anything that will give us the power to get us out of our suffering or to fix whatever is wrong.

Animism promises such power. Philip John Neimark—an American-born Jewish businessman who is also a priest of the animistic "Ifa" religion—says, "Religion is a marketplace. You have to deliver. And Ifa works" (Ifa, 4).

To the extent that we seek to manipulate spiritual powers—including God—for the "quick fix" or for our personal benefit, we are coming from an animistic rather than a biblical perspective. In that sense, we all have animistic tendencies.

Only when we serve and worship God solely for who He is—and not for what He can do for us—is our worship pure and free of animistic inclinations (see Steyne, 46–47).

COMMON ANIMISTIC BELIEFS AND PRACTICES

1. One God Beyond the Many Spirits

Most animistic religions teach that there is one Supreme Being who exists beyond the intermediate ancestors, spirits, and gods. This God

Spirit gate of an
Akha village,
northern Thailand.

is either by nature monistic (an impersonal oneness) or monotheistic (a personal Being). This Supreme Being is either too far removed from His creation or too abstract to be known. It might be that the Supreme Being uses the intermediate spirits to do His will and to serve as His representatives, but He still cannot be approached or known directly.

2. The Ultimate/Immediate Division

The animist views the "formal" religions—Christianity, Islam, Hinduism, etc.—as being relevant with respect to the *ultimate* issues, such as who is God, what is humanity's problem, and what happens after death. They see those religions as being irrelevant, however, when it comes to addressing the *immediate* issues of everyday life. This division between the ultimate and the immediate realms is why an animist can be a practicing Catholic, but also consult a *shaman* (an animistic priest who communicates with the spirits) in order to be healed.

3. The Spiritual Realm

According to animism, the spiritual realm with which we must deal consists of both personal spirit-beings and an impersonal spiritual energy.

A. *The Personal Spirit-Beings.* Animists believe there are two different kinds of spirit-beings: those that had been embodied (such as deceased ancestors) and those that had not (such as spirits and gods) (Van Rheenen, 259). The spirits are often seen as being mediators between us and God, able to intercede on our behalf. But to mediate on our behalf they must first be given homage (Henry, 8).

Spirit-beings possess specific powers and are localized geographically. Some spirits exert their powers over human endeavors (such as a business venture, a marriage, community relations, or war), while others exert their powers over aspects of nature (such as storms, the seas, or fields).

B. *An Impersonal Spiritual Force.* Besides the personal spirit-beings, animistic religions also teach that

A worshiper makes a food offering at an Asian temple.

there is an impersonal spiritual energy that infuses special objects, words, and rituals. Such energy gives these objects the power that people need to accomplish their desires.

Animists will often attribute magical powers to an object. For example, the following is a description of a technique for how those in folk Islam make a fetish out of the words of the *Qur'an*, their sacred scripture:

> One aspect of fetish-making involves writing a verse from the Koran that is relevant to the problem or concern of the person on a piece of paper in water-soluble ink. Before the paper is put inside the fetish, the marabout [a Muslim leader] dips it in water so the ink dissolves. Then the person who will wear the fetish drinks the water, thinking that by doing so the message will be internalized (Quicksall, 10–11).

4. The Concept of Sin

Animists are not concerned so much about offending the supreme God; instead, their concern is of a more immediate nature in that they are afraid of offending the local spirits. They realize that an offended spirit will inevitably exact retribution in the form of injury, sickness, failure, or interpersonal strife.

For example, Migene Gonzalez-Wippler, a follower of the animistic religion called Santeria, knew that Eleggua—the name of her god—required his followers to perform a simple offering to him every Monday morning. One Monday, however, Gonzalez-Wippler forgot to perform the ritual offering because she had just returned from a tiring trip and was busy unpacking. As she was walking around her apartment putting things away, she cut her leg on the sharp edge of the handle to the cabinet in which she kept her god. "When I pulled back my leg," writes Gonzalez-Wippler, "the door of the cabinet swung open, and there, looking up at me with aggrieved eyes, was Eleggua's image" (Gonzalez-Wippler, 236). Gonzalez-Wippler understood the cut to be the price that her god had inflicted on her for having neglected him.

Van Rheenen writes, "Animists live in continual fear of these [spiritual] powers" (Van Rheenen, 20).

5. Contacting the Spirits

Animists are more inclined than Westerners to attribute spiritual causes to their sickness or bad fortune. Divination, which is "the practice of giving information ... which is not available by natural means" (Henry, 71), is the means by which a person discovers either how he or she has offended some spirit or which person has cast a curse on him or her. Divination is also the means by which one discovers how to resolve the problem—either what the spirit requires or how to throw a counter-curse.

Methods of divination are numerous and varied; they include tarot cards, palm reading, the *I Ching*, tea-leaf reading, observing how feathers fall, the throwing of cowry shells, astrology, omens, dowsing (see Weldon), rituals, necromancy (contacting the dead), and interpreting dreams and visions. Divination can also be used to discover when it is the most fortuitous time to do such things as ask for someone's hand in marriage, begin constructing a building, sign a contract, or make an investment.

6. The Afterlife
There is no universal and consistent doctrine throughout the many animistic religions as to what happens to a person after death. Many see the person's spirit as continuing to exist after death either by being reincarnated into another life on earth or by "graduating" to a higher spiritual level.

The belief is also common that the person who dies becomes an ancestral spirit. The family must then continue to give offerings to that ancestor because it has the power either to protect or to plague the family.

SUGGESTIONS FOR EVANGELISM

1. Be Sensitive to the Animist's Perspective
In his book *Filipino Spirit World*, Rodney Henry talks about how an "informal conspiracy of silence" developed among the laity toward the clergy in the Philippines. By the phrase

Differences Between the Personal Spirit-Beings of Animism and the God of the Bible

THE PERSONAL SPIRIT-BEINGS OF ANIMISM	THE GOD OF THE BIBLE
Limited to one geographic location	Not limited geographically; God of all the earth and the universe (Acts 17:24)
Has power over various aspects of nature	Has power over all things (Acts 17:24)
Depends on our sacrifices	Doesn't depend on our sacrifices because He has created all things (Acts 17:25), and because He has provided on our behalf the "once and for all" sacrifice (Hebrews 9:24—10:14)

Differences Between the Impersonal Spiritual Force of Animism and the God of the Bible

THE IMPERSONAL SPIRITUAL FORCE OF ANIMISM	THE GOD OF THE BIBLE
The spiritual forces can be manipulated according to the person's will.	God is not moved or manipulated by charms or by rituals. That which moves God is a repentant and humble heart before Him (Psalm 51:16–17; Proverbs 21:3).
The spiritual forces can be used for either good or evil purposes.	God is holy and hates that which is evil (Psalm 5:4). The Bible says, moreover, that the "sacrifice of the wicked is detestable—how much more so when brought with evil intent!" (Proverbs 21:27).

Church belonging to the Indians of the Chiapas region, Mexico. Their religion syncretizes Catholicism and animism.

"conspiracy of silence," Henry is referring to the laypeople's reluctance to talk to the clergy about their problems with the spirits because the clergy didn't take such things seriously. For example, Henry described a situation in which a layperson was asked to deal with someone who was being "troubled by demons." This layperson said,

> I stopped to ask our American missionary to pray for me and for the situation with the student. When I explained the situation to him, he simply laughed at me and changed the subject. *That was the last time I ever talked to an American about the spirit-world* (Henry, 33; emphasis added).

The first principle, then, in dealing with someone who comes from an animistic perspective, is to refrain from scoffing at their view of the world. Such skepticism will only cause them to refrain from discussing that part of their lives with you, but it will not turn them from it.

2. Be Aware of the Influence of Secularistic Thinking in Our Lives

The Lausanne Committee for World Evangelization has stated that "the influence of the enlightenment in our education, which traces everything to natural causes, has further dulled our consciousness of the powers of darkness" (Lausanne, 2). We, as Western Christians, need to be aware of how naturalistic, empirical thinking has influenced our worldview to the extent that we have dismissed the influence of the spirit world altogether. Such a worldview, moreover, is not biblical.

3. Find Common Ground

Animism and Christianity share several concepts in common (see Tippett, 134–139), and the Christian can use them for building common ground.

First, both Christians and animists believe in the existence and the influence of the supernatural. Both Christianity and animism would stand together in their opposition to the naturalistic thinking that says only matter exists. Animists, like Christians, believe that, while we might plant the seeds and cultivate the soil, there is a supernatural element that causes the growth. Or, while the doctor is the one who dresses the wound and sets the broken arm, there is, again, a supernatural element that causes the healing.

Second, offending the supernatural carries consequences. With the animist, those consequences include things such as sickness, doing poorly in an exam, interpersonal strife, or financial ruin. With the Christian, the consequences of our offending—sinning against—God is that it causes our fellowship with Him to be broken.

Third, both Christians and animists have the hope that there is a way by which to escape the consequences of our transgressions.

Fourth, often the animist believes in some form of a Supreme Being who stands above the spirits and spiritual powers.

Asking the animist to talk about his or her concept of the Supreme Being and about his or her cultural traditions, legends, and practices often bears unexpected fruit. That fruit could be a redemptive analogy—a theological similarity with Christianity in picture or story form—that could be used to illustrate the Gospel. Ask such questions as:

- What is the supreme God like?
- Was there a time when God was close to humanity? What caused the original separation between humanity and God? Why does God seem distant now?
- How do we offend the gods, spirits, or ancestors?
- What are the consequences of such offenses?
- Is there a way by which to divert those consequences?
- Does God care about us now? If so, how?

4. Highlight the Differences

The key differences between animism and Christianity are, first, that in

> Animists, like Christians, believe that, while we plant the seeds and cultivate the soil, there is a supernatural element that causes the growth.

The Animistic and Biblical Worldviews Contrasted

	ANIMISM	CHRISTIANITY
GOD	God exists, but He is beyond our abilities to know Him or to communicate with Him.	God exists, and although He is beyond our comprehension, He is nevertheless knowable; and He has made himself known to us through Jesus Christ and through the Bible (Hebrews 1:1–2).
ULTIMATE/ IMMEDIATE ISSUES	Formal religions are concerned only with the ultimate issues of sin and salvation; but animism offers the power to cope with the immediate, everyday needs.	The God of Christianity is concerned both with the ultimate and the immediate issues. God desires to provide not only for our eternal needs but also for our daily needs (1 Peter 5:7).
THE SPIRITS	The spirits are seen as being either intermediaries between us and God or as representatives of God.	The spirits are deceptive; they seek to take the place of God in our lives.
THE POWER OF THE SPIRITS	The spirits and the instruments of magic have the power either to do harm to others or to bring benefit to us.	The spirits do have power, but our utilizing such power leads to bondage. God has demonstrated through Jesus Christ that He is greater than the spirits and magic, for "the one who is in you is greater than the one who is in the world" (1 John 4:4; see also Exodus 8:18) and He has "disarmed the powers and authorities" (Colossians 2:15). Submitting to God brings freedom (John 8:32–36) not bondage.

Christianity God has not remained distant and silent, but He has broken through to our world through Jesus Christ, through whom He has made himself known to us (John 1:1, 14, 18; Hebrews 1:1–2; 1 John 4:9–10).

Second, through the sacrificial death of Jesus Christ, God has paid for—removed, covered, taken care of—the consequences that we have incurred as a result of our offenses against Him. The gods, spirits, and ancestors of animism offer no such grace.

The "once and for all" nature of Christ's sacrifice, moreover, means that the matter of our sin is settled with God (see Hebrews 9:25–26; Isaiah 53:6; 2 Corinthians 5:21), and the path is cleared for us to have a personal relationship with God (Hebrews 4:16).

5. Model Trust in God Alone

The animist is coming from the perspective that God is distant and that He does not care about our everyday concerns or, if He does care, He can act only through the spirits. As a result, the animist takes his or her problems and concerns to a spirit to solve, or relies on the power of a ritual or an amulet to meet his or her needs.

For example, the following was written about a Catholic woman who placed her faith in a locket that had an image of St. Vincent De Paul on one side and a likeness of the Virgin Mary on the other:

> "Many times I was in danger of losing my life," said 74-year-old Barbara Trzos. "Maybe because of the locket I was spared."
>
> She clutched it in Krakow, where she was taken to a prison and sentenced to death. She clutched it in Auschwitz, where she performed slave labor. She clutched it in Dresden, where the bombs exploded around her. She clutched it in Bergen-Belsen, where disease and starvation almost finished her.
>
> "I do believe," she said, "the locket was just protecting me."
> (McCaffrey, B1).

Placing one's faith in such a thing as a locket is animism. Animists might interpret their clutching on to something, such as a locket, as clutching on to that which God has provided for them. In reality, however, that object has become a replacement for God; they are trusting in the supposed magical powers of the creation rather than in the Creator.

We as Christians need to encourage the animist to let go of whatever he or she is clutching for protection or prosperity and to cling instead to the only true and secure Source of our protection and prosperity.

The way to get the animist to question his or her object of trust is first to discuss how dependence on animistic powers is an addiction that leads to bondage. The more power we experience, the more we crave that power. Such powers eventually begin to "own" us.

Second, we need to demonstrate through our lives that God is intensely interested in every aspect of our lives. We can rest, therefore, in His power to provide for our needs. Peter exhorts, "Cast all your anxiety on him because he cares for you" (1 Peter 5:7). It is in the sense of casting all our anxieties on God that we are to be a "better animist than the animist," for we should take *every concern* to God. When a child gets sick, our first reaction should be to pray for him or her and to seek God's guidance concerning his or her care. If we're worried about our job, our primary response should be to take our concern to God.

Third, we must point the animist to Scripture. Go to Matthew 10:29–30, for example, and point out that Jesus

A St. Christopher medal. Placing one's faith in such a thing as a locket is a form of animism.

said that God is not only aware of each sparrow that falls to the ground but that He is even aware of the number of hairs on our heads. If God is concerned about such insignificant matters as sparrows and the hair on our heads, then how much more is He concerned about us, for we "are worth more than many sparrows" (Matthew 10:31).

Make it clear that approaching God through prayer is the answer to our problems, not depending on the power of some spirit or amulet. Also, we should pray for things with the animist. Ask the animist what concerns he or she has; and then pray for those concerns with him or her.

Then stand back and be prepared to see God work in ways that might be beyond our previous experience or limited expectations.

6. Be Ready for God to Work in Mighty Ways

Jesus made a connection between the demonstration of God's power over Satan's kingdom and the invasion of the kingdom of God into Satan's realm when He said, "If I drive out demons by the Spirit of God, then the kingdom of God has come upon you" (Matthew 12:28). Significantly, He made a similar connection between the conquering of demons and the invasion of His kingdom when He gave His pattern for prayer: "Our Father in heaven ... *your kingdom come*, your will be done on earth as it is in heaven ... *but deliver us from the evil one*" (Matthew 6:10, 13, emphasis added).

Because the Lord's Prayer is clearly still relevant for us today, God is demonstrating His power over Satan and his demons so as to confirm that the presence of His kingdom is also still active today. This is significant for us as we consider working with animists.

Because the power to cope with everyday issues is such an important matter to an animist, the animist will probably not be inclined to switch allegiance from the spirits to Jesus unless the power of Jesus is visibly

demonstrated to be greater than that of the spirits.

Moreover, God does not seem to be shy about showing His power to animists who are seeking after Him (Shetler). So, be ready to be amazed by the way in which God will work.

At the same time, though, we as Christians must walk a fine line between an *expectant* faith that believes God wishes to demonstrate His power to the animist and a *presumptuous* faith, whereby we make demands of how God is to demonstrate His power. God knows best what is important to a person in animism and which demonstration of His power will have the most effect in that person's life.

One Wycliffe missionary, for example, said that God did not work healings among the tribe with whom he was working. Instead, He validated His message by giving the people dreams. Such dreams worked better than healings because dreams were an important source of information for this particular people.

The point is that we need to seek the Holy Spirit's guidance in knowing how we should pray for an animist.

While, initially, God might demonstrate His power in amazing ways in order to get the attention of the animist, the issue will quickly change from that of power to that of trusting God and of becoming conformed to His character (see Shetler, 78–79). Malcolm Hartnell, a missionary to the animistic Digo people in Kenya, Africa, stated it well when he wrote,

> If Christianity, in the person of God, simply offered a better genie than the demonic powers, Digoland would have converted a long time ago. But, of course, it does no such thing. At the heart of the Christian faith is a personal relationship with God, akin to that of a child to its parent. God does promise to meet our needs, he does promise to guide us, he does promise to give us victory over sin and Satan. But the primary goal of our relationship with God is not to get everything we want

Traditional site of Jesus' Sermon on the Mount. Jesus said, "seek first my kingdom and righteousness and all these things will be given to you as well" (Matthew 6:28–33).

but to make us more like God himself and he answers our requests according to that purpose (excerpt from Hartnell's personal prayer letter).

We need to turn the animist's heart so he or she can see his or her need for such a relationship with God.

7. Turn Their Hearts Toward Desiring a Relationship With God

Animists need to understand that God can meet both their immediate and their ultimate needs. The most urgent issue, though, is their need to break their addiction to power—and to the "powers"—and to be in a relationship with God.

Jesus addressed the issue of how the believer is to meet his or her needs:

And why do you worry about clothes? See how the lilies of the field grow. They do not labor or spin. Yet I tell you that not even Solomon in all his splendor was dressed like one of these. If that is how God clothes the grass of the field, which is here today and tomorrow is thrown into the fire, will he not much more clothe you, O you of little faith? So do not worry, saying, "What shall we eat?" or "What shall we drink?" or "What shall we wear?" For the pagans run after all these things, and your heavenly Father knows that you need them. But seek first his kingdom and his righteousness and all these things will be given to you as well (Matthew 6:28–33).

There are three things to note in the passage above that are relevant to the animist.

A. Nature Reveals God's Glory.
God is the One who is active within nature, not the spirits, for "God clothes the grass of the field." The creation reveals *God's* handiwork and displays *His* glory (Psalm 19:1), not that of the spirits! The spirits are unworthy usurpers of His glory. We should give our worship and allegiance to God alone, not to some created spirit-being.

B. God Cares.
Jesus is talking in the above passage about people's everyday needs, and He is saying that God cares about meeting such needs.

When we trust things like spirit-beings, rituals, or charms, we are actually bringing into question the

Opposite: "The Light of the World" by the English artist Holman Hunt, who used the verse "Behold I stand at the door and knock" as his theme.

goodness of God's character, for we are doubting that He cares. Jesus is saying in the above passage that, of course, God cares (see 1 Peter 5:7); and because He cares, He will provide (see Acts 14:15–17). To believe anything else is to disparage God's character and to place our trust in the creation rather than the Creator, and that is an offense to God.

Animists are, in effect, saying that those things that are created are better able to handle our concerns than is the God who has created all things (see Acts 17:29–30), thereby placing the creation above the Creator. That is idolatry! The animist must understand that God is a jealous God and that He will not tolerate such idolatry (Exodus 34:14; Deuteronomy 4:23–24; 6:13–14), for He alone is worthy of our trust and worship. He cares for us more than any spirit or god, and He alone can accomplish all that He wills (Job 23:13; 42:2).

C. Seek God First.
Our lives are not to be consumed with temporal matters. Instead, our desires are to be for God's "kingdom and his righteousness." This is where almost everyone's thinking is upside down and backwards, for most of us believe that after we take care of the everyday matters, then we can concern ourselves with God.

Jesus is saying, however, that our desire to know the eternal One is to be our first priority; God will then take care of the temporal matters. The phrase "seek first his kingdom and his righteousness" denotes being in a right relationship with God; and it is at the point of being in a right relationship with God that the two realms—the ultimate and the immediate—meet. How? Because as our ultimate needs are met by being brought into a relationship with God through faith in Jesus Christ, then God will also provide for our immediate needs. God is not moved by charms, rituals, or fetishes. He is moved by a heart that is humbled before Him (Proverbs 21:3; Psalm 51:16–17; Isaiah 66:1–2; Hebrews 10:19–22).

8. Address Their Fears

Animists live in a state of fear. They are afraid of the retribution of the spirits because of an offense, or they fear the harm an enemy can inflict on them through some form of spiritual power. But God is greater than the spirits and the powers, and He will protect us (Colossians 2:15; 1 John 4:4).

Also, the good news is that as believers in Jesus Christ we no longer need to relate to God—or to the spiritual realm—out of fear of judgment or punishment, for through Jesus Christ God has removed that reason to fear Him (Romans 8:1). The Bible says, "Perfect love drives out fear, because fear has to do with punishment" (1 John 4:18). God demonstrated that perfect love in that "while we were still sinners, Christ died for us" (Romans 5:8). Based on our faith in Christ, we can now "approach the throne of grace with confidence, so that we may receive mercy and find grace to help us in our time of need" (Hebrews 4:16)—a relevant verse for the animist.

9. Be Clear About Who Christ Is and Who We Are in Him

Jesus Christ is the Creator of all things (John 1:1; 1 Corinthians 8:6; Colossians 1:16–17; Hebrews 1:2, 10). As such, He is infinitely greater and more powerful than Satan and his demons, for they are created beings.

The power of Jesus Christ over the demons is most clearly seen in the Gospel of Mark, for there are more cases of Jesus demonstrating His power over demons (1:24–27; 1:34, 39; 3:11–12; 5:1–13; 7:25–30; 9:17–29) in the Gospel of Mark than in any other Gospel. Mark, moreover, gives examples of Jesus demonstrating His power not only over the demons but also over disease (1:30–34, 40–42; 5:25–34; 6:56), physical handicaps and deformities (2:1–12; 3:1–5; 7:33–35; 8:22–25; 10:46–52), death (5:41–42), and nature (4:35–41; 6:30–44; 6:48; 8:1–8; 11:13–14, 20–21), which are also issues of concern for the animist.

THE
OF THE
LIGHT
WORLD

BEHOLD I STAND AT THE DOOR AND KNOCK IF ANY MAN
HEAR MY VOICE AND OPEN THE DOOR I WILL COME
IN TO HIM AND WILL SVP WITH HIM AND HE WITH ME.

This ancient tomb in Jerusalem has a rolling stone door similar to the tomb where Jesus was buried.

Invite your international friend to read through the Gospel of Mark with you so you can discuss with him or her the instances of Jesus' power. Also, consider together the passages in which are described the victory that Jesus has won over Satan (Mark 3:27; Colossians 1:13–14; 2:15; Hebrews 2:14–15; 1 John 3:8).

Moreover, when a person places his or her trust in Jesus, then the following becomes true: "We know that anyone born of God [the believer] does not continue to sin; the one who was born of God [Jesus Christ] keeps him safe, and the evil one cannot harm him" (1 John 5:18). This verse points out two things that are true of the believer.

First, having believed in Christ, we are secure in Him, knowing that "the evil one cannot harm him." What this means, as Paul explains in a similar passage, is that nothing, including "demons," can "separate us from the love of God that is in Christ Jesus our Lord" (Romans 8:39). Through faith in Jesus Christ, we are now

- "children of God" (John 1:12; Galatians 3:26; Ephesians 1:5),
- "justified freely by his grace" (Romans 3:24),
- freed from condemnation (Romans 8:1),
- secure in the "love of God" (Romans 8:39),
- "holy and blameless" (Ephesians 1:4),
- freed from slavery to sin (Ephesians 1:7),
- sealed by the Holy Spirit for eternal life (Ephesians 1:14).

Satan cannot touch such truths! The second truth about the believer is that since we are "born of God," meaning the Holy Spirit has given us new life, we now have the power to "not continue to sin." Because we live in a fallen world, we are still subject to the attacks and the temptations of the evil one (Ephesians 6:16). Through the power of the indwelling Holy Spirit, however, we have the power to resist Satan (Ephesians 6:13; James 4:7; 1 Peter 5:9).

10. Point Out the Deceptive Nature of the Spirits

Satan, the "prince of this world" (John 12:31) and the "god of this age" (2 Corinthians 4:4), is a natural-born liar. His evil nature, however, is not obvious. Instead, his deception is cloaked in apparent beauty and in the promise of power.

Satan's act of deceiving humanity with the lure of power began in the Garden of Eden when the serpent promised that "you will be like God" (Genesis 3:5). And the deception continues through today. Notice, for example, the message of the human and "angelic" authors in *Ask Your Angels:*

> Slowly, surely, we are collectively emerging from this illusion of evil. To do this means to hold firmly to the understanding of God as One Power, as One Ultimate Life Principle, from which all else emanates (Daniel, 29).

Such a message is appealing in its optimism, but it is fundamentally opposed to the Christian Gospel. The message of these "angels" is that evil is an illusion (thus dismissing the necessity of Christ's atoning death) and that we are emanations from the "One Power" (thus denying that our sin has separated us from God).

Satan's plans, moreover, are not for our good, but for our destruction (John 8:44; 10:10; Hebrews 2:14); and he will use the appearance of beauty and the promise of power to lure us into that destruction (Genesis 3:6; 2 Corinthians 11:14). If we think we can see through the deception of Satan and his spirits through our own natural abilities, then one of two things is true.

First, if we are able to see through the deception of the spirits, then we should not bother following them. Because since we can see through their schemes, they would be lesser beings than we.

Second, if we are unable to see through their deception, then we would be well-advised to stay away from them.

CONCLUSION

Satan will not let go of those in his kingdom without a struggle. So, be prepared in your own life to do spiritual battle when witnessing to an animist. Have others pray for you and with you.

But also be encouraged that many animists are ripe for accepting the Gospel. Diligently seek the guidance and the power of the Holy Spirit as you share the love of Christ with your animist friend.

BIBLIOGRAPHY AND RESOURCES

Barrett, David. "Annual Statistical Table on Global Mission: 1994." *International Bulletin of Missionary Research.* Gerald Anderson, ed. New Haven, Conn.: Overseas Ministries Study Center, January 1994.

Cimino, Richard, ed. "Japan's New Religions Stress Technique, Search for Authority." *Religion Watch.* North Bellmore, N.Y.: Richard Cimino, April 1993, Vol. 8, no. 6.

Daniel, Alma, Timothy Wyllie, and Andrew Ramer. *Ask Your Angels.* New York: Ballantine Books, 1992.

Gehman, Richard. *African Traditional Religion in Biblical Perspective.* Kijabe, Kenya: Kesho Publications, 1989.

Gonzalez-Wippler, Migene. *Santeria: The Religion.* New York: Harmony Books, 1989.

Gross, Edward. Miracles, *Demons, & Spiritual Warfare.* Grand Rapids, Mich.: Baker Book House, 1990.

Henry, Rodney L. *Filipino Spirit World: A Challenge to the Church.* Manila: OMF Publishers, 1986.

Ifa. "In the news..." Chicago: Ifa Foundation of North America, Inc., August 1993.

Konya, Alex. Demons: *A Biblically Based Perspective.* Schaumburg, Ill.: Regular Baptist Press, 1990.

Lausanne Committee for World Evangelization. "Press Release: Lausanne Committee Issues Statement on Spiritual Warfare." Wheaton, Ill.: LCWE, August 27, 1993.

McCaffrey, Ray. "Commentary: Woman parted from locket that protected her." *Gazette-Telegraph.* Colorado Springs: Freedom Communications Inc., August 7, 1995.

Montgomery, John, ed. *Demon Possession.* Minneapolis: Bethany House Publishers, 1976.

Musk, Bill. *The Unseen Face of Islam.* Eastbourne, E. Sussex, UK: MARC, 1989.

Myers, Bryant. "What's going on?" *MARC Newsletter.* Monrovia, Calif.: MARC Publications, September 1994, no. 94-3.

Quicksall, Brad. "Not Always What They Appear to Be." *The Quiet Miracle.* Columbus, Ohio: Bible Literature International, Spring 1992, Vol. 70, no. 1.

Shetler, Joanne, with Patricia Purvis. *And the Word Came with Power.* Portland, Ore.: Multnomah, 1992.

Steyne, Philip. Gods of Power: *A Study of the Beliefs and Practices of Animists.* Houston: Touch Publications, 1992.

Tippett, Alan. "The Evangelization of Animists." *Let the Earth Hear His Voice.* J. D. Douglas, ed. Minneapolis: World Wide Publications, 1975.

Tippett, Alan. "Possessing the Philosophy of Animism for Christ." *Crucial Issues in Missions Tomorrow.* Donald McGavran, ed. Chicago: Moody Press, 1972.

Van Rheenen, Gailyn. *Communicating Christ in Animistic Contexts.* Grand Rapids, Mich.: Baker Book House, 1991.

Weldon, John. "Dowsing: Divine Gift, Human Ability, or Occult Powers?" *Christian Research Journal.* Elliot Miller, ed. San Juan Capistrano, Calif.: Christian Research Institute, Spring 1992, Vol. 14, no. 4.

Buddhism

Dean C. Halverson

BUDDHISM AMONG THE NATIONS

It is estimated that the number of adherents to Buddhism comprise around 6% of the world's population (Barrett, 25), although this figure is difficult to gauge because of Buddhism's ability to assimilate itself into a culture and to influence that culture's underlying beliefs.

Theravada Buddhism (the distinctions between the major forms of Buddhism will be covered later) exists primarily in Myanmar, Cambodia, Laos, Sri Lanka, and Thailand.

Mahayana Buddhism exists primarily in mainland China, Hong Kong, Japan, Taiwan, and Vietnam.

Vajrayana, or Tantric, Buddhism exists primarily in Bhutan, Mongolia, and Tibet.

THE FOUNDING OF BUDDHISM

Buddhism was founded by Siddhartha Gautama during the sixth century B.C. His life (563–483 B.C.) coincides with the time when the people of Judah were exiled in Babylon.

Buddha's life can be divided into

Golden Buddha, Thailand, Asia.

three periods: enjoyment, enquiry, and enlightenment.

The Period of Enjoyment (563–534 B.C.)*

Siddhartha Gautama was born into the warrior caste of the Shakya tribe in the town of Kapilavastu, which was at that time northeastern India but is now part of Nepal.

Tradition says that Siddhartha's father sought to shelter his son in a palace so that he would never see any form of suffering, such as old age, sickness, death, or the poverty of an ascetic. One day, however, Siddhartha ventured away from the palace and encountered all four kinds of suffering. This experience had a profound effect on him. It caused him to become disillusioned with his wealth, and he became deeply concerned about the issue of suffering.

The Period of Enquiry (534–528 B.C.)

As a result of his encounter with suffering, Siddhartha left his family—including a wife and child—and his life of luxury. He committed himself to discovering the source of suffering and how to eliminate it.

Convicted by the ascetic he had seen, Siddhartha began to practice extreme asceticism. After six years, his body became so weak because of eating so little that he almost drowned while bathing in a river. He had to grab an overhanging branch to pull himself out of the water. He realized that extreme asceticism did not produce the enlightenment he was seeking concerning the source of suffering and how to eliminate it.

The Period of Enlightenment (528–483 B.C.)

Siddhartha then ate some food and walked to a city named Bodh Gaya, where he sat under a fig tree by the edge of a river. He vowed not to rise again until he had attained enlightenment, and subsequently went into a deep state of meditation.

During his meditation, Siddhartha was severely tempted by Mara, the evil one. Siddhartha resisted her temptations, though, and after a period of time (some say one night, others as many as forty-nine days) he attained enlightenment and became the Buddha, which means "the enlightened one." (From now on, we will refer to Siddhartha as Buddha.) Bodh Gaya is now the site of the holiest shrine in the Buddhist world, the Mahabodhi ("great enlightenment") Temple.

Buddha called his path to enlightenment the Middle Way, because it avoided the extremes of both affluence and asceticism, both of which had only caused him to suffer. Shortly after his enlightenment, Buddha traveled to Benares, and in the Deer Park there he preached his first sermon—the contents of which have come to be known as the Four Noble Truths. Eventually, he won thousands of followers, who formed communities called *sanghas*.

After forty-five years of spreading his message, Buddha died, probably as a result of food poisoning. His last words were, "Decay is inherent in all component things! Work out your salvation with diligence" (Humphreys, 41).

THE SPREAD OF AND THE SPLITS WITHIN BUDDHISM

For two centuries Buddhism did not spread beyond the borders of India. Then came King Ashoka, who ruled India from 274–232 B.C. Ashoka was a warrior-king who, during one battle, became so revolted by the bloodshed that he resolved to renounce all such fighting. He subsequently converted to Buddhism and devoted himself and his resources to its propagation. Ashoka commissioned Buddhist missionaries to go to the other parts of India, as well as to Syria, Egypt, Cyrene, Greece, Sri Lanka, Myanmar, and Thailand.

*Headings on this page taken from the lecture notes of Dr Alvin Low, ACTS, PO Box 62725, Colorado Springs, CO 80962.

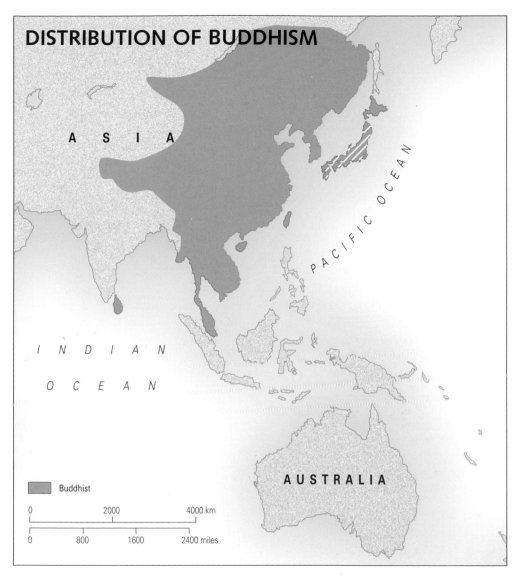

DISTRIBUTION OF BUDDHISM

A S I A

PACIFIC OCEAN

INDIAN

OCEAN

AUSTRALIA

Buddhist

0	2000	4000 km

0	800	1600	2400 miles

Around this same time a major division began to develop within Buddhism. The primary issue was whether enlightenment is accessible to everyone or to only a few. Those Buddhists who said enlightenment is accessible to everyone were called "Mahayana" ("the greater vehicle"), and those who said it is accessible to only the committed few (for instance, monks) were called "Hinayana" ("the lesser vehicle"). Being offended by the negative connotation of the term Hinayana, the latter began to refer to themselves as Theravada Buddhists, which means "the teaching of the elders."

The difference in emphasis between the two branches of Buddhism is illustrated in the difference between whether one strives to become a *bodhisattva* or an *arahat*. The *bodhisattva* (a Mahayana concept) is one who has attained enlightenment but, out of compassion for the unenlightened masses, refuses to enter *nirvana* in order to come back and guide others along the path.

The *arahat* (a Theravada concept), on the other hand, is one who is more concerned with his own enlightenment than with that of others. His primary concern is to attain enlightenment for himself by forsaking all illusion.

There are other differences between the two branches.

1. Theravada Buddhists see Buddha as being a man only and not a god. Conversely, Mahayana Buddhists view Buddha as a historical manifestation of a universal Absolute, or Buddha essence.

2. Theravada Buddhists insist there can be only one Buddha. Mahayana Buddhists say there have been many manifestations of the Buddha essence and that there will be at least one more, called the "Maitreya Buddha."

3. Whereas Theravada Buddhists teach that one must attain enlightenment solely through one's own efforts, Mahayana Buddhists teach that the *bodhisattvas* can help people along the path and can even transfer their own extra karmic merit to such seekers.

From India, Theravada Buddhism spread toward the southeastern regions of Asia, and Mahayana Buddhism spread toward the northeastern parts of Asia.

In the sixth century A.D., the Indian scholar Bodhidharma introduced Ch'an Buddhism to China (Powell, 88). Ch'an Buddhism is a technique for meditating on the "Vast Emptiness" within oneself. This form of meditation migrated to Japan in the twelfth century and was the predecessor to Zen Buddhism. Japanese scholar D. T. Suzuki was largely responsible for bringing Zen Buddhism to America during the early part of the twentieth century.

Another form of Japanese Buddhism is "Pure Land," or Jodo, Buddhism. The Pure Land is a transitional realm from which it is easier to attain *nirvana* than from the realm of the earth. One enters the Pure Land through faith in

Stone Buddha statue in a forest.

Amitabha—or Amida—Buddha and by repeating the *nembutsu* ("Namu-Amida-Butsu").

Besides the two branches of Theravada and Mahayana Buddhism, there is a third branch known as Vajrayana, or Tantra. Vajrayana Buddhism is derived from a form of Hinduism called *tantra*, which emphasizes occultic techniques for the development of spiritual power. "Vajrayana" means "the diamond vehicle," and the metaphor refers to the purity of the spiritual power being tapped into and the ability of the techniques to cut through illusions quickly so as to gain enlightenment (Yamamoto, 40).

The people of Tibet, where Vajrayana Buddhism is the predominant religion, have given the world what is probably today's most recognizable living symbol of Buddhism—the Dalai Lama. The Dalai Lama is Tibet's exiled spiritual and political leader. Tibetan Buddhists consider the Dalai Lama to be the fourteenth reincarnation of Avalokiteshvara, the *bodhisattva* of compassion (Hinnells, 336).

Besides the three branches of Buddhism mentioned above, there is also the distinction between the "official" version of Buddhism and the "folk" version. The two versions are very different from each other, and often those involved in the folk version know very little of the official version. Folk Buddhists are animistic (see chapter on animism) in that they believe spirits influence and control people's lives. They believe that people must appease the spirits in order to have success, and that they should seek the guidance of the spirits through various forms of divination.

Be aware, then, that when someone claims to be Buddhist, he or she could be referring to a folk version of Buddhism, which is animistic.

Buddhist temple, with guardian dragon, Thailand.

THE BELIEFS OF BUDDHISM

As we have already seen, there are obviously extreme variations within the religion known as Buddhism. Nevertheless, there are some beliefs that most Buddhists share. These common beliefs are contained in the most basic of Buddhist teachings: the Four Noble Truths.

The First Noble Truth
Life consists of suffering (*dukkha*). This concept of suffering includes the experiences of pain, misery, sorrow, and unfulfillment.

The Second Noble Truth
Everything is impermanent and ever-changing (the doctrine of *anicca*). We suffer because we desire those things that are impermanent.

The Third Noble Truth
The way to liberate oneself from suffering is by eliminating all desire. We must stop craving that which is impermanent.

The Fourth Noble Truth
Desire can be eliminated by following the Eightfold Path, which consists of eight points. These eight points can be categorized according to three major sections:

WISDOM (*Panna*)
1. Right Understanding
2. Right Thought

ETHICAL CONDUCT (*Sila*)
3. Right Speech
4. Right Action
5. Right Livelihood

MENTAL DISCIPLINE (*Samadhi*)
6. Right Effort
7. Right Awareness
8. Right Meditation

These eight points are not steps that must be done in sequential order. Instead, they are attitudes and actions that are to be developed simultaneously with each other (Rahula, 46).

The first two points, moreover, serve as the foundation from which the other points flow. When one has Right Understanding, for instance, he or she sees the universe as impermanent and illusory and is aware that the "I" does not, in reality, exist. Such a concept is known as the doctrine of anatta ("no self").

Right Thought follows Right Understanding in that it means to renounce all attachment to the desires and thoughts of our illusory selves.

As a person attains such a literally selfless perspective, he or she finds

Buddhist priests in yellow robes in procession, Thailand.

Buddhism and Christianity Contrasted

	THERAVADA BUDDHISM	MAHAYANA BUDDHISM	CHRISTIANITY
GOD	*Nirvana*, an abstract Void	*Nirvana*, an abstract Void, but also an undifferentiated Buddha essence	A personal God who is self-existent and changeless.
HUMANITY	An impermanent collection of aggregates	An impermanent collection of aggregates. For some, personal existence continues for a while in the Pure Land.	Made in God's image. Personal existence has value. We continue to exist as persons after death.
THE PROBLEM	We suffer because we desire that which is temporary, which causes us to continue in the illusion of the existence of individual self.	Same as Theravada	We suffer because of the consequences of our sin. But we also suffer because, being made in God's image, we are fulfilled only when we are in a relationship with our Creator God. Even though we are most fulfilled when in relationship with God, we have rebelled against Him, and are thus alienated from Him.
THE SOLUTION	To cease all desire in order to realize the nonexistence of the self, thus finding permanence	To become aware of the Buddha-nature within	To be forgiven by and reconciled with God. We find permanence in the immutability of God.
THE MEANS	*Self-reliance.* We must follow the Middle Path and accrue karmic merit.	*Self-reliance.* The means vary from that of following the Eightfold Path, to emptying the mind, to accruing merit by performing rituals, to realizing the Buddha-nature within, to depending on the merits of a *bodhisattva.*	*Reliance on God.* We must repent of our sins and trust in the saving work of Jesus Christ.
THE OUTCOME	To enter *nirvana* where the ego is extinguished	The outcome varies from that of returning as a *bodhisattva* in order to guide others, to entering *nirvana,* to living in a Pure Land from which one can enter *nirvana.*	Our existence as individuals survives death, and we are fulfilled as we are in eternal fellowship with a loving and personal God.

Contemplative head of a serene reclining Buddha, Myanmar (Burma).

the power to speak well of others (Right Speech), to obey Buddhism's moral commands or abstentions (Right Action), and to avoid making his or her living through an occupation that breaks the moral precepts of Buddhism (Right Livelihood).

At the basis of the concept of ethical conduct are the *sila*, or moral precepts. These precepts include the commands to refrain from:

1. the taking of life
   (all forms, not just human),
2. stealing,
3. immoral sexual behavior
   (monks must be celibate),
4. lying,
5. the taking of intoxicants.

While the *sila* address one's actions, the *samadhi* (mental discipline) addresses one's attitudes and state of awareness. *Samadhi* is defined as a deep state of consciousness "in which all sense of personal identity ceases" (Rice, 310). Through Right Effort one prevents evil thoughts from entering the mind; through Right Awareness

one is especially conscious of the events in one's life; and through Right Meditation one can attain the bliss of enlightenment.

Buddha's *immediate* goal was to eliminate the cause of suffering. His *ultimate* goal, though, was to become liberated from the cycle of death and rebirth (*samsara*) by teaching how we can cease craving and thereby eliminate our attachment to and beliefs in the existence of the illusory self. As we are successful in eliminating such attachment, then the effects of karma will have nothing to attach themselves to, which releases the individual from the realm of illusion. At that moment of enlightenment, the person achieves the state of *nirvana*—the ultimate goal for the Buddhist, and Buddhism's equivalent of salvation.

Buddha described *nirvana* (Pali, *nibbana*) with the following words:

There is a sphere which is neither earth, nor water, nor fire, nor air, which is not the sphere of the infinity of space, nor the sphere of the infinity of consciousness, the sphere of nothingness, the sphere of perception, or non-perception, which is neither this world, neither sun nor moon. I deny that it is coming or going, enduring, death, or birth. It is only the end of suffering (Powell, 28).

Nirvana does not mean that the person is annihilated when entering such a state, because, as Buddha reasoned, there never existed any person to be annihilated in the first place.

In regard to the *samsara* cycle (reincarnation), while Hinduism would posit an individual essence that is continuous from lifetime to lifetime, Buddhism does not teach that such a continuous essence exists. According to Buddha, no self exists that is continuous throughout the *samsara* cycle. Instead, each individual consists of a combination of five "aggregates," called *skandhas,* which include the physical body, emotions, perception, volition, and consciousness (Ch'en, 44). Death

causes these aggregates, or parts, to be dismantled, and, much like a car, it ceases to be a cohesive unit when it is taken apart piece by piece.

THE BUDDHIST SCRIPTURES

The issue of what was to be considered scripture marked another reason for the split between Theravada and Mahayana Buddhism. The Theravada Buddhists considered the canon to be closed with the Pali *Tripitaka.* "Pali" refers to the language in which it was written, and "*Tripitaka*" (also spelled *Tipitaka*) means the "three baskets" of teachings, which include Buddha's sermons, rules for monks, and philosophical teachings. The length of the *Tripitaka* is around seventy times that of the Bible (Rice, 388).

The Mahayana Buddhists, on the other hand, saw the canon as remaining open. Thus, they include in their scriptures writings from Indian,

Buddhist monk during meditation.

Wooden Buddhist temple.

Chinese, Japanese, and Tibetan sources. Some of the more popular Mahayana scriptures include the Lotus Sutra (*Saddharma-pundarika*) and the Perfection of Wisdom (*Prajna-paramita*), which in turn includes the Diamond Sutra and the Heart Sutra.

The sacred scriptures of Vajrayana Buddhism are the *Kanjur* (108 volumes) and the *Tanjur* (225 volumes; Powell, 124).

HINDRANCES TO EVANGELISM AND COMMON OBJECTIONS

1. Different Perspectives

The person influenced by Buddhism might have difficulties understanding some of the concepts of Christianity. Christians, for example, speak of a God who has emotions such as anger and love, but Buddhists see such emotions as a negative rather than something to be proud of. Such emotions indicate that such a person is still stuck in his or her attachment to the ego (Tsering, 157). By way of another example, the Christian speaks of eternal life, but the Buddhist interprets the hope of life after death as having its source in the separatistic ego, which continues to thirst after personal existence.

If the person who comes from a Buddhist background rejects your message, ask why. It might be more an issue of misunderstanding than of a conscious rejection. As one author wrote, "Most Buddhists have never heard the Gospel because they have misheard it" (Weerasingha, 62). It often takes several attempts to learn how to communicate the Gospel clearly to a Buddhist.

2. "Many Paths to God"

Most Buddhists believe that there are many paths to God. How should one address such a belief?

First, point out where the emphasis is placed in the statement, "Just as there are many paths to the top of the mountain, so there are many paths to God." The emphasis is placed on the path that we must walk. In other words, to the Buddhist, salvation is based on human effort. We are the ones who must strive to make it up the mountain. That's not good news.

Second, explain the biblical reasoning behind the exclusivity of the biblical way of salvation through the concept of reconciliation. Reconciliation refers to the restoring of a relationship that has been broken. You might pose the following question to your friend: "Assume that you are responsible for having broken a relationship with a friend because of a wrong that you committed against him or her. How many ways are there to restore that relationship?"

The answer is that there is really only one way for such a relationship to be restored: through confessing our guilt and requesting our friend's forgiveness.

In the same way, we have rebelled against the moral authority of God and have thus broken our relationship with Him. Salvation, then, is a matter of being reconciled to God (see Colossians 1:21–23). God has provided the means for reconciliation and forgiveness through Jesus Christ, as we confess our sins and place our trust in Him.

3. "Jesus Is Not Unique"

Your Buddhist friend might see Jesus as being a spiritual Master on a par with Buddha (Theravada Buddhism)

or as a *bodhisattva* (Mahayana Buddhism). Consider the differences, though, as outlined in the charts ("Buddha and Jesus" and "The *Bodhisattvas* and Jesus").

There are also several other approaches to use when addressing the issue of the uniqueness of Jesus.

1. Encourage your Buddhist friend to read the Book of John in order to learn for himself or herself who Jesus claimed to be.

2. Campus Crusade for Christ publishes a Bible study about Jesus' uniqueness: The *Uniqueness of Jesus* (San Bernardino, California: Campus Crusade for Christ International, 1983). Consider going through this study with your friend.

3. You could also encourage your friend to read *More Than a Carpenter,* by Josh McDowell.

SUGGESTIONS FOR EVANGELISM

1. Acknowledge and Affirm Your Common Ground
It is best to start with the common ground that you and your Buddhist friend have. Even though Christianity and Buddhism are irreconcilable in

Buddha and Jesus

THERAVADA BUDDHISM	CHRISTIANITY
1. Buddha did not claim to have a special relationship with God. In fact, Buddha did not consider the matter of God's existence to be important, because it did not pertain to the issue of how to escape suffering.	1. Jesus did claim to have a special relationship with God (John 3:16; 6:44; 10:30; 14:6, 9).
2. Buddha claimed to *point to the way* by which we could escape suffering and *attain* enlightenment.	2. Jesus claimed to *be the way* by which we could *receive* salvation and eternal life (John 14:6; 5:35).
3. Buddha taught that the way to eliminate suffering was by eliminating desire.	3. Jesus taught that the solution to suffering is found not in eliminating desire but in having right desire (Matthew 5:6).

The Bodhisattvas and Jesus

MAHAYANA BUDDHISM	CHRISTIANITY
1. There are many *bodhisattvas*.	1. There has been only one incarnation of the Son of God.
2. The *bodhisattvas* were motivated out of a sense of their own compassion for the world. Their compassion is not a reflection, however, of the Void's feelings toward the world.	2. Jesus is the unique demonstration of God's love for the world (John 3:16; Romans 5:8; 1 John 4:10).
3. The *bodhisattvas* view the physical world as an illusion to be escaped.	3. The Bible says that Jesus created the universe and that it was declared good (John 1:3; Genesis 1:31).
4. The *bodhisattvas* had to overcome their sin (i.e., attachment to the self, ignorance) during the process of going through numerous lifetimes.	4. Jesus was sinless from the very beginning; it did not take a process to make Him sinless (Matthew 27:4; Luke 23:41; 2 Corinthians 5:21; Hebrews 4:15).

their fundamental beliefs, there are some significant similarities on which you can build. Those similarities include the beliefs that

■ desire can cause suffering.
■ personal peace will be found when we abide in that which is permanent.
■ it is best to live a moral life.
■ self-discipline has spiritual value.
■ meditation and prayer are important.
■ compassion is a virtue that should be nurtured.

Buddhist sculptures, That Thanom, Thailand.

Offerings before a Buddhist altar, Thailand.

2. Pick Up on the Issue of Desire

Buddha taught that desire is the source of all suffering. Therefore, he contended, in order to eliminate suffering we must eliminate desire.

Such a goal is obviously difficult to attain, since it requires *desiring* to eliminate *desire*.

Gently point out that Jesus said, "Blessed are those who hunger and thirst for righteousness, for they will be filled" (Matthew 5:6). According to Jesus, then, the issue is having *right* desire, not eliminating desire altogether.

3. Be Open About Your Faith in a Personal God

One of the fundamental tenets that sets Christianity apart from Buddhism is that God is personal. Buddhists believe that ultimate reality is an impersonal Void or Emptiness (*sunyata*).

What are the implications or benefits of God's being personal? He is able to love us. He can also hear and answer our prayers. And He can empathize with our suffering (Exodus 3:7; Hebrews 4:15). A Void would not be able to do such things. Share how you have found peace and joy knowing that God loves you and that you can take your cares and concerns to Him.

4. Point to God's Permanence

Another benefit of God's being personal has to do with the issue of permanence. Buddha taught that permanence can be found only in the Void. As Christians, we can agree that we need to base our lives on that which is permanent.

The problem with the Buddhist concept of permanence, though, is that, when we find permanence in the Void, we as individuals cease to exist. Before we can find permanence, we must disappear into the Void.

Because in Christianity God is personal, we can find permanence in Him without the undesirable consequence of having to deny our value and existence as persons. The result of salvation is not the individual disappearing in the Void, but being joined in an interpersonal relationship with God.

The God of the Bible is permanent in two ways. First, He is permanent in that He is changeless in His character (Malachi 3:6; James 1:17). Second, He is permanent in that He is faithful in all that He promises (Lamentations 3:23; Hebrews 13:5).

How can we make God's permanence a part of our lives? Consider the following:

> Jesus answered .... "Do not work for food that spoils, but for food that endures to eternal life, which the Son of Man will give you. On him God the Father has placed his seal of approval."
>
> Then they asked him, "What must we do to do the works God requires?"
>
> Jesus answered, "The work of God is this: to believe in the one he has sent" (John 6:27–29).

In these verses, Jesus talks about working either "for food that spoils" (impermanence) or "for food that endures to eternal life" (permanence). We can receive the "food that endures" through faith in Jesus Christ.

5. Be Clear About the Matter of Sin and the Opportunity for Forgiveness

One thing that both Buddhism and Christianity have in common are moral precepts. The moral precepts of Buddhism, called *sila*, are similar to some of the Ten Commandments. The minimum number of *sila* mentioned among Buddhist sects is five, and they include abstaining from killing any form of life, stealing, sexually immoral behavior, lying, and the taking of intoxicants.

The difference, though, between Buddhism and Christianity is that in Buddhism when one sins—or breaks the moral precepts—the consequences have no vertical dimension. In Buddhism sin is a matter both of ignorance (a mental issue) and of karma (an issue of an impersonal moral principle, similar to a natural law). As such, sin carries no consequences with respect to breaking one's unconditional connection to the Void.

What are the implications of these two Buddhist approaches to sin—ignorance and karma?

First, because sin is a matter of ignorance, then sin is something that we alone must deal with. It's our problem, not God's. The Void is unable to be concerned about whether or not we suffer as a result of our ignorance. Moreover, the journey toward overcoming such ignorance takes innumerable lifetimes.

Second, because the law of karma is an impersonal principle similar to a law of nature, the consequences of our moral actions are inevitable. Sin, in other words, cannot be forgiven because there is no forgiver. Just as you don't ask forgiveness from the law of gravity—a natural law—neither is it possible for the law of karma to forgive.

According to Christianity, though, there is a vertical dimension to sin because God is transcendent, personal, and holy. Every relationship is governed by moral laws such as honesty, respect, and, often, fidelity. When those moral laws are broken, the relationship is strained and perhaps broken. The same is true of our relationship with God. Our sin is a reflection of our attitude of moral rebellion against the authority of a holy God (Isaiah 53:6). As such, the consequence of our sin is to cause our relationship with God to be broken.

What are the implications concerning the Christian approach to sin?

First, because God is personal He can be—and is—concerned about our suffering, and He longs for us to be in fellowship with Him.

Second, because God is personal He

is able to forgive us of our sins, which He has done through the sacrificial death of Jesus Christ.

Moreover, because the Bible says that "God is faithful [a form of permanence] and just and will forgive us our sins" (1 John 1:9) we can trust in and count on His forgiveness.

6. Use Bridges to the Good News

There are concepts within Buddhism that can be used as bridges to help Buddhists understand the Gospel.

One bridge has to do with the doctrine of the *bodhisattva*. A *bodhisattva* is one who, out of compassion, has refused to enter *nirvana* in order to assist others along the way to enlightenment. The part of this concept that is significant as a bridge to the Gospel is that the *bodhisattva* is able to transfer his extra karmic merit to the one who believes in him (Weerasingha, 75).

Another bridge is a story from Buddhist literature that could be used to illustrate the meaning of Christ's crucifixion:

Prince Mahanama, of the Shakya clan and a cousin of Buddha, had great faith in the teachings of Buddha and was one of the most faithful followers.

At the time a violent king named Virudaka of Kosala conquered the Shakya clan. Prince Mahanama went to the King and sought the lives of his people, but the King would not listen to him. He then proposed that the King let as many prisoners escape as could run away while he himself remained underwater in a nearby pond.

To this the King assented, thinking that the time would be very short for him to be able to stay underwater.

The gate of the castle was opened as Mahanama dived into the water and the people rushed for safety. But Mahanama did not come up, sacrificing his life for the lives of his people by tying his hair to the underwater root of a willow tree (*The Teaching of Buddha*, 254–255).

Note the images in the above story that illustrate the significance of Christ's sacrificial death:

Enslavement: The issue is that of enslavement—the Shakya clan was enslaved to a wicked king; humanity is enslaved to sin (John 8:34; Romans 6:6,16).

One Died for All: The death of one resulted in freedom for all—Mahanama's death resulted in the freedom of the Shakya clan from bondage to the king; Christ's death resulted in our freedom from bondage to sin (Matthew 20:28; Romans 5:18–19).

Motivated by Love: The act was freely chosen, and the motivation was that of love—as Mahanama voluntarily chose to die out of love for his people, so Christ also freely gave up His life out of love for all humanity (John 10:11–18; 13:1, 34).

Salvation Is Free: The salvation offered is free for the taking—those in the Shakya clan could receive their freedom from bondage simply by running from the kingdom; people can receive the gift of salvation simply by placing their faith in the atoning work of Jesus Christ (Romans 3:20–24; Ephesians 2:8–9).

GLOSSARY OF BUDDHISM

Anatta: "No self." The doctrine that no continuous self exists.

Anicca: The doctrine that says everything is impermanent, changing, and in a constant state of flux.

Lama (Tibetan): Teacher.

Mantra: "Thought form" (Rice, 247). A mental aid for meditation.

Nirvana (Pali, *nibbana*): Literally, "to extinguish," as in blowing out a flame; the goal of enlightenment.

Rinpoche (Tibetan): "Precious one." A word of honor that is often found at the end of the name of a Tibetan lama.

Samadhi: A state of concentration in which one loses the sense of the individual self.

Samsara: The cycle of life, death, and rebirth.

Satori: The state where, through Zen meditation, all thought ceases.

Skandhas: The combination of five elements, or aggregates, that come together to form a person.

Sunyata: The Buddhist concept of Void, or Emptiness, in which there is no substance, no concept of self, and no duality (*Teaching*, 118).

Tanha: The desire and craving that causes rebirth.

Tulku (Tibetan): Literally, "incarnation." A *tulku* "is a person who is a mystical emanation from a famous teacher or deity" (Tsering, 153).

Yana: A "vehicle" or a "way" of spiritual progress (as in Mahayana).

BIBLIOGRAPHY AND RESOURCES

Barrett, David. "Annual Statistical Table on Global Mission: 1994." *International Bulletin of Missionary Research.* Gerald Anderson, ed. New Haven, Conn.: Overseas Ministries Study Center, January 1994.

Ch'en, Kenneth K. S. *Buddhism.* Woodbury, N.Y.: Barron's Educational Series, Inc., 1968.

Hinnells, John R., ed. *A Handbook of Living Religions.* New York: Penguin, 1984.

Humphreys, Christmas. *Buddhism.* Baltimore, Md.: Penguin, 1951.

Lausanne Committee for World Evangelization. "Christian Witness to Buddhists." *Lausanne Occasional Papers,* no. 15. Wheaton, Ill.: LCWE, 1980.

McDowell, Josh. *More Than a Carpenter.* Wheaton, Ill.: Tyndale House Publishers, 1977.

McDowell, Josh and Don Stewart. *Understanding Non-Christian Religions.* San Bernardino, Calif.: Here's Life Publishers, 1982.

Powell, Andrew. *Living Buddhism.* New York: Harmony Books, 1989.

Rahula, Walpola. *What the Buddha Taught.* New York: Grove Press, 1974.

Rice, Edward. *Eastern Definitions.* Garden City, N.Y.: Anchors Books, 1980.

Seamonds, John. *Tell It Well: Communicating the Gospel Across Cultures.* Kansas City, Mo.: Beacon Hill Press, 1981.

The Teaching of Buddha. Tokyo: Buddhist Promoting Foundation, 1966.

Tsering, Marku. *Sharing Christ in the Tibetan Buddhist World.* Upper Darby, Penn.: Tibet Press, 1988.

Weerasingha, Tissa. "Concepts of Salvation in Buddhism." *Evangelical Review of Theology.* Exeter, Devon, U.K.: Paternoster Press; January 1991.

Yamamoto, J. Isamu. *Beyond Buddhism.* Downers Grove, Ill.: InterVarsity, 1982.

Yamamoto, J. Isamu. "Buddhism in America," a four-part series. *Christian Research Journal.* San Juan Capistrano, Calif.: Christian Research Institute, Spring/Summer 1994, Fall 1994, Winter 1995, Spring 1995.

ORGANIZATION

Jim Stephens
Sonrise Center for Buddhist Studies
P.O. Box 116
Sierra Madre, CA 91025
Phone: (626) 797-9008
http://www.sonrisecenter.org/contact.html

Confucianism
Thomas I. S. Leung

NUMBER OF ADHERENTS

Confucianism is not a formal religion in the conventional sense. It is a religious belief-system that forms the values that are implicit to most Asian people.

This massive group of people includes the Chinese, Japanese, Korean, and Vietnamese. It is estimated that there are 1.3 billion Chinese, 126 million Japanese, 26 million Koreans, and 74 million Vietnamese. If we take about 90% of this total who are consciously or unconsciously influenced by this Confucian worldview, the total number would be around a billion and a half.

East Asia is experiencing a resurgence of interest in Confucianism. Marxism is on the decline in China, and the people are looking for a spiritual foundation for their values that is both contemporary and Chinese. The rulers of China are not opposed to this resurgence of Confucianism because it emphasizes loyalty.

Statue of Confucius at Confucian temple, Jiangsu Province, Nanjing, China.

THE INFLUENCE OF CONFUCIANISM

The Confucian work ethic is regarded by many as the basis for the amazingly rapid economic growth in East Asia today. It is safe to say that approximately one quarter of the world's population lives under such a work ethic.

1. The Confucian work ethic is a strong commitment to the family. Loyalties in the family are established during the present lifetime and then continued after death.

2. It is founded on a strong moral ethic of practicing virtues, giving words of wisdom, doing good works, and having the attitudes of loyalty, trustworthiness, and respect.

3. It is oriented toward the "eternal" but in a temporal sense. Such an idea sounds contradictory, but the concept of the eternal in Confucianism is not that of the continuation of the person in a transcendent life in heaven. Instead, it is the continuation of the person's

ethical influence on the thoughts and values of his or her descendants. As Chan writes, the ancestors' "influence [is] exerted not through their power but through their moral example and inspiration" (Chan, 4).

THE FOUNDING PHILOSOPHY OF CONFUCIANISM

The challenge the ancient Chinese people faced was to unite and harmonize the various tribes that populated the vast plains along the Yellow River. During the Chou Dynasty (1122–897 B.C.), the Duke of Chou solved this problem by establishing the Ritual-Music Culture, which was a rationalistic/humanistic order that emphasized the need for harmony in human relationships (for further discussion on the Ritual-Music Culture, see "The History of Taoism" in the chapter on Taoism). In the ancient scripture called *The Book of Rites*, it was stated that "music can

Confucian temple, Taipei, Taiwan.

promote harmony." Yu Tze, one of Confucius' disciples, also stated that "the function of rites is harmony." The Ritual-Music Culture was a cultural order of harmony that lent itself to the integration of many different tribes co-existing with each other.

The political ideal that was hoped would be established by the Ritual-Music Culture was not realized, however, partly because the Duke of Lu failed to follow the prescribed norms.

By the time of Confucius (551–479 B.C.), this culture had collapsed, taking virtue and social order with it. This collapse gave rise to the problem of how to reconstruct the ideal cultural-political order.

Confucius, which is the Latinized version of the Chinese name K'ung Fu-tzu ("Grand Master K'ung"), was the prime minister of the *State of Lu* and a well-educated intellectual who was passionately committed to maintaining the Ritual-Music Culture. In an effort to restore the cultural-political order of the day, he left his home at the age of fifty-six and traveled extensively throughout China, hoping to persuade the lords and dukes to follow the rites of the Ritual-Music Culture. Confucius' hope was "to bring peace and security to the people." His quest to establish a cultural-political order in which there was such peace and security failed, however. So, at the age of sixty-eight he returned home to teach and to

Oldest surviving Confucian temple (1665), Tainan, Taiwan.

THE THREE ASPECTS OF JEN

THE GOAL	*Jen* is the goal of an ideal humanity that is symbolized in the *Analects* by the terms "superior man," "gentry intellectual," and a "person of *jen*." It refers to an ideal whereby the individual has actualized his or her full potential and is manifesting his or her moral perfection.
THE PROCESS	*Jen* is the human process that is needed to reach the goal of the ideal person. Included in this process are the practices of self-reflection, self-cultivation, and moral responsibility.
THE FOUNDATION	*Jen* is the true nature that resides within each person. According to Confucianism, this true nature is good.

THE EARLY CONFUCIANIST WORLDVIEW

TRUE HUMANITY	*Jen* ("true humanity") is the basic human quality that is originally good. It provides the source and foundation for all virtues and rites.
THE MANDATE FROM HEAVEN	*Jen* is the moral "mandate from heaven." The normal understanding of the phrase "mandate from heaven" would imply an anthropomorphic kind of God who makes moral decrees. Such is not the case in Confucianism, however. Instead, the mandate from "heaven" refers to the natural law or moral order within things.
THE BASIS FOR HARMONY	The harmonious way of living must be based on the person's realization and actualization of *jen*.

write. (At seventy-three, he died.)

As a result of the failure to change the culture, Confucius asked himself: Does the failure to reconstruct a harmonious cultural order mean that the concepts of virtue or goodness are not eternal and transcendent? Are good and evil merely relative? If not, what then are the foundations of virtue and goodness? Thus, the problem became a philosophical/metaphysical one: "What is the foundation of virtue and goodness in an age of confusion?"

While searching for an answer to this problem, Confucius went to a deep level with respect to human nature—the moral level—in order to establish harmony. In other words, Confucius called for each person to reflect seriously concerning his or her moral decisions and to act responsibly in the face of adversity.

This sense of moral responsibility served as the foundation for the Ritual-Music Culture, but that culture collapsed. Confucius was finding, though, that the foundation for such moral responsibility still existed in the moral consciousness of the individual, specifically in the *jen. Jen,* which can be translated simply as "humanity," refers to the ideal goodness—or "good nature"—that resides within each individual. This "good nature" is

the source from which all virtues flow. Through *jen* each individual has the potential to actualize his or her "good nature" and thereby to realize an ideal state of life.

Instead of striving to reestablish the entire cultural/political order in an effort to reconstruct the Ritual-Music Culture, Confucius aimed to communicate the need for each individual to transform himself or herself. He called for each individual to return to his or her original humanity—*jen*—and then to actualize it through moral practice and cultivation. Confucius, in other words, was humanistic in his orientation in that he found the solution to the cultural crisis in humanity itself, not in anything religious or spiritual. Chan writes, Confucius "was looking to ideal men rather than to a supernatural being for inspiration" (Chan, 15).

Following Confucius, Mencius (372–289 B.C.) developed concepts such as *hsin* ("heart-mind") and *hsing* ("human nature"). When those two terms are combined as *hsin-hsing* ("heart-mind nature"), they refer to the original goodness that resides within all humans. Through self-reflection and self-cultivation one can realize his or her good nature and hence discover "heaven" in the

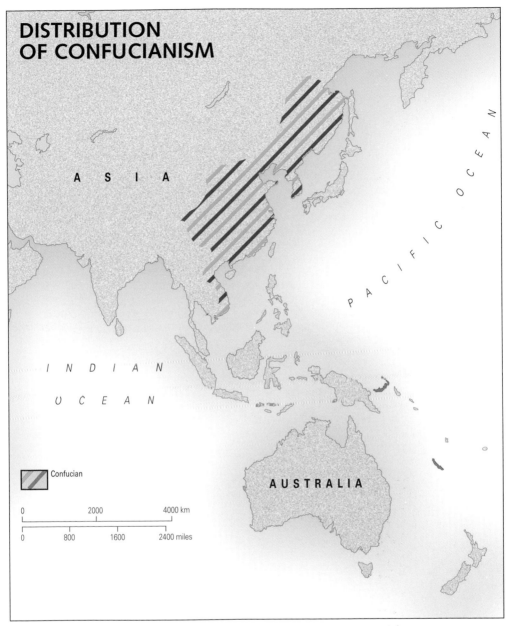

DISTRIBUTION OF CONFUCIANISM

A S I A

PACIFIC OCEAN

I N D I A N   O C E A N

Confucian

| 0 | 2000 | 4000 km |

| 0 | 800 | 1600 | 2400 miles |

AUSTRALIA

"heart-mind nature." For Confucianists, this is the way by which to approach Ultimate Reality.

Instead of the Western way of proving the existence of an external and transcendent God, Mencius provided an inward way of knowing "heaven." If human beings continue to extend and to nourish this goodness, "heaven" can be served and peace can be achieved on earth.

With respect to humanity's being by nature good, Mencius emphasized that teaching to an even greater extent than did Confucius. He wrote, "Man's nature is naturally good just as water naturally flows downward" (Chan, 52), and "If you let people follow their feelings (original nature), they will be able to do good" (Chan, 54).

The early Confucianist worldview, is summarized in the chart on page 70.

In the second century B.C., the Emperor Han Wu-Ti adopted Confucianism as the official ideology of China. All other schools of thought were considered to be heretical and were therefore excluded. Confucianism became part of the imperial order, and Confucianists became the literate elite who entered the monarchy and became advisers in the royal court.

The imperial academy was founded in 124 B.C. The Confucian Code of Conduct became the theme used for education.

Under imperial Confucianism, the literate elite became the ruling class in China. Culture and politics were integrated together in that the Confucian culture justified the political system, and the political system protected the culture.

After Buddhism was introduced into China in the second century A.D., it spread rapidly and dominated the religious thoughts of the Chinese people from A.D. 500–850. Confucian ideology, although still holding the ruling power, was severely challenged.

In the Sung Dynasty (A.D. 960–1368), there arose a Confucian revival movement known as Neo-Confucianism. Neo-Confucian philosophers integrated Buddhist teaching into Confucianism.

By way of responding to the Buddhist teaching on the "ontology of Emptiness" (Ultimate Reality is a nothingness), however, the Neo-Confucianists developed the concept of *Tien-li* ("the Heavenly Principle"). *Tien-li* is the innate moral nature and the source of moral goodness in *hsin-hsing* ("heart-mind nature"). The Neo-Confucianists were saying that the being of humanity and the world is not empty, but it is, instead, a world of creativity with the principle of goodness as its foundation.

The Neo-Confucianists reaffirmed Confucius as the Sage, and then brought Mencius into the status of orthodoxy, recognizing him as the Second Sage. Confucianism was

thereby reestablished as the orthodox ideology until the early 1900s, the beginning of the Republic of China in 1911.

During the early twentieth century, frustrated Chinese intellectuals blamed Confucianism for China's failure to modernize. This fact became especially evident during the May Fourth Movement of 1919. At that time, when Chinese intellectuals were looking for a new ideology to replace Confucianism, Mao entered the scene and introduced his Communist ideology.

After the feverish pitch of the 1949 Revolution and the birth of the People's Republic of China, everyone in China embraced the new Communist ideology. Confucianism was criticized as counter-revolutionary and as a feudalistic poison.

The honeymoon with Mao's Communist ideology was relatively short-lived, however, mostly because of the painful experience of the Cultural Revolution during the 1960s. Reflections on traditional Chinese values became a new trend during the 1980s. Then, in the early 1990s, many scholars reaffirmed Confucianism and proclaimed that the stage was set for a new cultural revival in China.

THE CONFUCIAN CANON

The canon of Confucianism begins with the Five Classics: *I-Ching* ("The Book of Changes"), *Shi* ("The Book of Poetry and Songs"), *Shu* ("The Book of Documents"), *Li* ("The Book of Rites"), and *Chun-Chiu* ("The Book of Spring and Autumn," or "The Chronicles of History").

Since *The Book of Rites* and *The Book of Spring and Autumn* contain three books of commentary each, the total number of classics is nine. Adding another four books—the *Analects, Meng-Zi* ("The Book of Mencius"), *Erh-Ya* ("The Book of Ancient Words"), and *Hsiao-Ching* ("The Book of Filial Piety")—makes for the grand total of thirteen classics,

THE CONFUCIANIST WORLDVIEW

GOD	Before the time of Confucius, God was spoken of as a personal Being and was called *Ti* or *Shang-ti*. Confucius, however, spoke of Ultimate Reality as T'ien, which had the less personal meaning of "Heaven" (Chan, 16).
THE MANDATE FROM "HEAVEN"	The moral order of things within nature. If there is to be harmony within a culture, humanity will strive to abide by this moral order.
CENTRAL CONCERN	The central concern of Confucianism is to affirm humanity's inherent goodness and to look for a way to actualize it.
HUMAN NATURE	Human nature is considered to be basically good and potentially perfect. Evil comes only when we are forced to act in an evil way or when we allow our minds to fall toward such an evil inclination.
THE WAY TO ACTUALIZATION	The way to actualize this goodness is through education, self-reflection, self-cultivation, and by behaving in accordance with the established norms of culture.
THE WORLD	The world is perceived as a place where one's purpose is to practice goodness, to love one another, and to work hard so as to nourish the earth. A person who actualizes his or her inner goodness will be a co-worker of "heaven." He or she will also be a person who is creative in bringing goodness to human beings and to other things. Such a person will then realize the harmony that is supposed to exist between humanity and nature.
HEAVEN	The attaining of heaven in the Christian sense is not a concern in Confucianism. Instead, heaven exists only as the foundation for the creativity that manifests itself in the whole world. Heaven is sometimes perceived as personal, but at other times it is simply a creative moral power and an impersonal principle.

or thirteen scriptures. These constitute the canon of Confucian scripture.

The neo-Confucianists of the thirteenth century considered the books *Meng-Zi, Chung Yung,* and *Da Hsueh* as the orthodox interpretation of Confucius' thoughts. Chu Hsi, a Neo-Confucian teacher, grouped these three books with the *Analects* (the collections of the sayings of Confucius), and, by doing so, provided a program for learning and self-cultivation. This collection was known as *The Four Books,* and they became the official standard for educators after the fourteenth century A.D. Chan writes,

These four books and Chu Hsi's commentaries on them were the basis of the civil service examinations from 1313 till 1905, replacing other Classics in importance and influence (Chan, 51).

SUGGESTIONS FOR EVANGELISM

The following is a suggested method for sharing the Gospel with those influenced by Confucianism. It has several characteristics. First, it comes from a standpoint of *humility* in that it appreciates the wisdom that is to be found in Confucianism.

Second, it is *comprehensive,* which is important to the Asian people. Why? Because the Asian standard of truth is based more on the comprehensiveness of a worldview than on how tight is its logic. The Asian people consider logic to be on the lower levels of understanding with respect to truth. Reality is perceived instead as being holistic. The more comprehensive a theory is the closer it is to the truth. Christian faith is more comprehensive because it goes beyond the "earthly" to the characteristics of heaven and it provides an explanation for why we can't live up to the moral standard that is set forth in Confucianism.

Third, the evangelistic approach given below intends to *fulfill* the Asian tradition of wisdom, not to discredit it.

Fourth, this approach *invites* the Asian to open his or her mind critically, to transcend his or her own spiritual horizon, and to enter into an experience of redemption through Jesus Christ.

Dragon on roof of Confucian temple, Taipei, Taiwan.

Here is the approach:

1. Humanity's Moral Goodness
Start from the description of the Confucian experience of the moral goodness of human nature, and the common human quest for justice. Mencius said, "The feeling of right and wrong is found in all men" (Chan, 54).

He also said, "All men have the mind which cannot bear [to see the suffering of] others" (Chan, 65). The implication of this statement, which expresses the feeling of sympathy common to all persons, is drawn out in the next point.

2. The Transcendent Root of Humanity's Goodness
The implication of humanity's goodness, quest for justice, and the "feeling of right and wrong" is that such things are rooted in something transcendent, something beyond and other than ourselves. Such things have little moral force or substance if they are founded only in personal

Teacher Day, celebrating the birth of Confucius, Taiwan.

preference or social mores.

Also, what is the metaphysical root of our sympathy for the suffering of others, which Mencius said "All men have"? If heaven is an impersonal principle, then is not our suffering the result of our living against the moral laws, or the moral order, of the universe? In other words, do we not reap what we have sown? Heaven, then, would not care about our suffering.

Is not our sense of sympathy better rooted in a personal God who is capable of caring about the suffering of others?

3. Evidences for God Being Personal

The nature of the transcendent on which human goodness and justice is founded is best characterized as personal, for an impersonal principle is not able to make such moral distinctions.

Confucius had depersonalized the Ultimate by speaking of that Ultimate in terms of *T'ien* ("heaven") rather than in terms of *Ti* or *Shang-ti*. Nevertheless, there are indications in the *Analects* that show that Confucius still considered the Ultimate to have personal attributes. For example, the following is written in the *Analects:*

> Confucius said, "Alas! No one knows me!" Tzu-kung said, "Why is there no one that knows you?" Confucius said, "I do not complain against Heaven. I do not blame men. I study things on the lower level but my understanding penetrates the higher level. It is Heaven that knows me" (Chan, 43).

To "know" someone is one of the characteristics of a personal Being, but not of an impersonal principle. In this regard, then, Confucius was attributing to "heaven" personal characteristics.

Another way to point to God as being personal is by noting how the harmony talked about in Confucianism is based on the five basic relationships. The five relationships are:

- ruler to subject,
- parent to child,
- husband to wife,

■ older to younger,
■ friend to friend.

The point is that Confucianism is saying that the context for meaning in life has to do with our relationships with each other. It is unthinkable for a Confucianist to consider life outside of such relationships.

If, though, these relationships supply the context for meaning on the human level, then how could it be that the greatest context—that of our relationship to Ultimate Reality— would be anything less than personal? If God were less than personal, would that not detract from the importance of even the personal relationships here on earth? If God *is* personal, do not the relationships on earth take on even greater meaning in that they point to the various ways—loyalty, respect, obedience, honesty, fidelity—in which we are to relate to God?

4. The Nature of Humanity Was Originally Good

Confucius and especially Mencius taught that humanity is by nature good. The term they used to refer to this original goodness is *hsin-hsing* ("heart-mind nature").

As Christians, we can agree with Confucianism in the idea that humanity was *originally* good. In other words, at the point of creation God created humanity in His image and declared His human creation, along with the rest of creation, to be good (Genesis 1:31).

5. The Silent God

Confucianists consider heaven to be silent:

Confucius said, "I do not wish to say anything." Tzu-kung said, "If you do not say anything, what can we little disciples ever learn to pass on to others?" Confucius said, "Does Heaven (*T'ien*, Nature) say anything? The four seasons run their course and all things are produced. Does Heaven say anything?" (Chan, 47).

In other words, just as Confucius

could teach even though he said nothing, so heaven can teach, even though it is silent. Mencius, too, taught that "Heaven does not speak" (Chan, 77).

Such a "silent God" is the biblical equivalent of general revelation, whereby "the heavens declare the glory of God; the skies proclaim the work of his hands" (Psalm 19:1).

While teaching can indeed take place through silence, neither Confucius nor Mencius used only silence to teach. After all, Confucius used speech to say that he would be silent. If Confucius and Mencius used speech to teach, which they did, then why did they feel it was necessary to say that heaven—or God—could teach *only* through silence?

Invite the Confucianist to consider the possibility that God could speak to humanity, especially if He is personal; and that a loving God would desire to do so.

Also, help the Confucianist become aware that as Christians we believe God has spoken to us through the incarnation of Jesus Christ (John 1:1; Hebrews 1:1–2) and through the Bible (2 Timothy 3:16; 2 Peter 1:21).

6. Humanity Is Not Only Good

While we experience that humanity is good, we do not experience that humanity is *only* good. We also experience that humanity is bad. Our experience of the badness of humanity does not square with the most fundamental premise of Confucianism, which is that humanity is in its very nature good. If it is true that humanity is by nature good, then wouldn't the doing of that which is good come more naturally and easily to us?

Does our experience confirm such natural goodness? For example, do our thoughts naturally tend toward kindness when people speak evil of us? Do we automatically desire to love those who have wronged us? If someone has been promoted ahead of us, do we immediately consider them more worthy than we and want to congratulate them?

Confucius said, "I have never seen one who really loves humanity" (Chan, 26). Why is that? If our nature is good, then love should come naturally.

Even Confucius acknowledged that "the way of the superior man is threefold, *but I have not been able to attain it*" (Chan, 42, emphasis added). Similarly, Mencius said, "No one can develop his original endowment to the fullest extent" (Chan, 54). Why, though, is such attainment so difficult if, as Confucius writes, "Man is born with uprightness" (Chan, 29)?

Mencius gives two reasons why we do evil and why attaining the standard of goodness is difficult.

First, he says we are forced to do evil:

> Man's nature is naturally good just as water naturally flows downward. There is no man without this good nature; neither is there water that does not flow downward. Now you can strike water and cause it to splash upward over your forehead, and by damming and leading it, you can force it uphill. Is this the nature of water? It is the forced circumstance that makes it do so. Man can be made to do evil, for his nature can be treated in the same way (Chan, 52).

Second, we do evil because we allow our minds to fall into it:

> In good years most of the young people behave well. In bad years most of them

Opposite: Hand-carved wooden figurine of Confucius, Taipei, Taiwan.

abandon themselves to evil. This is not due to any difference in the natural capacity endowed by Heaven. The abandonment is due to the fact that the mind is allowed to fall into evil (Chan, 55).

Notice how Mencius's two explanations work against each other. In the former, Mencius says our natural inclination is to do good and that we do evil only when forced; in the latter, he says that if we allow our mind to go in the way that is natural, it will be inclined to "fall into evil."

Which is it? Do we naturally tend toward goodness or toward evil? If it is toward goodness, then why did Confucius have to give us his version of the Golden Rule: "Do not do to others what you do not want them to do to you" (Chan, 39). If we were by nature good, why would we even need such a reminder?

Consider with your friend the struggle that Paul experienced: "I have the desire to do what is good, but I cannot carry it out" (Romans 7:18). Which idea better describes our internal state: the idea that we are by nature good and that doing the good comes easily and naturally to us, or that we are torn between the good and the bad and that we often disappoint ourselves in our inability to do the good?

On June 4, 1989, evidence for the truth of the Christian perspective was made painfully clear in the way the Communist government responded in such a brutal way to the demonstrators for democracy in Tiananmen Square. One Chinese student said, "Christianity is a very realistic religion because unlike our traditional Chinese religions, it starts from the premise that what is wrong with the world is mankind, not circumstances—this attracts us!" (MacMillan, 3). A Chinese professor concurred, "June 4 has impressed upon the people that man is bad; but all the Chinese religions teach that man is good, so they have to turn to Christianity. It is the only realistic religion" (MacMillan, 3).

7. Humanity's Core Problem

Why do we experience such a dichotomy of "natures"—desiring to do good but doing the opposite? Perhaps it is because we are made in the image of a holy God, but we have rebelled against God. As a result, it is that rebellion that is at the core of who we are. Seeking to be independent from God is what drives us, not the good nature within.

As a result, we are no longer intent on seeking after God or even following after the image of God, which is the pattern for goodness within us. Instead, our quest is for mortal things and for finding our satisfaction and security in created things—money, education, and success—rather than in God. These are not wrong in themselves, but they are wrong when they replace our relationship with God.

Confucius said, "He who commits a sin against Heaven has no god to pray to" (3:12; Chan, 25). The implication is that we have no God to pray to because through our sin we have separated ourselves from Him (see Colossians 1:21).

Humanity's core problem is that we have chosen to separate ourselves from God.

8. The Need for Reconciliation

Because our core problem is a broken relationship with God—the result of evil choices on our part—what is needed is to restore that relationship. Such a reconciliation cannot be accomplished through our own human effort. God, who has been wronged, cannot be forced to be reconciled. He must choose to reveal himself to us.

9. The Speaking God

In this sense, human beings need a "speaking God"—One who reveals His plan of forgiveness and reconciliation to humanity. Such a plan cannot be discovered through human means alone.

Confucius, however, did not offer the possibility of forgiveness. Instead, he said, "Man is born with

uprightness. If one loses it he will be lucky if he escapes with his life" (Chan, 29). Similarly, Mencius said, "Humanity [*jen*] is man's mind and righteousness is man's path. Pity the man who abandons the path and does not follow it" (Chan, 58). Such statements do not speak of forgiveness.

God, on the contrary, has revealed His plan for forgiveness and reconciliation, which was provided for us through the death and resurrection of Jesus Christ:

> God was reconciling the world to himself in Christ, not counting men's sins against them (2 Corinthians 5:19).

> This is love: not that we loved God, but that he loved us and sent his Son as an atoning sacrifice for our sins (1 John 4:10).

> If we confess our sins, he is faithful and just and will forgive us our sins and purify us from all unrighteousness (1 John 1:9).

OBJECTIONS TO CHRISTIANITY RAISED BY EAST ASIAN PEOPLE

Objection 1: "If humanity can only be saved by Christ, then it excludes the possibility of non-Christians to achieve a good personality. It is obvious, however, that certain Chinese non-Christians do in fact achieve good personalities through self-cultivation and self-reflection with the methods of their traditional philosophy and cultural wisdom."

Suggested Response: Distinguishing between creation and redemption, we see that a non-Christian might be able to achieve a certain level of personal goodness by actualizing certain good principles in creation. They cannot, however, be deemed to be "saved," for the experience of being saved is of the highest level (righteous) and can be actualized only through the redemption of God, which was accomplished through Jesus Christ.

Conversely, the term "not-yet-saved" does not mean that Christians are to look down on the experience of non-Christians. We must differentiate between actualizing goodness and being saved. "Being saved" is an experience of *faith,* whereas "actualizing goodness" is an issue of *behavior.* The former is an interpersonal experience with God; the latter is a human/moral experience not directly related to God.

Objection 2: "The distinction between general revelation and special revelation is unfair to other religions, and it also projects an imperialistic image of Christianity perceiving itself as being spiritually higher and more special."

Suggested Response: Replace the distinction between "general" and "special" revelation with a distinction between the "silent God" and the "speaking God." This will eliminate the emotional implications of these two terms.

Objection 3: "From a cultural point of view, Christianity, as a guest in East Asian countries, should be humble, and certainly should not seek to proclaim itself as higher than the host."

Suggested Response: We as Christians must demonstrate through our lives that we are humble enough to open our minds to appreciate the wisdom that is found in Confucianism. Only then can we credibly invite non-Christians to open their minds and to enter into the experience of redemption through faith in Jesus Christ, that is, to accept Christ as their own personal Savior.

Objection 4: "The concept of *T'ien* (Heaven) is both transcendent and immanent, which is more comprehensive than the Christian God, who is only transcendent but not immanent."

Suggested Response: The God of the Bible is not only transcendent but also immanent. God "sustains all things by

his powerful word" (Hebrews 1:3; see also John 1:1–3; Colossians 1:17). He is immanent because He is present to all things; there is no place where we can hide from God: "For he is not far from each one of us. For in him we live and move and have our being" (Acts 17:27–28).

In an even greater way, God is immanent through the Holy Spirit who indwells those who believe (2 Timothy 1:14; see also Romans 8:9–11; 1 Corinthians 6:19).

If a Confucianist questions the immanence of the Christian God, the Christian could in turn question the transcendence of the Confucian *T'ien*. Confucianists define *T'ien* as the moral order within things. In what way is *T'ien* transcendent and therefore more comprehensive? If the Confucianist acknowledges that *T'ien* is transcendent, or other than his creation, then it would seem that he or she would not be far from being able to understand that God is personal and that we have separated ourselves from God through sin.

CONSIDERING THE ISSUE OF ANCESTOR WORSHIP

From classical records, it is found that Chinese people worshiped the *Ti* (Creator) even before the Spring and Autumn periods (771–221 B.C.). God the Creator, however, seemed to be too far away from the human world. Therefore, philosophers like Confucius and Mencius transformed the concept of God to the idea of *T'ien* ("heaven"), which is the creative ground for all things, including humanity.

For the common person (the non-philosophers), they perceived that their ancestors were transcendent figures who were seen as living somewhere close to God. The rise of

ancestral worship shows how the ancient Chinese people were searching for a mediator to bridge the gap between themselves and God.

The original philosophical wisdom behind ancestral worship, according to Confucius, was to promote a sense of respectfulness toward the ancestors rather than to worship some invisible ghost or spirit. The distortion of this wisdom developed later when Buddhism introduced the cosmology of reincarnation.

As they began to view the deceased as those who continued on after death, they started to believe that ancestors existed somewhere as spirits. They also began to see them as being able to give blessings or curses. As a result, their fortunes became tied to the graces of their ancestors. Since then, ancestral worship has become a behavior based on superstition and appeasement.

From the Christian point of view, the original Confucian wisdom that emphasized the sense of respectfulness is not contradictory to biblical teachings. Christians also respect and remember their ancestors. It is not against biblical principles that some sort of memorial service for ancestors and parents can be developed in churches for Asian people.

Christians, however, cannot worship their ancestors and perceive them as gods or spirits who must be appeased. To do so is not only superstitious, it is disrespectful to the deceased.

The only true mediator between God and mankind is Jesus Christ (1 Timothy 2:5). Through Him, we can become children of God (John 1:12). A transcendent ethical relationship can then be developed, and the quest of Confucius, that ancient sage, is then fulfilled.

GLOSSARY OF COMMON CONFUCIAN TERMS

Chi (qì): The vital force. Originally means "breath" or "air." It is considered to be the dynamic principle that manifests all material things.

Hsin (xīn): The human heart-mind.

Hsing (xing): The nature of all things. When phrased with *Hsin,* as in *hsin-hsing*, it means "human nature" and is perceived as originally good.

Li (lǐ): The rites, the norms of behavior, especially in social relationships.

Jen (rén): Humanity, heavenly principle in the human heart-mind. *Jen* is the foundation for the virtues such as love, respectfulness, loyalty, forgiveness, etc.

Tai-Chi (tài jí): The Great Ultimate, the impersonal source of creativity that manifests the *yin-yang* forces and subsequently all things in the universe.

Tao (dāo): The Way, or the principle of everything; also the way of sage-rulership.

T'ien (tiān): Heaven, the source of all value and human goodness. It is sometimes referred to as the silent, personal God. Mostly, it is referred to as the ultimate creative force, and thus impersonal, from which all things flow.

Yin-yang (yīn yáng): The two forms of the force called *Tai-Chi,* the interaction of which results in the manifestation of all things, all situations, and all events in this universe.

BIBLIOGRAPHY AND RESOURCES

A. CLASSICAL TEXTS

The Analects
Translated by Lau, D. C.
  Harmandsworth: Penguin
  Books, 1979.
Translated by Legge, J. in the
  Chinese Classics, Vol. 1.
  Oxford: Clarendon Press,
  1893, pp. 137–354.

Centrality and Commonality
An essay on Chung-Yung,
  translated and commented on
  by Tu, Wei-ming. Honolulu:
  The University of Hawaii
  Press, 1976.

Chung Yung
Reflections on Things at Hand,
  translated by Chan, Wing-tsit.
  New York: Columbia
  University Press, 1967.

I Ching and I Chuan
Translated by Leger, J. New
  York: Dover, 1963.
Translated by Wilhelm, R. and
  rendered into English by
  Bayness, C. F. New York:
  Princeton, 1950.

B. CHINESE PHILOSOPHY AND RELIGION IN GENERAL

Bieler, Stacey and Dick Andrews.
  China at Your Doorstep:
  Christian Friendships with
  Mainland Chinese. Downers
  Grove, Ill.: InterVarsity Press,
  1987.
Chan, Wing-Tsit. *A Source Book*
  in Chinese Philosophy.
  Princeton, N.J.: Princeton
  University Press, 1963.
Chang, Hao. "New
  Confucianism and the
  Intellectual Crisis in

Contemporary China." *Limits*
  of Change: Essay on
  Conservative Alternatives in
  Republican China. C. Furth,
  ed. Boston: Harvard
  University Press, 1976.
Fang, Thom'e H. *Chinese*
  Philosophy: Its Spirit and
  Development. Taipei: Linking,
  1981.
Feng, Yu-lan. *A History of*
  Chinese Philosophy.
  D. Boddes, trans. 2 Vols.
  Princeton: Princeton
  University Press, 1952–1953.
Feng, Yu-lan. *A History of*
  Chinese Philosophy, A New
  Edition, 3 Vols. Peking:
  People Publishers, 1980-
  1986.
Feng, Yu-lan. *The Spirit of*
  Chinese Philosophy. E. R.
  Hughes, trans. London: Kegan
  Paul, 1947.
Fingarette, H. *Confucius—The*
  Secular As Sacred. New York:
  Harper & Row, 1972.
Fu, Charles Wei-hsun.
  "Lingarette and Munro on
  Early Confucianism: A
  Methodological Examination."
  Philosophy East and West.
  April 1978, Vol. 28, no. 2, pp.
  181–198.
Kong, R. L. "Metaphysics and
  East-West Philosophy:
  Applying the Chinese Ti-Yung
  Paradigm." *Philosophy East*
  and West. January 1979, Vol.
  29, no. 1, pp. 49–57.
Leung, In-sing. *Spiritual Journey*
  to Different Realms of
  Philosophy and Wisdom.
  Taipei: Cosmic Light, 1982.
Leung, In-sing. *Interpenetration*
  and Transformation: Dialogue
  With Contemporary New
  Confucianist. Taipei: Cosmic
  Light, 1985.
Leung, In-sing. "Communication

and Hermeneutics, A
  Confucian Postmodern Point
  of View." *Journal of Chinese*
  Philosophy. Vol. 19, 1992,
  pp. 404–422.
Liu Shu-hsien. "A Philosophic
  Analysis of the Confucian
  Approach to Ethics."
  Philosophy East and West,
  Vol. 22, no. 4, October 1972,
  pp. 417–425.
Liu Shu-hsien. "The Use of
  Analogy and Symbolism in
  Traditional Chinese
  Philosophy." *Essays in East-*
  West Philosophy: An Attempt
  at World Philosophical
  Synthesis. Honolulu:
  University of Hawaii Press,
  1951.
MacMillan, Ron. "China's
  University Students Embracing
  Christianity." *News Network*
  International. Santa Ana,
  Calif.: News Network
  International; January 17,
  1990.
Munro, K. J. *The Concept of*
  Man in Early China. Stanford,
  California: Stanford University
  Press, 1969.
Nakamura, Hagime. *The Ways*
  of Thinking of Eastern People.
  Tokyo: Japanese Government
  Press, 1960.
Taylor, Rodney. *The Religious*
  Dimensions of Confucianism.
  New York: State University of
  New York Press, 1990.

Hinduism

Dean C. Halverson

HINDUISM AMONG THE NATIONS

It is estimated that adherents to Hinduism make up around 13% of the world's population. Such a figure must not be taken as "hard and fast," however, because the influence of Hinduism's teachings go far beyond those who would actually label themselves as Hindu.

The vast majority of Hindus—some 700 million—live in India, where they account for 82% of the population.

Hindus also comprise a significant portion of the population in seven other countries: Bangladesh (11%), Bhutan (25%), Fiji (41%), Mauritius (50%), Nepal (89%), Sri Lanka (15%), Surinam (27%), and Trinidad (25%) (Johnstone). More than two million Hindus live on the Indonesian island of Bali, although the country of Indonesia as a whole is predominantly Muslim.

Nepal is the only nation where Hinduism is the state religion.

There are more than one million Hindus in North America.

INTRODUCING HINDUISM

The origins of Hinduism can be traced back to around 1500 B.C. in what is

Elaborately carved stone towers of Hindu temple, Java, Indonesia.

Decorated statues to mark a Hindu celebration.

now India. It began as a polytheistic and ritualistic religion. The rituals were at first simple enough to be performed by the head of the household. As the centuries passed, however, they became increasingly complex. As a result, it became necessary to create a priestly class and to train those priests to perform the rituals correctly. During this time, the *Vedas* were written to give the priests instructions as to how to perform the rituals.

As a result of the emphasis on the rituals, the priests became the sole means by which the people could approach and appease the gods. Because of their position as mediators with the gods, the priests gained an increasing amount of power and control over the lives of the people. Finally, around 600 B.C., the people revolted. The form of Hinduism that emerged after the revolt emphasized the importance of internal meditation as opposed to the external rituals.

Between 800 to 300 B.C. the *Upanishads* were written. The *Upanishads,* also called *Vedanta* ("the end or conclusion of the *Vedas*"), are the Hindu equivalent of the New

Testament. The *Upanishads* expound the idea that behind the many gods stands one Reality, which is called *Brahman. Brahman* is an impersonal, monistic ("all is one") force. The highest form of *Brahman* is called *nirguna,* which means "without attributes or qualities."

Even after the *Upanishads* were written, the Hindu concept of God continued to develop. It developed in the direction of God being personal. *Nirguna Brahman* became *saguna Brahman,* which is *Brahman* "with attributes." This personified form of *Brahman* is also called *Ishvara.*

According to Hindu tradition, *Ishvara* became known to humanity through the *Trimurti* (literally, "three manifestations") of *Brahman.* Those manifestations include *Brahma* (the Creator), *Vishnu* (the Preserver), and *Siva* (the Destroyer). Each of the three deities has at least one *devi,* or divine spouse.

Ishvara became personified even further through the ten mythical incarnations of *Vishnu,* called *avatars.* The forms of these incarnations include that of animals (for example, a fish, tortoise, and boar) and of persons

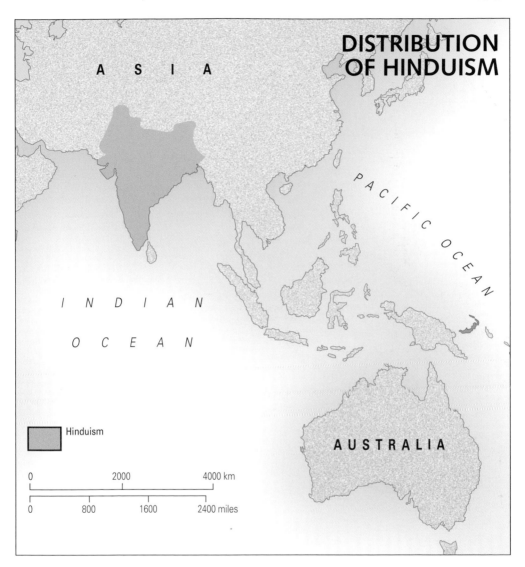

DISTRIBUTION OF HINDUISM

A S I A

P A C I F I C   O C E A N

I N D I A N

O C E A N

Hinduism

| 0 | 2000 | 4000 km |

| 0 | 800 | 1600 | 2400 miles |

AUSTRALIA

(for example, Rama, Krishna, Buddha). Epics such as the *Ramayana* and the *Mahabharata*, which includes the popular *Bhagavad-Gita*, tell the stories of these myths. Beyond the principal deities of the *Trimurti* and the *avatars*, it is estimated that there are 330 million other gods in Hinduism.

Besides the religion's various concepts of God, Hinduism can also be divided along the lines of whether the physical universe is considered to be real or illusory (*maya*). The nondualists (*advaita*) see *Brahman* alone as being real and the world as illusory. The qualified nondualists (*vishishtadvaita*) affirm the reality of both *Brahman* and the universe in that the universe is extended from the Being of *Brahman*. And the dualists (*dvaita*) see *Brahman* and the universe as being two distinct realities.

In the course of its history, Hinduism has spawned three other religious movements that have since become world religions: Jainism, Buddhism, and Sikhism.

Although Hinduism is tremendously diverse, most Hindus hold to the following beliefs:

THE BELIEFS OF HINDUISM

1. The Impersonal Nature of Brahman

Hindus see ultimate Reality, *Brahman*, as being an impersonal oneness that is beyond all distinctions, including personal and moral distinctions. Since Hindus also consider *Brahman* to be an impersonal force of existence, the universe is seen by most Hindus as being continuous with and extended from the Being of *Brahman*.

2. The Brahman/Atman Unity

Most adherents of Hinduism believe that they are in their true selves (*atman*) extended from and one with *Brahman*. Just as the air inside an open jar is identical to the air surrounding that jar, so our essence is identical to that of the essence of *Brahman*. This is expressed through the phrase *Tat tvam asi*, "That thou art."

3. The Law of Karma

Humanity's primary problem, according to Hinduism, is that we are ignorant of our divine nature. We have forgotten that we are extended from *Brahman* and that we have mistakenly attached ourselves to the desires of our separate selves, or egos, and thereby to the consequences of its actions.

Because of the ego's attachments to its desires and individualistic existence, we have become subject to the law of karma. The law of karma is the moral equivalent of the natural law of cause and effect. In essence, it says that we reap what we sow. The effects of our actions, moreover, follow us not only in the present lifetime but from lifetime to lifetime, which is why there is reincarnation.

4. Samsara (Reincarnation)

Samsara refers to the ever-revolving wheel of life, death, and rebirth (Rice,

Statue of the Hindu deity Ganesha.

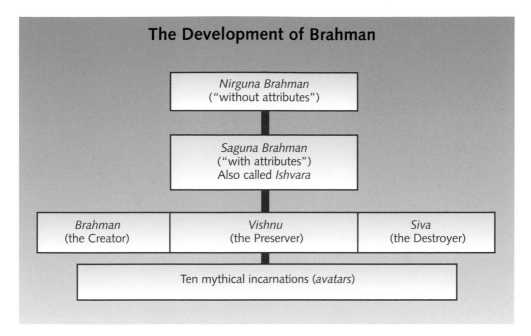

The Development of Brahman

Nirguna Brahman ("without attributes")		
Saguna Brahman ("with attributes") Also called *Ishvara*		
Brahman (the Creator)	*Vishnu* (the Preserver)	*Siva* (the Destroyer)
Ten mythical incarnations (*avatars*)		

310). We are reaping in this lifetime the consequences of the deeds we committed in previous lifetimes. A person's karma determines the kind of body—whether human, animal, or insect—into which he or she will be reincarnated in the next lifetime.

5. Moksha (Liberation)

The solution in Hinduism is to be liberated (*moksha*) from the wheel of life, death, and rebirth. Such liberation is attained through realizing that the concept of the individual self is an illusion and that only the undifferentiated oneness of *Brahman* is real. With such a realization in mind, one must strive to detach oneself from the desires of the ego and thereby attain enlightenment.

Hinduism offers at least three paths by which to attain enlightenment. They include *karma marga* (the way of action and ritual), *jnana marga* (the way of knowledge and meditation), and *bhakti marga* (the way of devotion).

By way of contrast, the direction of the Hindu way to enlightenment is *from humanity to God*, and it is *based on one's own effort*. The direction of the biblical way of salvation, on the other hand, is *from God to humanity* in that it is *based on God's grace*, and it is a gift to be received through faith (Ephesians 2:8–9; 1 John 4:10).

Also, according to the *Upanishads*, the goal of enlightenment *is for the individual self to lose its separate identity* in the universal Self. The end result of biblical *salvation*, on the other hand, is to have an everlasting *relationship* with God. Eternal life means to be in relational *communion* with a personal God, not in an undifferentiated *union* with an impersonal oneness.

THE HINDU SCRIPTURES

The earliest of the Hindu scriptures are the *Vedas*. *Veda* means "knowledge," and it has the same root as the English word "wisdom" and the Greek *oida* ("to know") (Noss, 86).

There are four *Vedas*: the *Rig Veda*, the *Sama Veda*, the *Yajur Veda*, and the *Atharva Veda*. Each *Veda*, moreover, is divided into four parts: the *Mantras* (the basic verses or hymns sung during the rituals, also called *Samhitas*), the *Brahmanas* (explanations of the verses), the

Karma and Sin Compared and Contrasted

THE SIMILARITIES

Both involve moral issues.

Both affirm the existence of a cause-and-effect relationship between our actions and the results they produce in our present lives (see Proverbs 11:18; 22:8).

THE DIFFERENCES

KARMA (HINDU CONCEPT)	SIN (CHRISTIAN CONCEPT)
Karma does not affect one's relationship with *Brahman*, which is the essence of existence within all things. Whether one's karma is good or bad makes no difference to the fact that we are unconditionally extended from the oneness of *Brahman*.	Sin does affect our relationship with God in that we become alienated from Him. One of the attributes of God is absolute moral holiness, and our sin reveals an attitude of rebellion against His moral authority.
The law of karma, which makes morality like a law of nature, does not allow for the possibility of forgiveness. Its consequences are inevitable and inescapable.	Because God is personal, and because persons can forgive, God can forgive us of our sins. Moreover, He has done so through Jesus Christ.

Aran-yakas (reflections on their meaning), and the *Upanishads* (mystical interpretations of the verses). These scriptures are called *shruti*, which means "that which is heard." *Shruti* literature is the Hindu equivalent to scripture that is revealed.

Besides such primary scriptures, there are also secondary ones that are considered *smriti*, or "remembered." Included in the *smriti* scriptures are the popular *Ramayana* ("Rama's way") and *Mahabharata* ("the great story") epics. Within the

The cow is a sacred animal in Hinduism, and allowed to roam freely.

Mahabharata epic is the most popular of all Hindu scriptures—the *Bhagavad-Gita*, the main character of which is Krishna. While the *smriti* scriptures are not as authoritative as the *shruti* scriptures, they have nevertheless exerted much more influence on the culture of India because of their popularity.

Other *smriti* scriptures include the *Vedangas* (codes of law, such as the *Laws of Manu*), the *Puranas* (the genealogies and legends of the gods), the *Darshanas* (philosophical writings), *Sutras* (rules of ritual and social conduct), and the *Tantras* (writings on attaining occultic power) (Organ, 180).

SUGGESTIONS FOR EVANGELISM

1. Offer Jesus' Forgiveness

Bakht Singh, a convert from Hinduism and an Indian evangelist, once said, "I have never yet failed to get a hearing if I talk to them about forgiveness of sins and peace and rest in your heart" (Hesselgrave, 169). Forgiveness is a real need for Hindus because it is not

Hinduism and Christianity Contrasted

	HINDUISM	CHRISTIANITY
GOD	Impersonal	Personal
HUMANITY	Continuous in the sense of being extended from the Being of God	Discontinuous in the sense of being separate from the Being of God; continuous in the sense of being made in God's image
HUMANITY'S PROBLEM	Ignorance	Moral rebellion
THE SOLUTION	Liberation from illusion and ignorance	Forgiveness of sin and reconciliation with the personal holy God
THE MEANS	Striving to detach oneself from the separated ego and seeking to be aware of one's unity with the divine through self effort	Repenting of sin and trusting in the completed and substitutionary work of Jesus Christ
THE OUTCOME	Merge into the Oneness; the individual disappears	Eternal fellowship with God; the person is fulfilled in a loving relationship with God

available in their belief-system, which is based on the law of karma.

The fact that forgiveness is not available in Hinduism troubles many Hindus, for they are aware that the actions that bind them to this illusory realm keep accumulating and the prospect of escape is hopelessly remote.

A biblical passage that is good to use with a Hindu is:

Come to me, all you who are weary and burdened, and I will give you rest. Take my yoke upon you and learn from me, for I am gentle and humble in heart, and you will find rest for your souls. For my yoke is easy and my burden is light (Matthew 11:28–30).

The kind of people that Jesus had in mind when He spoke those words were those who felt burdened by the effort that it took to attain salvation.

Jesus offers rest in place of the feeling of being "weary and burdened" beyond hope. We find such rest by coming to Him, which means believing in Him (see also John 6:35).

The reason Jesus could say that His yoke is "easy" and His burden is "light" (v. 30) is that He has accomplished the work of salvation on our behalf. He has taken the burden of our sin upon His own shoulders. His disciples follow One who is not a taskmaster but who is "gentle and humble in heart" (v. 29).

2. Keep God's Personhood in Mind

When discussing your beliefs and those of your Hindu friend, keep God's personhood in mind at all times. This has several benefits.

Richly-colored sculpture of a Hindu goddess.

First, it will help you find ways to illustrate the Christian perspective on spiritual issues by using images that are familiar to everyone because they have to do with interpersonal relationships. Through such images you can illustrate the following aspects of sin:

- the meaning of sin (sin is the rejection of God's moral authority),
- the consequences of sin (interpersonal alienation),
- the resolution of sin (confession and forgiveness),
- the hope of eternal life (everlasting fellowship with a personal and loving God).

The above examples of illustrating sin through interpersonal relationships were taken from the parable of the prodigal son (Luke 15). Obviously this parable can be useful to illustrate for the Hindu the Christian understanding of sin and forgiveness.

One drawback of that parable, however, is the killing of the fattened calf to celebrate the son's return. Such an image is offensive to Hindus, who consider the cow to be sacred. Be careful to point out that the main theme is not the killing of the calf but the alienation and then the reconciliation of the son to his father, and the joy of the father, who represents God, at the return of his son.

Second, the fact that God is personal will provide ways for you to move your friend's thinking toward the Christian Gospel. For example, if God is personal by nature, then He is able to be aware of and empathize with our suffering (Exodus 3:7; Hebrews 4:15). Is the Hindu *Brahman* able to be as concerned for us?

Another example of using the fact that God is personal has to do with the destiny of the individual after death. To "know" the impersonal *Brahman* of Hinduism is to lose your identity as a distinct and separate person. There is a drive within each of us, however, that wants to cling with all our might to our existence as personal beings. Is such a drive nothing more than the ignorance of our separatistic egos, as Hinduism would contend?

Is it not true that we are most fulfilled when we are in a relationship of friendship or love? How much more fulfilled would we be if we were in fellowship with a personal, holy, and loving God?

Such a fulfilling relationship is precisely what the God of the Bible offers for eternity (see John 14:2–3; 17:3; Revelation 21:3).

3. Ask and Listen

Hinduism is a vastly diverse religion. Some beliefs unify the religion, but it has no specific doctrinal creed. As such, it is very tolerant, allowing each person to choose his or her own set of beliefs.

Don't assume you know what your Hindu friend believes. Ask questions about his or her beliefs concerning God, man, sin, and salvation, and listen carefully to his or her answers.

Listen closely, for example, to the words that your Hindu friend uses to describe the way to enlightenment. He or she might very well use words such as "achieve," "attain," "overcome," and "strive." Such words are significant because they reveal how enlightenment—the Hindu equivalent of salvation—is based on human effort rather than on God's grace.

You might discuss with your friend such passages as Romans 3:19–24 and Ephesians 2:8–9, which speak of the futility of attempting to earn one's salvation and of how salvation is a gift from God to be received by faith.

4. Have a Humble Spirit

Don't approach a Hindu with a spirit of superiority. With respect to our eating of meat and our attachment to materialism, Hindus see Christians as spiritually inferior. Live your life as an open book. Let them see the peace of mind you have because you are assured of forgiveness in Jesus Christ and of your destiny after death.

5. Focus on Jesus

Present your Hindu friend with a New Testament and ask him or her to discover who Jesus is. Let your friend know that even Gandhi said, "I shall say to the Hindus that your lives will be incomplete unless you reverently study the teachings of Jesus" (Hingorani, 23). Such a quote carries a lot of weight with most Hindus.

Encourage your friend to read the books of Luke and John.

Snakes in a Hindu snake temple.

Hindu sculpture, India.

6. Be Aware of Differing Definitions

Be aware of terminology or concepts that could be misunderstood by followers of Hinduism. For example, Hindus would understand being "born again" as referring to reincarnation, which is something from which they want to be liberated. In Christian terminology, however, being "born again" is to be made new or to be regenerated by the transforming power of the Holy Spirit.

RESPONDING TO HINDRANCES AND OBJECTIONS

1. Cultural Barriers

There are several cultural factors that might prevent Hindus from considering Christianity.

a. Hinduism is intertwined with the culture of India, the home of most Hindus. Radhakrishnan, a renowned Indian scholar and statesman, once said, "Hinduism is more a culture than a creed" (Beaver, 170). Thus, many Hindus think they must reject their culture before they can accept Christianity.

b. There is a cultural/religious pride among educated Hindus that prevents them from considering other religions.

c. Christianity has been associated, at least in the Indian's mind, with "materialistic civilization and imperialistic exploitation" (Hingorani, 32).

d. The Indian family is very close. The actions of one member of the family affect the rest of the family. Mahendra Singhal, a Hindu who came to Christ, wrote,

My dilemma [with respect to his conversion] had another dimension. My acceptance of Jesus Christ would make my parents lose respect and position in the community. My brothers and sisters would suffer disgrace. Even though I was working away from home in a different environment, I was not really free to make my own decisions (Singhal, 3).

Each of these issues is difficult to deal with, but with God they are not insurmountable. We must keep the focus on Jesus Christ and His salvation and separate the message as much as possible from Western culture. Christianity, after all, has its roots in Asia, not in the West.

Also, as Christians we must affirm with Gandhi that "conversion must not mean denationalization" (Hingorani, 15). While Christianity certainly speaks to the polytheistic aspects of the Indian culture, it does not require, for instance, that a believer eat meat. Indians can be Christian and still be proud of their national heritage.

The price for accepting Christ might indeed be high, but Jesus has promised that those who pay such a price "will receive a hundred times as much and will inherit eternal life" (Matthew 19:29).

2. "There Are Many Paths to God"

Probably the most common Hindu objection to Christianity is the belief that there are many ways to God. Each person can choose the way best suited for him or her. The Hindu sees ultimate Reality, *Brahman,* as being an undifferentiated oneness. If that view of God is accurate, then it would indeed be true that there are many ways to God, because God would be the underlying force within each person. Such an idea was reflected in *Hinduism Today* when it printed a chart of the major world religions entitled "Truth Is One, Paths Are Many."

By way of response, you must continually set before your Hindu friend the image of a God who is personal. If God is by nature personal, then the issues of how to know God are different from those of knowing an impersonal, undifferentiated force. With a personal God, the issues are similar to those of relating to a friend or parent. To be more specific, there are issues of morality, obedience, and trust.

If God is personal, sin is not a matter of ignorance but of moral rejection and disobedience, which causes the relationship to be broken.

If our primary problem is that we have broken our relationship with the Person of God, then it is understandable why there is only one

Ferocious Hindu temple demon, Bali, Indonesia.

Vishnu and Jesus:
The Differences Between Their Incarnations

VISHNU	JESUS
At least ten incarnations (some claim more) in both animal and human form	One incarnation in human form
While the stories of the *avatars*, or incarnations, of *Vishnu* might have a core of truth, their historicity is not essential, for they are primarily mythical in nature. If it were shown that there were no historical basis to the stories, it would have no effect on their meaning and influence. One Hindu tradition even asserts that when the avatars walked, they left no footprints.	The historicity of Jesus' life is very important to the veracity of Jesus' claims and to the salvation that He accomplished on our behalf (1 Corinthians 15:14, 17; 1 John 1:1-3). If Christ did not actually live, die, and rise from the dead in history, then Christianity is built on a lie and the Gospel is without foundation.
The purpose of *Vishnu*'s incarnation was "for destruction of evil-doers" (*Bhagavad-Gita* 4:8; Edgerton, 23).	The purpose of Jesus' incarnation was to "seek and to save what was lost" (Luke 19:10). "For God did not send his Son into the world to condemn the world, but to save the world through him" (John 3:17; see also John 10:10).
The *avatars* pointed to *a way* by which we can *attain* enlightenment over a period of many lifetimes: "But *striving zealously*, with sins cleansed, the disciplined man, *perfected through many rebirths,* then (finally) goes to the highest goal" (Bhagavad-Gita 6:45; Edgerton, 37, emphasis added).	Jesus points to himself as *the way* by which to *receive* eternal life immediately (John 6:29, 40; 10:9–10; 11:25–26; 14:6).
Vishnu incarnates periodically as an *avatar* when the need arises, and then the *avatar* dies and is reabsorbed back into *Brahman*. Hinduism makes no claims concerning the bodily resurrection of the *avatars*.	Jesus' incarnation was a unique event. His sacrifice was "once for all" (Hebrews 9:26–28); He died and rose from the dead; and His individual identity is maintained before, as well as after, the incarnation.

way to God. You can illustrate this for your Hindu friend by asking: How many ways are there to restore a relationship that you have broken? The answer, of course, is that there is only one way: through confessing your guilt and requesting forgiveness.

Also, share with your Hindu friend the *inclusiveness* of Jesus Christ toward others:

■ Christ beckons *"all* who are weary and heavy laden" (Matthew 11:28, emphasis added) to come to Him.
■ He commends a variety of people. For example, he commends the faith of the Roman centurion (Matthew 8:5–13), the kindness of the Samaritan (Luke 10:29–37), and the repentance of the tax collector (Luke 18:9–14) and the sinful woman (Luke 7:36–50).
■ The inclusive Christ associates with the social outcast (Luke 19:1–10) and the sinner (Luke 15:1–7).
■ The Gospels portray Jesus meeting everyone at his or her point of need. For example, He is the provider for the physically hungry (Matthew 14:13–21) and the spiritually hungry (John 6:35); the healer of the leper, the lame, the blind, the deaf, and the mute; the seeker of the lost (Matthew 18:10–14; Luke 19:10); the lover of the children (Matthew 19:14); "a light for revelation to the Gentiles" (Luke 2:32; John 8:12); the physician of the spiritually sick (Matthew 9:12–13); and the gate through whom one passes to receive eternal life (John 10:9).

The Gospel of Jesus Christ, moreover, is intended for the *whole* world. As John wrote concerning the end: "I looked and there before me was a great multitude that no one could count, *from every nation, tribe, people and language*, standing before the throne and in front of the Lamb" (Revelation 7:9, emphasis added). Such an all-embracing Christ will naturally appeal to the Hindu (Sudhakar, 3).

3. "Jesus Christ Is Not Unique"
The Hindus see their gods and *avatars*

(incarnations) as manifestations of the impersonal *Brahman*. They view Jesus as merely one of those avatars. Your Hindu friend might be willing to incorporate Jesus into his or her pantheon, but he or she would be unwilling to accept Jesus as the exclusive incarnation of God.

Gandhi represented typical Hindu thinking when he said,

I . . . do not take as literally true the text that Jesus is the only begotten son of God. God cannot be the exclusive Father and I cannot ascribe exclusive divinity to Jesus. He is as divine as Krishna or Rama or Mohammed or Zoroaster (Hingorani, 53).

But was the incarnation of Jesus really the same as *Vishnu's*

Statue of Hindu deity Shiva.

Opposite: Statue of Ganesha.

Colorful statue of Ganesha, Delhi, India.

incarnations, which included Krishna and Rama? No, there were distinct differences. (See the "*Vishnu* and Jesus" chart).

If the objection of Jesus' uniqueness comes up, encourage your Hindu friend to read through the Gospel of John and then to judge the issue for himself or herself. One former Hindu wrote, "At the urging of my classmate . . . I began to read the New Testament to learn more about Jesus. He totally captivated me. Here was someone who struck me as different from anyone else who ever lived" (Sairsingh, 5–6).

4. "I Must Pay for My Own Karmic Debt"

Hindus are deeply influenced in their thinking by the law of karma. Their tendency, then, is to believe that actions have consequences both now and in subsequent lives, and that each person bears the consequences of his or her own actions alone. Typically, therefore, Hindus have difficulty understanding the concept of Jesus' substitutionary death on our behalf. How could Jesus suffer in our place and pay for our debt, while we receive forgiveness and salvation as a free gift? To the Hindu, it doesn't make sense.

The law of karma has validity: The Christian can acknowledge that the law of karma is true in this lifetime in that one who sins will personally reap the consequences of that sin, such as shame, the loss of a friend's trust, ill health, a jail sentence, or a failed marriage. Even Paul wrote, "A man reaps what he sows" (Galatians 6:7).

Sin hurts God: Sin, or karma, doesn't involve just the person who committed the act, however; it also involves the victim . . . and God. If, for instance, I commit a violent act against a daughter, the parents will be hurt as well—because they love her. In the same way, God is hurt when we sin against those He loves. In a very real sense, God is the primary One who is hurt by our sin. David wrote after committing the sins of both murder and adultery, "Against you, you only, have I sinned" (Psalm 51:4). As a result of our sin, our fellowship with Him is broken. And until restitution is made, that fellowship will continue to be broken.

Forgiveness is possible: While the bad news is that such sin results in our alienation from God, the good news is that, with a personal God, forgiveness is possible, just as it is possible for any person to forgive another person for a wrong he or she committed.

Richly decorated detail of a Hindu temple.

ourselves their karma.

That is precisely what Jesus accomplished on the cross. Being God, He was sinless and represented the One who had been sinned against. Being man, He was qualified to bear on our behalf the consequences of our sin, which was death. He paid for our karma in that He took the penalty of death that we deserved and paid it on our behalf. Because of what Jesus Christ did on our behalf, forgiveness from God has become available.

5. "The Crucifixion Goes Against Nonviolence to All Life"

Some Hindus have difficulty understanding the significance of Christ's crucifixion because of their conviction that one must act with nonviolence toward all life, which is the Hindu doctrine of *ahimsa.* What needs to be explained to them is that the crucifixion of Christ was the graphic consequence of "the wages of sin" (Romans 6:23) and the direct result of Christ's having taken our sins upon himself.

The following word picture might help your Hindu friend understand the meaning of the cross. Have him or her imagine a loved one—perhaps a daughter—becoming involved with drugs. At first the daughter experiments with marijuana. She does it for the enjoyment of the experience, and she's able to control it. But within a few weeks she becomes involved with heavier drugs such as cocaine. The highs and lows become more intense, and she develops a craving for the drugs. They begin to control her; she becomes addicted. Her parents see what the drugs are doing to their daughter: her grades plummet, she hangs out with the wrong crowd, she gets in trouble with the law, she becomes distant in her relationship with them. Then, one tragic day, they find their daughter dead as the result of a drug overdose.

Now ask: As the parent of this daughter, what would your attitude be toward the drugs? Would you be upset only with the death of your

If God were an impersonal force, moral law would become more like the laws of nature. Forgiveness would not be possible, for an impersonal law cannot forgive.

Forgiveness has its price: Forgiveness is not without cost. When we forgive the one who has wronged us, we bear *on ourselves* the hurt and the consequences caused by that person's action. In a sense, we have chosen to take on the consequences of their actions; we have taken on

daughter and would you have no conviction concerning the effects of drugs? Or, would you be motivated to warn others about the dangers of doing drugs?

Explain to your friend that God feels even more strongly than he or she does about the death of a person. Death grieves Him; He abhors it. But that is precisely why He hates sin—because sin, like drugs, destroys people. And that is why He was motivated to give His one and only Son as a sacrifice for our sins. Christ's death does not uphold killing; instead, it demonstrates the extent to which God loved us (Romans 5:8). It shows how much He desires that we have life (John 3:16–17; 10:10) and to make a way for us to have a relationship with Him (John 17:3).

Dr. Mahendra Singhal, a former Hindu, said,

> Hindus believe in going to the extremes to demonstrate their love for someone. A mother, for example, would go hungry to feed her children. A father would deprive himself of everything so that his children could go to school. The image of Jesus Christ that made the strongest appeal to me was the limit to which He was willing to go to show His love toward me, and I did not even know Him at the time. I have discovered in my witnessing to Hindus that they are generally moved by the depiction of Jesus on the cross to validate His love toward us.

BIBLIOGRAPHY AND RESOURCES

Beaver, R. Pierce, et al. eds. *Eerdman's Handbook to the World's Religions*. Grand Rapids, Mich.: Wm. B. Eerdman's Publishing Co., 1982.

Edgerton, Franklin, trans. *The Bhagavad Gita*. Cambridge, Mass.: Harvard University Press, 1975.

Heim, S. Mark. *Is Christ the Only Way?: Christian Faith in a Pluralistic World*. Valley Forge, Penn.: Judson Press, 1985.

Hesselgrave, David. *Communicating Christ Cross-Culturally*. Grand Rapids, Mich.: Zondervan, 1978.

Hingorani, Anand, ed. *The Message of Jesus Christ by M. K. Gandhi*. Bombay: Bharatiya Vidya Bhavan, 1964.

Johnstone, Patrick. *Operation World*. Pasadena, Calif.: William Carey Library, 1986.

Lewis, James and William Travis. *Religious Traditions of the World*. Grand Rapids, Mich.: Zondervan, 1991.

Maharaj, Rabindranath, with Dave Hunt. *Death of a Guru*. New York: A. J. Holman Co., 1977.

McDowell, Josh and Don Stewart. *Understanding Non-Christian Religions*. San Bernardino, Calif.: Here's Life Publishers, 1982.

Noss, John B. *Man's Religions*, 5th ed. New York: MacMillan Publishing Co., Inc., 1974.

Organ, Troy Wilson. *Hinduism: Its Historical Development*. New York: Barron's Educational Series, 1974.

Rice, Edward. *Eastern Definitions*. Garden City, N.Y.: Doubleday & Company, Inc., 1980.

Sairsingh, Krister. *A Hindu's Quest for the Holy*. Colorado Springs, Colo.: International Students, Inc., 1987.

Singhal, Mahendra. "The Choice and the Price." *SCP Newsletter*. Berkeley, Calif.: Spiritual Counterfeits Project, 1987, Vol. 12, no. 3.

Stott, John. *The Cross of Christ*. Downers Grove, Ill.: InterVarsity Press, 1986.

Sudhakar, Paul. "Mission to the Average Hindu." Unpublished paper, no date.

GLOSSARY OF COMMON HINDU TERMS

Ahimsa: The doctrine of nonviolence to all life, which is the basis for a Hindu being vegetarian.

Asanas: The physical postures or ways of sitting in order to do yoga.

Avatar: The incarnation of a deity.

Bhakti: A form of yoga in which a person loses one's self through devotion to a personal concept of God, either Krishna or Rama.

Brahmin: The priestly caste of Hinduism, which is to be differentiated from the term *Brahman,* which is Hinduism's word for ultimate Reality.

Dharma: The Hindu word for "religion." It is the way a Hindu should live, especially with respect to performing the duties of one's caste. To live according to the *dharma* is to live in harmony with the universe.

Karma: The law of cause and effect active in the moral realm.

Mantra: "Thought form." A single or multisyllable phrase (usually in Sanskrit) on which one meditates. Each *mantra* is identified with a particular deity to the extent that the correctly pronounced *mantra* embodies that deity. The point of repeating the *mantra* is to invoke the powers of that deity and to invite it to enter you (Rice, 247).

Maya: The doctrine that the visible world is an illusion that clouds the reality of absolute oneness. *Maya* may also be considered to be the divine play of the gods.

Nirvana: Refers to the individual self merging into the impersonal and undifferentiated oneness of the Ultimate Self. *Nirvana* is the goal of enlightenment.

OM: The *mantra* that contains all the primal vibrations of the universe. It is considered to be the queen of the *mantras* (Rice, 279).

Puja: The term for the worship of deities at an altar.

Samadhi: A focusing of the mind with the goal of emptying it of all thoughts and of attaining one's absorption in the ultimate Oneness.

Yoga: A physical and mental discipline that is practiced for the purpose of spiritual liberation or empowerment.

ORGANIZATIONS

Dr. Mahendra Singhal
Hinduism International Ministries, Inc.
P.O. Box 602
Zion, IL 60099
Phone/Fax: (847) 872-7022

Rabi Maharaj
East/West Gospel Ministries
Box 2191
La Habra, CA 90632

Hinduism S.T.P. (Summer Training Program)
International Missions, Incorporated

P.O. Box 14866
Reading, PA 19612-4866
Phone: (610) 375-0300

HIS (Helping International Students)
1711 Pendleton St.
Columbia, SC 29201
Phone: (803) 779-2852
Fax: (803) 779-8533

Islam

Dean C. Halverson

ISLAM AMONG THE NATIONS

Islam makes up around 20% of the world's population. It is the second largest religion in the world, trailing only Christianity.

Muslims (followers of Islam) are spread primarily over the areas of North Africa, the Middle East, South-Central Asia, and Indonesia.

Although Islam began in Saudi Arabia, non-Arab Muslims now outnumber Arab Muslims by a ratio of almost three to one. Also, the four nations with the largest number of Muslims today are all outside the Middle East. Indonesia—166 million, 88% of the population; Pakistan—111 million, 97%; Bangladesh—97 million, 85%; India—93 million, 11%.

Roughly one-fifth of the more than 530,000 international students in the United States come from 40 Islamic countries. Most of these countries have a minimal number of Christians in their populations (0–2%). Moreover, governments have either closed the countries' borders to missionaries, or have made evangelism illegal, or both.

THE FOUNDING OF ISLAM

In A.D. 570, Muhammad was born into an Arabian tribe called the Quraysh. The Quraysh were influential because they controlled the city of Mecca. Mecca was important economically because it served as a convenient resting place for trading caravans. It was important religiously because the *Ka'bah* was located there.

The *Ka'bah is* a cubic structure that, at the time of Muhammad, contained 360 deities. Each Arabian tribe had hand-picked its own deity and came to Mecca each year to pay homage to its god.

It was the custom of those who were spiritually-minded to retreat to a place of solitude once a year. Muhammad observed this practice for several years in a cave in Mount Hira. In the year 610, at age 40,

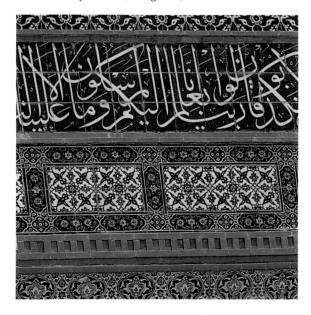

Inscribed tiles forming part of the Dome of the Rock, Islam's third holiest site, Jerusalem, Israel.

103

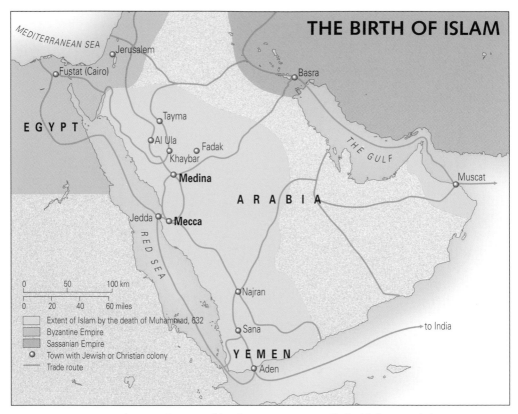

THE BIRTH OF ISLAM

MEDITERRANEAN SEA

Jerusalem

Fustat (Cairo)

Basra

EGYPT

Tayma

Al Ula

Fadak

Khaybar

Medina

THE GULF

Muscat

ARABIA

Jedda

Mecca

RED SEA

0   50   100 km

0   20   40   60 miles

Najran

to India

Extent of Islam by the death of Muhammad, 632
Byzantine Empire
Sassanian Empire
Town with Jewish or Christian colony
Trade route

Sana

YEMEN

Aden

Muhammad received his first revelation from the angel Gabriel. This was the beginning of a series of revelations that were eventually compiled in Islam's sacred scripture, the *Qur'an*, which means "recitations."

Muhammad is said to have doubted initially the origin of these new revelations. He thought that perhaps he had been possessed by *jinn*, or demons. His wife Khadijah, however, reassured him that his visions were of divine origin, and she encouraged him to teach that which had been revealed to him.

As Muhammad began to preach more publicly, the leaders of his own tribe pressured him to keep quiet about his message of strict monotheism. They viewed such a teaching as a threat to their polytheistic religion and especially to the source of their livelihood, since they benefited economically from the pilgrimages the tribes made to the *Ka'bah*. Muhammad, however, refused to stop preaching, and he began to accrue a significant following.

As he continued to preach against polytheism, persecution increased against the followers of this new religion. Eventually, around 100 Muslim families were forced to flee to a city named Yathrib (now called Medina), which is around 200 miles north of Mecca.

Muhammad followed these families shortly thereafter, fleeing Mecca in the year 622. Muslims now look to the year of his flight to Yathrib as the beginning of the Muslim calendar. This event is known as the Hijrah (also spelled *Hegira*), which means "a series of migrations."

After several successful sieges and military victories against Mecca, and after making treaties with the Quraysh tribe, Muhammad and his army took control of Mecca in 630 without a struggle. Upon entering the city, he personally destroyed the idols in the *Ka'bah*. Within a year of Mecca's submission to Muhammad, he was able to unify all the tribes of the Arabian peninsula under the religion of Islam.

On June 8, 632, Muhammad died.

THE SECTS OF ISLAM

The two major sects of Islam, Sunni and Shi'ite, were divided originally over a dispute as to who should serve as the first *caliph,* or successor, to Muhammad, who had failed to appoint one before his death. The Sunni Muslims insisted that Muhammad's successor should be elected. The Shi'te (or Shia'h) Muslims thought he should come through Muhammad's blood. line, which would have meant that Ali, Muhammad's cousin and son-in-law would have been his successor. The Sunnis were the ones who got their way.

The Sunnis now comprise 80% of the Muslim population, and they differ from the Shi'ites in other ways besides that of a dispute over who was to be the original successor.

Characteristic Muslim minaret, from which the call to prayer is made daily.

The Red Mosque, Delhi, India. Islam rapidly spread as far as Spain in the West and India in the East.

For example, the Sunnis and the Shi'ites differ with respect to their source of authority. The Sunnis emphasize the authority of the written traditions, which include not only the *Qur'an* but also the *Sunna* ("custom") from which the Sunnis derive their name. The *Sunna* includes the *Hadith* in which the sayings and conduct of Muhammad and his companions are recorded. The *Sunna* fills in many areas where the *Qur'an* is silent. The Sunnis also receive guidance from the principles arrived at by a consensus of the elders, or religious scholars (*ulama*), who derive their decisions based on the *Qur'an*, the *Sunna*, and subsequent rulings.

The Shi'ites, on the other hand, are more authority-oriented (rather than consensus-oriented). When their movement began, they believed that God spoke through an *Imam*, the Muslim equivalent of the Catholic Pope. In the ninth century, however, the twelfth *Imam* occultated, or became hidden, and the source of authority was passed on to the *ulama*, who considered themselves collectively to be the general representatives of the hidden *Imam*. *The* Shi'ites await

the return of the twelfth *Imam*, called the *Mahdi*, similar to the way Christians look for the return of Christ. Shi'ites are typically more authority-oriented than consensus oriented—the Ayatollah Khomeini of Iran, for example, was a Shi'ite leader.

Another difference between the two sects is that the Sunnis believe there should be a separation between civil and religious authorities, whereas, the Shi'ites maintain that the religious authorities should exercise both political and religious power.

Sufism is the mystical third wing of Islam. The goal of the Sufi is to renounce worldly attachments, to see only God in all things, and to attain assimilation of the self into the vast Being of God.

There are also several minor Muslim sects, including the *Wahhabis* (primarily in Saudi Arabia), the *Druze* (primarily in Lebanon, Syria, and northern Israel), the *Alawites* (primarily in Syria), and the *Ahmadiyas* (primarily in Pakistan). Beyond the major and minor sects, Islam has also been a contributing factor in two religions: Sikhism and Baha'i.

Islam and Christianity Contrasted

	ISLAM	CHRISTIANITY
GOD	A singular unity. No partner is to be associated with God.	A compound, or complex, unity — one in essence, three in person
HUMANITY	Good by nature	Sinful by nature
SIN	Sin is thought of in terms of rejecting right guidance. It can be forgiven through repentance. No atonement is necessary	Sin is serious in that it is spoken of as causing spiritual death (Romans 6.23; Ephesians 2:1). It is serious because it reflects an attitude of moral rebellion against the holy God, which causes us to be alienated from Him. An atonement is necessary before our relationship with God can be restored.
SALVATION	The standard for salvation is having one's good deeds outweigh one's bad deeds. Therefore, it is based on human effort.	The standard for salvation is the absolute holiness of God (Matthew 5:48). Therefore, it can only be offered as a gift by God, based on His grace and Jesus' atoning work, and it can be received through faith. Salvation cannot be earned.
JESUS	One of the major prophets. To associate Jesus with God (for instance, to call Him the Son of God) is blasphemy. Muslims affirm the virgin birth of Jesus and the miracles that He performed.	The one and only Son of God. John wrote, "Who is the liar? It is the man who denies that Jesus is the Christ. Such a man is the antichrist—he denies the Father and the Son" (1 John 2:22).
THE DEATH OF JESUS	According to the Islamic tradition, Jesus did not die on the cross. Instead, He ascended to heaven, and Judas died in His place on the cross. Muslims believe that it is disrespectful to believe that God would allow one of His prophets—and especially one of the most honored of the prophets—to be crucified.	Jesus died a physical death and gave His life as the substitutionary atonement for our sins. He then rose from the dead in a physical but immortal body and appeared to hundreds of witnesses (1 Corinthians 15). God's specific purpose for sending Jesus into the world was for Him to be crucified and to die for our sins (Matthew 20:28; John 3:16; Romans 83; 2 Corinthians 5:21; 1 Peter 1:19–20). Jesus voluntarily gave His life for us (John 6:51; 10:11–17). The end was not that of dishonor but that of the highest exaltation (Acts 2:29–33; 5:30–31; Philippians 2:8–11).
THE BIBLE	Corrupted. Abrogated by the *Qur'an*.	Authentic. Divinely inspired. The final authority in all matters of faith and truth.

The golden-roofed Dome of the Rock, Jerusalem.

THE BELIEFS AND OBLIGATIONS OF ISLAM

The term "Islam" means "submission" to the will of God, and the person who submits is called a "Muslim." The religion of Islam can he divided into beliefs (*iman*) and obligations (*deen*).

The major beliefs of Islam include the following:
    1. *God.* The central doctrine of Islam is that God is one and that no partner is to be associated with Him. To associate a partner with God is to commit the sin of *ishrak* (also spelled *shirk*), for which the *Qur'an* offers no forgiveness (*Surah* 4:48).* Obviously, as a result of this central doctrine of Islam, the doctrine of the Trinity is offensive to Muslims.
    2. *Angels.* In the gap between the God of the *Qur'an* and humankind exists a hierarchy of angels. The archangel Gabriel is of the highest rank, succeeded by the rest of the angels.
    Each person has two angels assigned to him or her, one to record the person's good deeds and the other to record the bad deeds.
    At the bottom of the hierarchy are the *jinn*, from which we get the word

"genie." Muslims believe that the host of *jinn* were created from fire, are usually bad, and are able to possess people.
    3. *The Prophets of God.* According to the *Qur'an*, God has sent a prophet to every nation to preach the message of there being only one God. In all, 124,000 prophets have been sent, according to tradition. Most are unknown, but many include biblical characters such as Adam, Noah, Abraham, Moses, David, Solomon, Jonah, John the Baptist, and Jesus.
    Each prophet was given for a particular age, but Muhammad is the only prophet who is for all time. He is considered to be the "Seal of the Prophets."
    4. *The Holy Books.* Four of the highest-ranking prophets were given books of divine revelation. Those four are Moses, who was given the *Tawrat* (Torah), David, who was given the *Zabur* (Psalms), Jesus, who was given the *Injil* (Gospel), and Muhammad, who was given the *Qur'an*. Of those four books, Muslims contend that only the *Qur'an* has been preserved in an uncorrupted state.
    5. *The Day of Judgment.* The God of the *Qur'an* has decreed that there will be a day when all will stand before Him in judgment. On that day,

* References will vary several verses on either side depending on the translation you are using. Most references in this chapter are taken from 'Abdullah Yusuf 'Ali's translation.

EVANGELISTIC DO'S AND DON'TS WITH MUSLIMS

The "Do's"

• Love and respect your Muslim friend(s).
• Pray with them, with their permission, and pray for them.

• Consult the Bible often to explain and support what you believe. This will expose your Muslim friend(s) to the Bible's ring of authority and authenticity. At an appropriate time, offer to study the Gospel of John with them.

• Meet with them individually. Witnessing to Muslims is best done one-to-one. When you meet with Muslims in a group, they will dutifully defend their religion in front of others so as not to expose the doubts they might have.

• Point to Jesus as often as you can without being offensive. A former Muslim said, "It is vital for the Muslim to see Christianity not as a religion but as a living, new relationship with God."

•Use Jesus' parables and stories. Muslims are more influenced by stories and parables than they are by logical arguments.

•Read at least a few portions, if not all, of the Qur'an so that you will become familiar with the Muslim concept of God and with themes of their religion.

• Be patient, persistent, and prayerful. Muslims are notoriously slow in turning to Jesus Christ for salvation.

• Handle the Bible with respect. The custom in Islamic countries is to not lower the Qur'an below the waist. Muslims also keep the Qur'an on the highest shelf in the house, for nothing should be placed upon the Qur'an. Also, they consider it a sign of disrespect to write in the Qur'an or the Bible.

The "Don'ts"

•Don't be critical of Islam, the Qur'an, or Muhammad. In fact, try to avoid such subjects altogether. Instead, accentuate the Good News of the Gospel.

• Don't take your Muslim friend(s) to church until you know they are ready for it. There is much that happens at a church service that the typical Muslim would find dishonoring to God and therefore offensive to him or her (for example, men and women sit together and casually touch each other). If you do take a Muslim to church, discuss with him or her what to expect beforehand. It is best to introduce a Muslim slowly to the Christian culture by taking him or her to an informal Bible study.

• Don't argue with your Muslim friend. Understand that a Muslim cannot lose an argument, because he or she would then lose face. Try to sensitively stimulate your friend's thinking instead.

Muslim men in their habitual prayer position.

each person's deeds will be weighed in the balance. Those whose good deeds outweigh their bad deeds will be rewarded with Paradise; and those whose bad deeds outweigh their good will be judged to hell. Whether one's good deeds outweigh one's bad deeds is a subjective matter, though, known only by God. As a result, a Muslim has no assurance that he or she will he accepted by God.

The obligations of Islam include the following:

1. *To Recite the Shahadah.* The word *shahadah* means to bear witness. When reciting the *shahadah,* one says, "I bear witness that there is no God but Allah and that Muhammad is His messenger." Saying the *shahadah* with sincerity is all it takes to become a Muslim.

2. *To Pray (Salat).* A Muslim is required to say seventeen cycles (*rak'a*) of prayer each day. These cycles are usually spread over five times per day—dawn, noon, midafternoon, dusk, and two hours after sunset (Hamada 102). Muslims may pray either individually or in a group. They wash themselves in a prescribed manner before praying, which is called ablution or *wudu'.* When they pray, they must face toward Mecca. The direction of prayer *(qibla) is* marked by the niche, or *mihrab,* in the mosque. *(Hinnells, 142).* The noon service on Friday is the only time when Muslims are expected to gather together at the mosque.

3. *To Fast (Sawm).* In commemoration of Muhammad's receiving the *Qur'an* during the ninth lunar month of *Ramadhan,* Muslims are expected to fast during the daylight hours that month. During the fast, they must abstain from eating, drinking, smoking, and sexual relations. After sundown, Muslims are allowed to partake of all those things again until sunrise.

4. *To Give Alms (Zakat).* Muslims are commanded to give one-fortieth (2.5%) of their income primarily to the poor and needy.

5. *To Make the Pilgrimage (Hajj).* Every Muslim must make the trip to Mecca at least once during his or her lifetime, provided he or she is able with respect to health and finances. Each pilgrim must wear the white garments called *ihram,* which have the effect of eliminating all class or status distinctions during the *Hajj.*

Muslim women at prayer.

The process of visiting several sacred sites usually takes more than a week. After the pilgrimage, the pilgrim is entitled to be referred to as a *Hajj*.

CONCERNING GOD

Many people assume that the God of the *Qur'an* is the same as the God of the Bible. But is that a correct assumption? The following lists compare and contrast the two concepts of God.

The God of the Qur'an and the God of the Bible

THE SIMILARITIES

■ Both are One.
■ Both are transcendent Creators of the universe.
■ Both are sovereign.
■ Both are omnipotent.
■ Both have spoken to humanity through messengers or prophets, through angels, and through the written word.
■ Both know in intimate detail the thoughts and deeds of men.
■ Both will judge the wicked.

THE DIFFERENCES

■ The God of the *Qur'an* is a singular unity; but the God of the Bible is a compound unity who is one in essence and three in persons (Matthew 28:19; John 10:30; Acts 5:3–4).
■ The God of the *Qur'an* is not a father, and he has begotten no sons (*Surahs* 19:88–92; 112:3); but the God of the Bible is a tri-unity who has eternally existed as Father, Son, and Holy Spirit (Matthew 28:19; Luke 3:21–22; John 5:18).
■ Through the *Qur'an*, God broke into history through a word that is written; but, through Jesus Christ, God broke into history through the Word who is a Person (John 1:1, 14; Colossians 1:15–20; Hebrews 1:2–3; 1 John 1:1–3; 4:9–10).
■ The God of the *Qur'an* "loves not the prodigals" (*Surahs* 6:142; 7:31, Ali; 'Ali has "wasters"); but Jesus tells the story of a father, a metaphor for God the Father, who longs for the return of his prodigal son (Luke 15:11–24).
■ "Allah loves not those that do wrong" (*Surah* 3:140, Ali), and neither does He love "him who is

Domes of the Blue Mosque, Amman, Jordan.

treacherous, sinful" (*Surah* 4:107, Ali); but "God demonstrates his own love for us in this: While we were still sinners, Christ died for us" (Romans 5:8).

■ "Allah desires to afflict them for some of their sins" (*Surah* 5:49, Ali; also see *Surahs* 4:168–169; 7:179; 9:2; 40:10); but the God of the Bible does not "take any pleasure in the death of the wicked" (Ezekiel 18:23) and is "not wanting anyone to perish, but everyone to come to repentance" (2 Peter 3:9).

■ The standard for judgment for the God of the *Qur'an* is that our good deeds must outweigh our bad deeds (*Surahs* 7:8–9; 21:47); but the standard of the God of the Bible is nothing less than complete perfection as measured by the holy character of God (Matthew 5:48; Romans 3:23).

■ The God of the *Qur'an* provided a messenger, Muhammad, who warned of Allah's impending judgment (*Surahs* 2:119; 5:19; 7:184, 188; 15:89–90) and who declared that "No bearer of a burden can bear the burden of another" (*Surahs* 17:15; 35:18, Ali); but the God of the Bible provided a sinless Savior, Jesus, who took our sins upon himself and bore God's wrath in our stead (Matthew 20:28; 26:28; Luke 22:37; John 3:16; 10:9–11; 2 Corinthians 5:21; Galatians 3:13; 1 Thessalonians 5:9–10) .

ANSWERING THE OBJECTIONS COMMONLY RAISED BY MUSLIMS

1. "The Bible Has Been Corrupted"

Muslims have been taught that the early texts of the Bible were corrupted by the Jews and the Christians. This is known as the doctrine of *tahrif*, or alteration.

As support for this doctrine, Muslims point to the following passages:

A party of them heard the Word of Allah, and perverted [Ali has "altered"] it knowingly after they understood it (*Surah* 2:75, 'Ali).

Center of the Whirling Dervishes, a mystical Islamic sect, Konya, Turkey.

The domes and minarets of one of the great mosques of Cairo, Egypt.

And there are among them [the Jews] illiterates, who know not the Book, but (see therein their own) desires, and they do nothing but conjecture. Then woe to those who write the Book with their own hands, and then say: "This is from Allah," to traffic with it for a miserable price! (*Surah* 2:78–79, 'Ali).

These *Qur'anic* passages, however, speak of *misinterpreting* Scripture and of *passing something off as Scripture* that is not Scripture, but they *do not speak of altering the actual biblical manuscripts* themselves (Parrinder, 147).

Significantly, the *Qur'an* itself considers the previous revelations contained in "the Book" to be authoritative and authentic revelations from God (*Surah* 2:136; 4:163). The *Qur'an* encourages Jews and Christians to "stand fast by the Law, the Gospel, and all the revelation that has come to you from your Lord" (*Surah* 5:68). It uses the Torah and the Gospel to authenticate Muhammad as the prophet (*Surah* 7:157), and it encourages those who doubt Muhammad's teachings to "ask those who have been reading the Book from before thee" (*Surah* 10:94). The *Qur'an* also urges people to believe in the previous Scriptures (*Surah* 4:136).

Clearly, it would be inconsistent for the *Qur'an* to, on the one hand, advise people to consult the previous Scriptures and to believe in them, and then, on the other hand, teach that those Scriptures are corrupted and therefore untrustworthy.

With as much as the *Qur'an* talks about the previous Scriptures as being revealed from God, the Muslim contention that Jews and Christians have altered those Scriptures flies in the face of the *Qur'an's* own statement that, "None can change His words" (*Surah* 6:115; also see 6:34; 10:64). Considering such a statement in the *Qur'an*, are Muslims willing to admit that their doctrine of *tahrif* in fact questions the power of God to protect His revealed word? Would not such questioning be an affront to God?

Consider also the impossibility of corrupting the biblical texts. To accomplish such a feat would have meant that the worldwide community of Jews had agreed to the textual

The towering minaret of one of the mosques in Alexandria, Egypt.

changes that the remote and relatively insignificant Jewish community in Medina was suggesting. Then it would also have meant that the Christians of the world, who also possessed the Torah, assented to the changes among the Jews, even though the Christians were not even agreeing among themselves at that time about certain doctrinal issues.

Furthermore, the manuscript evidence does not support the accusation of textual corruption. With respect to the authenticity of the Old Testament, the Dead Sea Scrolls,

which date from 100 B.C., confirm in an astounding way the accuracy of the Masoretic manuscripts, which date from A.D. 900 (Geisler & Nix, 405, 408). The significance of those dates is that they show that the manuscripts that existed *after* the Muslim accusation of *tahrif* are identical to those that existed long *before* Muhammad even lived.

With respect to the authenticity of the New Testament, biblical scholars have found 3,157 Greek manuscripts that contain either portions or all of the New Testament and that date from the second century on (Geisler & Nix, 466). Of the variants (textual differences) between these manuscripts, 95% have to do with trivialities, such as a letter being deleted by mistake. In response to the accusation by Muslims that the variants significantly changed Christian doctrine, it must be stated that no Christian doctrine rests solely on, or is even affected by, a debatable text (Bruce, 20; Geisler & Nix, 474).

2. The Doctrine of the Trinity

In light of the Muslim sin of *ishrak*—associating a partner with God—Muslims raise several objections to the doctrine of the Trinity.

Objection No. 1: "Christians worship three gods." There are several ways to approach this objection.
1. Affirm your agreement with your Muslim friend(s) that there is only one God. Read with them the biblical passages that assert as much (Deuteronomy 6:4; Mark 12:29–32; 1 Corinthians 8:4).
2. Point out that the Bible speaks at times of a compound or complex unity rather than a simple, undivided unity. In other words, the word "one" often means there is a plurality in the oneness (Genesis 2:24; Exodus 24:3; Judges 20:1, 8, 11; Romans 12:5).
3. Explain that it is not surprising that we, as God's creatures, would not be able to fully understand the nature of our Creator. The difficulty of understanding and explaining the concept of the Trinity is, in fact, evidence *for* its divine origin. It is unlikely that such a concept would be invented by mere humans.

One staff member of International Students, Inc., uses an illustration called "Flatland" to explain this point. Flatland is a two-dimensional realm, and in Flatland reside Mr. and Mrs. Flat. It would be just as difficult for Mr. and Mrs. Flat to comprehend us and our world in which there are three dimensions as it is for us to comprehend the nature of God, who exists in several dimensions beyond ours.
4. Clarify the makeup of the Trinity—that it consists of the Father, Son, and Holy Spirit. Because of the following verse, some Muslims believe that the Trinity consists of God, Jesus, *and* Mary: "And when Allah will say: O

Ritual fountain outside the El Aksa Mosque, Jerusalem, Israel. Muslims wash carefully before worship.

WORLDWIDE DISTRIBUTION OF ISLAM

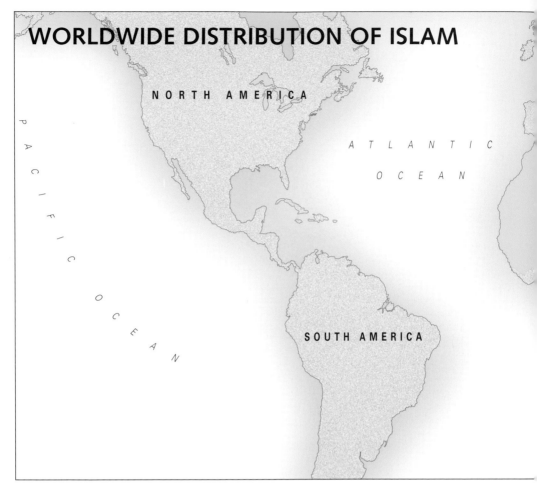

NORTH AMERICA

ATLANTIC

OCEAN

PACIFIC

OCEAN

SOUTH AMERICA

Jesus, son of Mary, didst thou say to men, Take me and my mother for two gods besides Allah?" (*Surah* 5:116, Ali).

5. Consider together with your Muslim friend the biblical evidence for the tri-unity of God. In the Bible, the Father is referred to as God (Matthew 11:25; John 6:27; 8:54; Ephesians 4:6), Jesus is recognized as God (Luke 5:17–26; John 1:1; 20:28), and the Holy Spirit is identified as God (Acts 5:3–4). Even though each is referred to as God, the Bible does not speak of three gods but of the three as being one: "baptizing them in the name (singular) of the Father and of the Son and of the Holy Spirit" (Matthew 28:19).

Plus, the Father, Son, and Holy Spirit are all identified as having attributes unique to God. For example, each Person of the Trinity existed before anything was created, and each was active in the creation of all things (God: Psalm 146:5–6; Mark 13:19; Acts 4:24; Jesus: John 1:1–3, 14; 1 Corinthians 8:6; Colossians 1:16–17; Holy Spirit: Genesis 1:1–3).

Moreover, each Person possesses the attribute of omnipresence, or being present to all things (God: Jeremiah 23:24; Acts 17:24–25; Jesus: Matthew 18:20; 28:20; Ephesians 1:23; Holy Spirit: Psalm 139:7–8).

Objection No. 2: "God has no sons." The second objection that arises from the doctrine of the Trinity has to do with Christians referring to Jesus as the Son of God. When Muslims hear

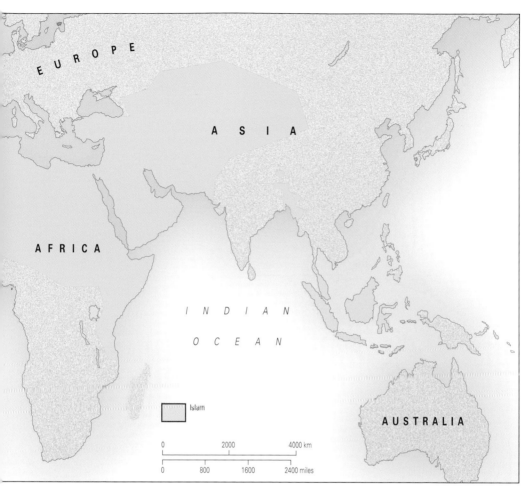

Islam

the phrase "Son of God," they understand it to imply that God had physical relations with a woman in order to have a son. The Qur'an says, "Such (was) Jesus the son of Mary: (It is) a statement of truth, about which they (vainly) dispute. It is not befitting to (the majesty of) Allah that He should beget a son" (*Surah* 19:34–35).

In the Arabic language there are two words for expressing "son of": *walad* and *ibn*. *Walad* definitely denotes becoming a son through the union of a male with a female. We as Christians would agree that Jesus was not a *waladdu'llah*—"son of God"— in that sense. The Bible says Jesus was born of the virgin Mary (Matthew 1:23; Luke 1:34). Moreover, the

Qur'an itself does not deny the virgin birth of Jesus (*Surah* 3:47).

Unlike *walad*, however, the word *ibn* can be used in a metaphorical sense. For example, Arabs themselves talk about a traveler as being an *ibnu'ssabil*—"son of the road" (Fellowship, 6). They obviously do not mean by such a phrase that one has had sexual relations with the road. It is in this wider metaphorical sense that Jesus is understood as being the Son of God.

When Jesus referred to God as "My Father" and to himself as "the Son" (Matthew 11:27; John 5:17, 22–23), He was not talking about His physical birth. Instead, He was claiming to have a special relationship with God that referred to His identity and equality. To be the "son of" someone is to be of the same order as and to have the same qualities as that person.

The Jews of Jesus' day made it clear that this idea of the sameness of order and quality is how they understood Jesus' statement when they said, "He was even calling God his own Father, *making himself equal with God*" (John 5:18, emphasis added). In another instance, Jesus said, "I and the Father are one" (John 10:30). For making that statement, the Jews picked up stones to kill Jesus "for blasphemy, because you, a mere man, *claim to be God*" (John 10:33, emphasis added).

One Iranian Christian says that he deals with this controversial issue by specifying that Jesus is "the *spiritual* Son of God." This is not to deny Jesus' humanity, but such a phrase will be less offensive to the Muslim.

Another approach is to ask your Muslim friend, "Are you not limiting God by saying that He is unable to express himself through human form? Are you not saying that something is then impossible with God? Remember that the angel declared to Mary that 'nothing is impossible with God' (Luke 1:37)."

This subject also includes the issue of the best way God could have communicated to humanity. By way of an illustration, the Vietnam War caused a family to be separated. The father was forced to stay in Vietnam, while the wife and two boys were able to come to the United States. For seventeen years, they communicated with each other only through letters and pictures. The father could see his boys grow up only from a distance. Then finally the governments of Vietnam and the United States made an agreement that allowed the father to come to the States to see his family. But what if the father said, "I don't really see any need to come see to you in person. Communicating through letters and pictures has been sufficient for seventeen years, so it will continue to be sufficient for me." What would you think of such a father?

What would you think of a God who, if it were at all possible, would refuse to communicate with His creation in person?

Objection No. 3: "The doctrine of the Trinity contradicts itself." Muslims often claim that the doctrine of the Trinity contradicts itself. After all, how can something be both three and one?

In response, for a statement to contradict itself it must both affirm and deny the same thing in the same respect. Does the doctrine of the Trinity do that? The answer is "no," because the doctrine states that God is *one in essence* (or being, or substance) and *three in person*. Essence and personhood are different. God is three in person in that each Person of the Trinity is distinct within the Godhead; God is one in that each Person of the Godhead shares the

The Islamic palace of Alhambra, Granada, Andalusia, Spain, built by the Muslim Moors.

same self-existing essence and other qualities unique to God.

This simultaneous distinction and sameness is seen in John 1:1, "In the beginning was the Word, and the Word was with God, and the Word was God." The word "with" indicates a distinction and a relationship between the Persons of the Son (the Word) and the Father (God), while at the same time the phrase "the Word *was* God"—a verb of being— indicates the sameness of essence between the two Persons.

Another way to approach the doctrine of the Trinity is by pointing out how practical it is in that it meets each person's felt needs, such as:

Love: God the Father demonstrated His love for us historically by sending His Son to save us (John 3:16; Romans 5:8; 1 John 4:9–10).

Freedom from guilt and sin: God the Son took our sins upon himself, paid the penalty of death on our behalf, and rose from the dead to give us victory over sin and death (Romans 5:8, 1 Corinthians 5:21; 15:3–4). Through Jesus we can receive the forgiveness of sins and freedom from guilt (1 John 1:9).

Empathy: Because the Word became flesh and lived among us, we know that *God, through Jesus*, is able to empathize with our suffering (Philippians 2:6–8; Hebrews 4:15).

Hope: Because *Jesus* physically rose from the dead, we have the hope of personal survival after death. Moreover, because of the life-giving power of *the Holy Spirit*, we have the assurance of eternal life (Romans 8:11; see also 2 Corinthians 1:22; 5:5; Ephesians 1:13–14).

Transformation: God the Holy Spirit indwells us (Romans 8:9–11; 1 Corinthians 3:16); makes our spirit, which was dead, alive (John 3:3–7; 2 Corinthians 5:17; Titus 3:5); and gives us the power to submit to God (Romans 8:5–17).

Communication with God: We can have a personal relationship with God because Jesus has broken the barriers between us and God (Ephesians 2:12–18; Colossians 1:21–22);

because He serves as our mediator with God (1 Timothy 2:5); and because *the Holy Spirit* assists us in our communication with God (Romans 8:26–27).

Interior of the mosque at Acre, on the Israeli coast.

3. The Crucifixion

Muslims believe that the God of the *Qur'an* would not dishonor his chosen prophet by allowing him to be crucified. One Iranian student said, "Do we not honor [Jesus] more than you do when we refuse to believe that God would permit Him to suffer death on the cross? Rather, we believe that God took Him to heaven" (Woodberry, 164). Muslims, therefore, deny that Jesus was crucified. They believe instead that He was caught up into heaven and that someone (some say Judas) took His place on the cross.

The following is the primary passage that Muslims use to deny the crucifixion:

Opposite: Richly decorated interior of a mosque. Blue is a characteristic Muslim color.

That they said (in boast), "We killed Christ Jesus the son of Mary, the Messenger of Allah"—but they killed him not, nor crucified him, but so it was made to appear to them, and those who differ therein are full of doubts, with no (certain) knowledge, but only conjecture to follow, for of a surety they killed him not—nay, Allah raised him up unto Himself (*Surah* 4:157–158).

A careful reading of the above passage, however, shows that it does not deny that Jesus was crucified, but it instead *denies that the Jews caused Jesus to be crucified.* In point of fact, the Jews did not crucify Jesus, but the Romans did (John 18:31).

Even more importantly, God was ultimately responsible for Jesus' being crucified (Romans 8:3–4; 1 Peter 1:18–20). Even the *Qur'an* alludes to that fact in the following verse:

When Allah said: "O Jesus, *I will cause thee to die and exalt thee in My presence* and clear thee of those who disbelieve and make those who follow thee above those who disbelieve to the day of Resurrection" (Surah 3:54, Ali, emphasis added).

In light of the above passage, it is effective to have the Muslim also read Isaiah 53:4–11 to see why God caused Jesus to die. Following that, consider together the story of God ordering Abraham to sacrifice his son in *Surah* 37:101–107 (although the passage is not explicit, Muslims understand the son to be Ishmael):

So we gave him the good news of a boy ready to suffer and forbear. Then, when (the son) reached (the age of) (serious) work with him, he said: [Abraham] "O my son! I see in vision that I offer thee in sacrifice: Now see what is thy view!" (The son) said: "O my father! Do as thou art commanded: thou will find me, if Allah so wills one practicing patience and constancy!" So when they had both submitted their wills (to Allah) and he had laid him prostrate on his forehead (for sacrifice), We called out to him, "O Abraham!

Thou hast already fulfilled the vision!"—thus indeed do We reward those who do right. For this was obviously a trial—and we ransomed him with a momentous sacrifice" ('Ali).

There are three questions to ask a Muslim with respect to the above passage:

■ If salvation is only a matter of rewarding those who do good, and if God's purpose was only to test Abraham's obedience, why then was there a need for "a momentous sacrifice"? Was it not sufficient that Abraham went as far as he did?
■ Who provided the "momentous sacrifice"?
■ Is a goat enough to "ransom" humanity for our sins?

In light of the above passage from the *Qur'an* and the three questions, read what Jesus said concerning His mission: "The Son of Man [Jesus] did not come to be served, but to serve, and to give his life as a ransom for many" (Matthew 20:28). Jesus is the great sacrifice, and God is the One who sent Him (John 3:16).

A former Muslim who wrestled with the issue of Jesus' crucifixion said that one thing that really affected him was to see that Jesus "over and over mentioned and predicted His death, and it happened—it really happened." It is helpful, then, to point out the verses in which Jesus predicted His death (Matthew 12:39–40; 16:4, 21; 17:22–23; 20:17–19; 26:2; Mark 8:31; 9:31; 10:33–34; Luke 9:22, 44; John 10:11, 17–18; 12:32–33).

Rather than seeing the Crucifixion as dishonoring Christ, Muslims should see it not only as resulting in the greatest of honors but also as manifesting the epitome of what it means to be a Muslim. How is that? Consider the following:

And being found in appearance as a man, he humbled himself and *became obedient to death*—even death on a cross! Therefore *God exalted him to the*

highest place and gave him the name that is above every name (Philippians 2:8–9, emphasis added).

The word "Islam" means "obedience, submission." And it is obedience to God that Jesus demonstrated all the way to the Cross! Muslims should honor Him for such obedience!

Concerning the issue of God dishonoring one of His chosen prophets, the passage is clear that Christ's obedience led to God's exalting Him with the greatest of exaltations (also see Acts 2:29–33; 5:30–31).

Who, moreover, is being disrespectful? Those who say God would deceive by replacing Jesus with someone who looks like Him, or those who say God is able to raise His Prophet from the dead and to thereby conquer sin for all humanity?

Ultimately, the argument concerning the significance of the Cross of Christ must not be a theological one, but a personal one— what Jesus' death means to you. The Muslim must be shown the difference between the uncertainty of salvation by attempting to live up to the law versus the certainty of salvation by receiving God's grace through faith in Jesus Christ.

BIBLIOGRAPHY AND RESOURCES

Abdul-Haqq, Abdiyah Akbar. *Sharing Your Faith With a Muslim.* Minneapolis: Bethany House Publishers, 1980.

Adelphi, Ghiyathuddin and Ernest Hahn. *The Integrity of the Bible According to the Qur'an and the Hadith.* Hyderabad, India: Henry Martyn Institute of Islamic Studies, 1977.

Ali, Maulana Muhammad. *The Holy Qur'an.* Chicago: Specialty Promotions Co., Inc., 1985.

'Ali, 'Abdullah Yusuf. *The Meaning of the Holy Qur'an.* Brentwood, Md.: Amana Corporation, 1993.

Bruce, F. F. *The New Testament Documents: Are They Reliable?* Downers Grove, Ill.: InterVarsity Press, 1978.

Campbell, William. *The Gospel of Barnabas: Its True Value.* Rawalpindi, Pakistan: Christian Study Centre, 1989.

Esther, Gulshan and Thelma Sangster. *The Torn Veil: The Story of Sister Gulshan Esther.* Hants, United Kingdom: Marshall Pickering, 1984.

Farah, Caesar. *Islam: Beliefs and Observances,* 4th ed. New York: Barron's Educational Series, Inc., 1987.

Fellowship of Faith for Muslims. *Questions Muslims Ask.* Toronto: Fellowship of Faith for Muslims.

Geisler, Norman and William Nix. *A General Introduction to the Bible.* Chicago: Moody Press, 1986.

Ghaffari, Ebrahim and Marie. *Strategies for Sharing the Gospel With Muslim University Students in the U.S.* Colorado Springs, Colo.: Iranian Christians International, Inc., 1984.

Hahn, Ernest. *How to Share Your Christian Faith With Muslims.* Toronto: Fellowship of Faith for Muslims, 1988.

Hahn, Ernest. *Understanding Some Muslim Misunderstandings.* Toronto: Fellowship of Faith for Muslims.

Hamada, Louis. *Understanding the Arab World.* Nashville: Thomas Nelson Publishers, 1990.

Hinnells, John, ed. *A Handbook of Living Religions.* New York: Viking Penguin, Inc., 1984.

Hourani, Albert. *A History of the Arab Peoples.* Cambridge, Mass.: Harvard University Press, 1991.

Kershaw, R. Max. *How to Share the Good News With Your Muslim Friend.* Colorado Springs, Colo.: International Students, Inc., 1990.

Lewis, James and William Travis. *Religious Traditions of the World.* Grand Rapids, Mich.: Zondervan, 1991.

Marsh, C. R. *Share Your Faith With a Muslim.* Chicago: Moody Press, 1975.

McGrath, Alister. *Understanding the Trinity.* Grand Rapids, Mich.: Zondervan Publishing House, 1988.

Miller, William M. *A Christian's Response to Islam.* Phillipsburg, N.J.: Presbyterian and Reformed Publishing Co., 1976.

Momen, Moojan. *An Introduction to Shi'i Islam.* New Haven, Conn.: Yale University Press, 1985.

Parrinder, Geoffrey. *Jesus in the Qur'an.* London: Sheldon Press, 1965.

Parshall, Phil. *Bridges to Islam: A Christian Perspective on Folk Islam.* Grand Rapids, Mich.: Baker Book House, 1983.

Pfander, C. G. *The Mizan-Ul-Haqq: Balance of Truth.* Villach, Austria: Light of Life, 1986.

Saal, William. *Reaching Muslims for Christ.* Chicago: Moody Press, 1991.

Sell, Canon. *The Historical Development of the Qur'an.* Chicago: People International.

Sheikh, Bilquis, with Richard Schneider. *I Dared to Call Him Father.* Old Tappan, N.J.: Fleming H. Revell Co., 1978.

Shorrosh, Anis. *Islam Revealed: A Christian Arab's View of Islam.* Nashville: Thomas Nelson Publishers, 1988.

Sproul, R. C. *The Mystery of the Holy Spirit.* Wheaton, Ill.: Tyndale House Publishers, Inc., 1990.

Waddy, Chris. *The Muslim Mind.* New York: New Amsterdam Books, 1990.

Woodberry, J. Dudley, ed. *Muslims & Christians on the Emmaus Road.* Monrovia, Calif.: Missions Advanced Research and Communications Center, 1989.

ORGANIZATIONS

Arab World Ministries
P.O. Box 96
Upper Darby, PA 19082
Phone: (800) 447-3566
email: www.awm.org

Fellowship of Faith for Muslims
P.O. Box 65214
Toronto, Ontario M4K 3Z2
CANADA

Friends of Turkey
508 Fruitvale Ct.
Grand Junction, CO 81504
Phone: (970) 434-1942
Fax: (970) 434-1461

HIS (Helping International Students)
1711 Pendleton St.
Columbia, SC 29201
Phone: (803) 779-2852
Fax: (803) 779-8533

Horizons Multicultural Communications
Box 18478
Boulder, CO 80308-8478
Phone: (303) 442-3333

Iranian Christians International, Inc.
P.O. Box 25607
Colorado Springs, CO 80936
Phone: (719) 596-0010

Samuel Zwemer Institute
Box 365
Altadena, CA 91001
Phone: (818) 794-1121

Al-Nour
P.O. Box 985
Colorado Springs, CO 80901
Fax: (719) 574-6075

Judaism and the Jewish People

Richard Robinson

NUMBER OF ADHERENTS

There is a distinction between the Jewish people and the religion of Judaism. Not all Jewish people consider themselves to be religious. Many profess to be atheists, agnostics, or secular. While not all Jewish people follow the religion of Judaism, when Jews choose to be religious, they generally choose some variety of Judaism rather than another religion. They consider Judaism "our" religion, available for those Jews who choose to adhere. In contrast, most Jewish people would consider Christianity to be "their" religion, that is, a religion appropriate for non-Jews.

With this in mind we can say that there are 12.8 million Jewish people in the world today. In a 1990 census of American (United States) Jews, 76% claimed to adhere to some Jewish religious affiliation, while 20% were secular.

The 1993 *American Jewish Yearbook* gives the following population statistics as of 1991: Of the 12.8 million Jews, 4.1 million are in Israel, 6.3 million in North and South America, and 868,000 in the former Soviet Union. In the United States, there were 5.8 million Jews in 1992. Because of the rapid changes in

Young Jews at Jerusalem's Western Wall, parts of which date back to Herod's Temple.

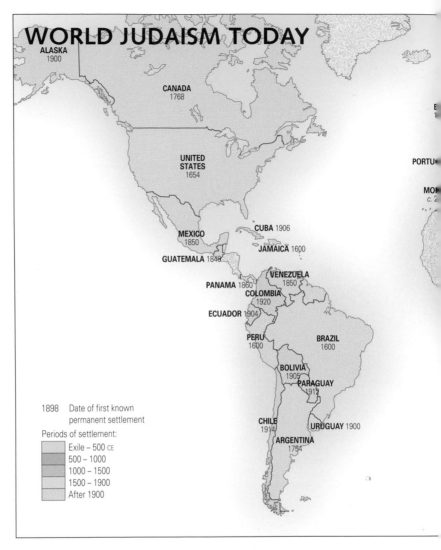

WORLD JUDAISM TODAY

ALASKA
1900

CANADA
1768

UNITED
STATES
1654

PORTU⬤

MO▮
c. 2

CUBA 1906

MEXICO
1850

JAMAICA 1600

GUATEMALA 1848

VENEZUELA
1850

PANAMA 1860
COLOMBIA
1920

ECUADOR 1904

PERU
1600

BRAZIL
1600

BOLIVIA
1905

PARAGUAY
1912

CHILE
1914

URUGUAY 1900

ARGENTINA
1754

1898   Date of first known
       permanent settlement

Periods of settlement:

Exile – 500 CE
500 – 1000
1000 – 1500
1500 – 1900
After 1900

the former Soviet Union, such numbers are highly susceptible to change.

INTRODUCING JUDAISM

The term "Judaism" is sometimes loosely used to include not only the faith of modern Jews but also that of the Old Testament. Sometimes it is used to include the entire Jewish way of life. It is best, however, to use the term "Judaism" to refer to the religion of the rabbis that developed from about 200 B.C. onward and crystallized following the destruction

of the Temple in A.D. 70. In this way Christianity is not described as a daughter religion of Judaism, but more correctly as a sister: both branched out from Old Testament faith.

THE DEVELOPMENT OF JUDAISM

From around 200 B.C. onward, new institutions and ways of life developed that distinguished rabbinic Judaism from the religion of ancient (Old Testament) Israel. New institutions

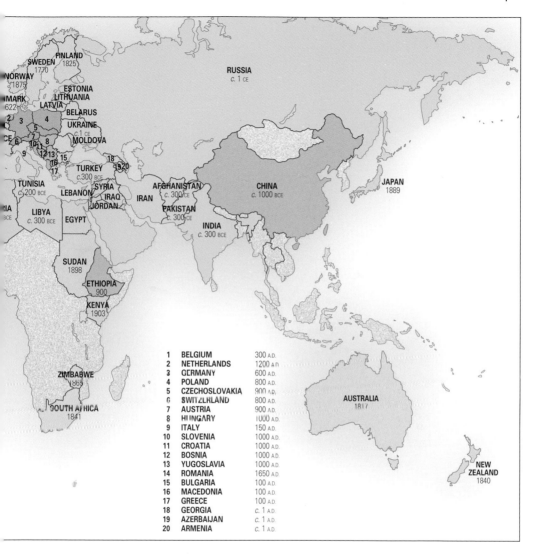

1	BELGIUM	300 A.D.
2	NETHERLANDS	1200 A.D.
3	GERMANY	600 A.D.
4	POLAND	800 A.D.
5	CZECHOSLOVAKIA	900 A.D.
6	SWITZERLAND	800 A.D.
7	AUSTRIA	900 A.D.
8	HUNGARY	1000 A.D.
9	ITALY	150 A.D.
10	SLOVENIA	1000 A.D.
11	CROATIA	1000 A.D.
12	BOSNIA	1000 A.D.
13	YUGOSLAVIA	1000 A.D.
14	ROMANIA	1650 A.D.
15	BULGARIA	100 A.D.
16	MACEDONIA	100 A.D.
17	GREECE	100 A.D.
18	GEORGIA	c. 1 A.D.
19	AZERBAIJAN	c. 1 A.D.
20	ARMENIA	c. 1 A.D.

arose such as the synagogue (the house of worship and study), the *yeshivot* (religious academies for the training of rabbis), and the office of the rabbi (a leader holding religious authority).

One of the greatest catalysts in the development of Judaism was the destruction of the Temple in A.D. 70, which resulted in the abolition of sacrifices and the priesthood. Rather than being guided by priests, prophets, or kings, the rabbis became the authorities who established various laws and practices that had normative authority.

Before the eighteenth century, there was basically one kind of Judaism. In contrast, one of the distinguishing features of modern Judaism is the existence of the three main movements or "branches." These branches are not quite equivalent to what Christians understand by denominations, where one's identity is often tied strongly to a particular denomination, and in which one's affiliation is often determined simply by family tradition. The branches of Judaism are more like voluntary associations, with classifications according to cultural and doctrinal

Orthodox Jews pray at the Western Wall, sometimes called the Wailing Wall.

formulas (like denominations) but with adherence to a particular branch often governed by personal preference, nearness of a given synagogue, or one's agreement with the rabbi's style and views (like voluntary associations).

Within each branch you will find adherents with varying degrees of observance. Many Jewish people formulate their own informal version of Judaism and do not fit exactly into any one of these categories. Nevertheless, knowing the distinctions between the branches and to which branch your Jewish friends adhere can be helpful in most witnessing situations.

Orthodox Judaism. There was only one kind of Judaism until the Age of the Enlightenment in the eighteenth century. Only later, to differentiate it from the other branches of Judaism, was this called "Orthodox." Today, Orthodox Judaism is characterized by an emphasis on tradition and strict observance of the Law of Moses as interpreted by the rabbis.

Reform Judaism. Reform Judaism began in Germany in the eighteenth century at the time of the Enlightenment, or *Haskalah*. It sought to modernize what were considered outmoded ways of thinking and doing and to thus prevent the increasing assimilation of German Jewry. Reform Judaism emphasizes ethics and the precepts of the prophets.

Conservative Judaism. This branch developed from nineteenth-century German roots as a middle-ground branch.

HOW TO THINK ABOUT THE THREE BRANCHES OF JUDAISM

It can be helpful to compare Orthodox Judaism with Roman Catholicism or Greek Orthodoxy, where there is a heavy emphasis on tradition. Reform Judaism can be compared with Unitarianism, emphasizing humanism. Conservative Judaism can be compared to modern

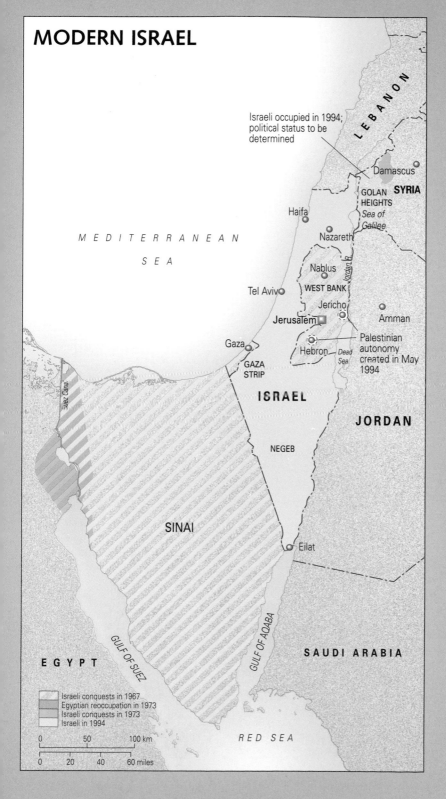

MODERN ISRAEL

Israeli occupied in 1994;
political status to be
determined

M E D I T E R R A N E A N

S E A

LEBANON

Damascus

GOLAN
HEIGHTS

SYRIA

*Sea of
Galilee*

Haifa

Nazareth

Jordan R.

Nablus

WEST BANK

Tel Aviv

Jericho

Jerusalem

Amman

Gaza

Palestinian
autonomy
created in May
1994

Hebron

*Dead
Sea*

GAZA
STRIP

ISRAEL

JORDAN

NEGEB

SINAI

Eilat

Suez Canal

GULF OF SUEZ

GULF OF AQABA

SAUDI ARABIA

E G Y P T

Israeli conquests in 1967
Egyptian reoccupation in 1973
Israeli conquests in 1973
Israeli in 1994

0   50   100 km

0   20   40   60 miles

RED SEA

The Three Branches of Judaism

CATEGORY	ORTHODOX	CONSERVATIVE	REFORM
HISTORY	Orthodoxy dates back to the days of the Talmud (second to fifth centuries A.D.). It was the only form of Jewish practice prior to the eighteenth century and the emergence of Reform Judaism. Orthodoxy today seeks to preserve classical or traditional Judaism.	Conservative Judaism is an American movement with roots in nineteenth century Germany. It arose as a reaction to what some viewed as the extreme assimilationist tendencies of Reform Judaism. It tried to be a middle ground, attempting to maintain basic traditions while adapting to modern life.	Reform Judaism emerged following the emancipation from ghetto life in the late eighteenth century. It sought to modernize Judaism and thus stem the tide of assimilation threatening German Jewry. It was thought that Jewish identity could be best maintained by modernization, but others saw this as in fact contributing to assimilation and the loss of Jewish identity.
OTHER TERMS	Traditional or Torah Judaism	Historical Judaism	Liberal or Progressive Judaism
U.S. MEMBERSHIP*	6% of all American Jews	35% of all American Jews	38% of all American Jews
VIEW OF SCRIPTURE	Torah, meaning essentially the teaching of the Five Books of Moses, is truth. A person must have faith in its essential, revealed character. A true Jew believes in revelation and the divine origin of the oral and written Torah. "Oral Torah" refers to various interpretations of the written Torah believed to have been given to Moses along with the written Torah. The Torah is accorded a higher place than the rest of the Hebrew Bible.	The Bible, both the Torah and the other books, is the word of God and man. It is not inspired in the traditional sense, but rather dynamically inspired. Revelation is an ongoing process.	The Bible is a human document preserving the history, culture, legends and hopes of a people. It is valuable for deriving moral and ethical insights. Revelation is an ongoing process.
VIEW OF GOD	God is spirit rather than form. He is a personal God—omnipotent, omniscient, omnipresent, eternal, and compassionate.	The concept of God is nondogmatic and flexible. There is less atheism in Conservative Judaism than in Reform, but most often God is considered impersonal and ineffable.	Reform Judaism allows a varied interpretation of the "God concept" with wide latitude for naturalists, mystics, super-naturalists, or religious humanists. It holds that "the truth is that we do not know the truth."

*(Source: 1992 American Jewish Yearbook)

CATEGORY	ORTHODOX	CONSERVATIVE	REFORM
VIEW OF HUMAN-KIND	Humanity is morally neutral, with a good and an evil inclination. He or she can overcome his or her evil bent and be perfected by his or her own efforts in observance of the Law.	This group tends toward the Reform view, though it is not as likely to espouse humanism. Perfectibility can come through enlightenment. Humanity is "in partnership" with God.	Humanity's nature is basically good. Through education, encouragement, and evolution he or she can actualize the potential already existing within him or her.
VIEW OF TRADITION OF THE LAW	The Law is the basis of Judaism. It is authoritative and gives structure and meaning to life. The life of total dedication to *Halakhah* (body of Jewish law) leads to a nearness to God.	Adaptation to contemporary situations is inevitable. The demands of morality are absolute; the specific laws are relative.	The law is an evolving, ever-dynamic religious code that adapts to every age. It is maintained that if religious observances clash with the just demands of civilized society they must be dropped.
VIEW OF SIN	Orthodox Jews do not believe in "original sin." Rather one commits sin by breaking the commandments of the Law.	Conservative Jews do not believe in "original sin." The individual can sin in moral or social actions.	Reform Jews do not believe in "original sin." Sin is interpreted as the ills of society. Humanity is sometimes held to have a "divine spark" within.
VIEW OF SALVATION	Repentance (belief in God's mercy), prayer, and obedience to the Law are necessary for a proper relationship with God. "Salvation" is not considered to be a Jewish concept, inasmuch as Jewish people presume a standing with God.	Conservative Jews tend toward the Reform view, but include the necessity of maintaining Jewish identity.	"Salvation" is obtained through the betterment of self and society. It is social improvement.
VIEW OF THE MESSIAH	The Messiah is a human being who is not divine. He will restore the Jewish kingdom and extend his righteous rule over the earth. He will execute judgment and right all wrongs.	Conservative Jews hold much the same view as the Reform.	Instead of belief in Messiah as a person or divine being, Reform Jews favor the concept of a Utopian age toward which humankind is progressing, sometimes called the "Messianic age."
VIEW OF LIFE AFTER DEATH	There will be a physical resurrection. The righteous will exist forever with God in the "World to Come." The unrighteous will suffer, but disagreement exists over their ultimate destiny.	Conservative Jews tend toward the Reform view, but are less influenced by nontraditional ideas such as Eastern mysticism.	Generally, Reform Judaism has no concept of personal life after death. It is said that a person lives on in the accomplishments or in the minds of others. Some are influenced by Eastern mystical thought, where souls merge into one great impersonal life force.

The Three Branches of Judaism (continued)

CATEGORY	ORTHODOX	CONSERVATIVE	REFORM
DISTINCTIVES IN SYNAGOGUE WORSHIP	The synagogue is a house of prayer as well as study; social aspects are incidental. All prayers are recited in Hebrew. Men and women sit separately. The officiants face the same direction as the congregants.	The synagogue is viewed as the basic institution of Jewish life. Alterations listed under Reform are found to a lesser degree in Conservative worship.	The synagogue is known as a "Temple." The service has been modernized and abbreviated. English, as well as Hebrew, is used. Men and women sit together. Reform temples use choirs and organs in their worship services.
BOOKS TO READ	Herman Wouk, *This Is My God*, orig. 1961. A. Cohen, *Everyman's Talmud*, orig. 1932.	S. Schechter, Some *Aspects of Rabbinic Theology*, orig. 1923. *Emet Ve-emunah: Statement of Principles of Conservative Judaism*, 1988. Marshall Sklare, *Conservative Judaism*, 1972.	Eugene B. Borowitz, *Reform Judaism Today*, 1983. *Liberal Judaism*, 1984.

liberal Protestantism, emphasizing form over doctrinal content.

Notice that there is no equivalent to evangelical Christianity, emphasizing a personal relationship with God. Orthodox Judaism is sometimes mistaken for this, but it is more concerned with living according to the traditional understandings than with a personal relationship with God.

The "Three Branches of Judaism" chart highlights the main distinctives of the three branches. In using this chart, it is important to understand that Judaism, in all its branches, is *a religion of deed, not creed.* It is possible to be an atheist and yet an Orthodox Jew! One may identify oneself as Orthodox because of attending an Orthodox congregation or because one keeps a traditional Jewish lifestyle (observing the Sabbath strictly, keeping kosher, etc.). What one believes about God, sin, or the afterlife is not nearly as important as living a proper life here and now, as defined by the branch to which one belongs. We can say that it is probable that someone who is Orthodox will in fact believe in God, while an atheist would be more likely

to align with the Reform branch, if any. But there are many exceptions. Though one can pair doctrinal positions with the three branches, doctrine is not taught in Judaism as it is in Christianity, and one may easily adhere to a particular branch without adopting the doctrines of that branch.

In other words, one can surmise correctly what an individual's lifestyle is likely to be on the basis of the branch to which he or she adheres. The only way to find out what a Jewish friend believes, however, is to ask. Do not assume what his or her beliefs are on the basis of the branch with which he or she affiliates.

Other Kinds of Judaism

The following are not major branches but should be known:

Reconstructionist. Reconstructionist Judaism is an American offshoot of Conservative Judaism. It maintains that Judaism is a "religious civilization" that must constantly adapt to contemporary life.

Hasidic. Hasidic Judaism, usually called Hasidism, is an ultra-Orthodox movement characterized by strict observance of the Law of Moses, mystical teachings, and is socially separatist. Several different Hasidic groups exist. Each finds its identity in its leader, called the *rebbe,* who is the dynastic head of the particular Hasidic group in which leadership is passed down through the generations from father to son.

Zionist. Zionism is listed here because it is sometimes mistaken as a form of Judaism. In reality it is a political movement dating from the late nineteenth century, concerned with the return of Jews to the land of Israel.

THE BELIEFS OF JUDAISM

Above we referred to the fact that Judaism is a religion of deed, not creed. If there is any religious principle (what Christians would call a "doctrine") that Judaism explicitly affirms and teaches, it is the "unity of God." Deuteronomy 6:4 called the Sh'ma—proclaims: "Hear O Israel, the

Lord our God, the Lord is one."

Beyond the affirmation of the *Sh'ma,* there have been attempts at compiling various statements of faith (such as the Thirteen Principles of Maimonides), but they have been few and not widely studied or accepted as binding.

The three branches do have their more or less "official" doctrinal

A silver pointer is used to mark the place in the Hebrew Scriptures.

Interior of a Sepphardic synagogue, the Old City, Jerusalem.

A Jewish boy reads from the Hebrew scriptures at his bar mitzvah in Jerusalem.

positions on various matters such as the person of God or the nature of humankind. These are described in the chart of "The Three Branches of Judaism." In no way, however, are they binding on any Jewish person.

THE PRACTICES OF JUDAISM

The Annual Holiday Cycle. Almost all Jewish people, regardless of the branch to which they belong, observe at least some of the Jewish holidays.

Two notes on terminology: Jewish people usually speak of "observing" the holidays rather than "celebrating" them. And while it is common for Christians to speak of the "feasts of Israel," they are spoken of by Jewish people as the "Jewish holidays." The major holidays in Judaism are explained in the chart entitled "Jewish Holidays."

The Life Cycle. Besides the annual holidays, there are various distinctive lifestyle events that characterize the lives of most Jewish people. Three of them are mentioned here. Consult resources in the bibliography to learn about the others.

■ Circumcision of sons on the eighth day. The accompanying ceremony is called *brit milah.*
■ *Bar mitzvah* (for boys) and *bat mitzvah* (for girls—not traditional). The coming-of-age ceremony at age thirteen. Generally consists of a synagogue service followed by an extended and elaborate reception with full meal.
■ Jewish weddings are typically characterized by the ceremony under a canopy—the *chuppah,* (rhymes with "look a"; the "ch" is pronounced gutturally as in German) and the smashing of a glass wrapped in a cloth to symbolize the destruction of the Temple.
■ Jewish mourning practices following a funeral include the family *sitting shiva,* or mourning for seven days (traditionally) or fewer.

Daily Lifestyle. Some other distinctive practices of Judaism include the following. The term "traditional Jews" in the material below is usually synonymous with "Orthodox." Some, however, from the other branches may choose to live more "traditionally" as an attempt to connect with their heritage.

■ Observing the Sabbath. Traditional Jews will abstain from work, from driving, and from lighting a fire on the Sabbath. Many who do not follow traditional observance will at least prepare a special family meal for the beginning of the Sabbath on Friday evening.

■ Donning *tefillin* (phylacteries), small black boxes containing Scripture portions that must be wrapped around the arm and forehead according to a set time and pattern. This is practiced today only by traditional Jews.

■ Placing a *mezuzah* on the doorposts of one's home. The *mezuzah* is a small rectangular box containing various Scripture portions. Though a traditional practice, many Jews have adopted it as a way of affirming their Jewishness, not necessarily related to any religious beliefs.

■ Keeping the dietary laws (keeping kosher). The most well-known dietary law is the prohibition of mixing meat and milk at one meal. Strictly observed by Orthodox Jews. Many other Jews will keep kosher to a limited degree out of customary ways of doing things rather than religious conviction. For example, even among nonreligious Jews who do not believe

the dietary laws are binding, it would be most unusual to find a baked ham served for dinner; chicken or beef would be customary instead.

Hebrew Scriptures.

THE JEWISH SCRIPTURES

The Old Testament portion of the Bible is the Scripture of Judaism. Some Jewish people prefer the term the "Hebrew Bible" so as not to imply that they accord any validity to the idea of a "new" covenant in contrast to an "old" one. In practice, however, many do use the term "Old

Jerusalem's Shrine of the Book, built to house some of the Dead Sea Scrolls.

Jewish Holidays

HOLIDAY	TIME OF YEAR	OBSERVANCE	RELATING TO JEWISH FRIENDS
Rosh Hashanah (the Jewish New Year). In the U.S., most often pronounced as "Russia Shunna."	September or October	Joyful atmosphere. Many attend synagogue services. Marks the first part of a ten-day period known as the High Holy Days or, less commonly, the Days of Awe.	Send a Jewish New Year greeting card, found in most card shops at this time of year. An appropriate greeting: "Happy New Year."
Yom Kippur (the Day of Atonement). Pronounced most often in the U.S. as "Yum Kipper" (rhymes with "some slipper"). 	September or October, ten days after *Rosh Hashanah*	The most solemn day of the year on the Jewish calendar. Even many less religious Jews will attend synagogue and recite prayers asking God to forgive their sin. Many will also fast for twenty-four hours.	There is no greeting. Nor is this an occasion for sending cards. If you have a Jewish co-worker, it would be thoughtful to say before inviting them to lunch, "We're heading out to lunch, but I thought you might be fasting today for *Yom Kippur*—or else you're welcome to join us." This shows that you know and recognize that they are Jewish.
Sukkot or *Sukkos*. Most often pronounced to rhyme with "took us." Also called Tabernacles or Booths. 	September or October, five days after *Yom Kippur*	A festive holiday. Traditionally, a temporary booth (*sukkah*, rhymes with "cook a") is constructed in backyards or behind the synagogue. Fruit is hung from the roof. Customs include waving the traditional *lulav* (branches of various plants) and *ethrog* (citron).	Not observed by many Jewish people. There is no generally used greeting.

HOLIDAY	TIME OF YEAR	OBSERVANCE	RELATING TO JEWISH FRIENDS
Hanukkah. Most often pronounced to rhyme with "onica" as in the name Veronica. 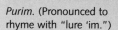	November or December. Lasts eight days.	A festive holiday that commemorates the victory of the Maccabees over the Syrian armies of Antiochus Epiphanes (ca. 175 B.C.). Characterized by lighting a *menorah* (lampstand) over a period of eight days, spinning the *dreidel* (a top—rhymes with "*wait'll*"), and eating potato pancakes called *latkes* (rhymes with "pot kiss").	Send a *Hanukkah* greeting card. An appropriate greeting: "Happy *Hanukkah*."
Purim. (Pronounced to rhyme with "lure 'im.")	February or March. Considered a minor holiday, but popular.	A partylike atmosphere can prevail. *Purim* recounts the story of the book of Esther, which is read. *Purim* plays in which the entire story is enacted in comedic style are popular.	No particular greeting
Passover 	March or April. Lasts a week, but the ceremonial meal called the *seder* is held only on the first two nights.	The most popular of all Jewish holidays, this is an occasion for the family to gather, making it something like a Jewish Thanksgiving. The events of the book of Exodus are recounted by reading through the *Haggadah* which is done at the *seder*. Unleavened bread (*matzo*, rhymes with "lotsa") is eaten for the entire week.	Send a Passover greeting card. An appropriate greeting: "Happy Passover." If a Jewish friend invites you to a *seder*, accept the invitation! The service is easy to follow in the *Haggadah*, and the food will be great.
Shavuot or *Shavuos.* Most often pronounced to rhyme with "ya knew us." Also called the Festival of Weeks.	May or June	Not widely observed. When it is, it has themes associated with springtime and harvest. Traditionally this holiday was the day when the Law was given at Mount Sinai.	No particular greeting

Testament." It should be noted that even though many Jews do not consider the Old Testament to be the Word of God and inspired, it is generally accorded respect as part of Jewish tradition and history.

There are other books, such as the Talmud, considered by Orthodox Jews to possess divine authority. The Talmud consists of the *Mishnah* and the *Gemara.* The *Mishnah* consists in large part of various legal rulings and was compiled around A.D. 200. The *Gemara* elaborates and comments on the discussions in the *Mishnah* and was compiled around A.D. 550. Most Jewish people consider the Talmud and other rabbinic interpretations to be useful for ethics and instructive for life but not binding as divine authority.

APPROACHING THE JEWISH PEOPLE WITH THE GOSPEL

How Jewish People View the Gospel

"Christianity is for the Gentiles." Christianity is considered to be "their" religion. It is perfectly fine for Gentiles to believe in Jesus. Jews, however, neither need to nor should they consider Christ. If a Jewish person is considering any religion, it should be Judaism. Furthermore, a Christian is considered to be any Westerner or churchgoer who is a Gentile. Since Jews are Jewish by virtue of birth, they assume that Christians are those born into a Christian home. The idea of a personal faith commitment is not understood.

You can respond by explaining that even though you were born a Gentile, you became a Christian by personal faith in Jesus. A Christian does not mean a follower of a Gentile religion but rather someone who is a follower of the Jewish Messiah—and "Christ" is Greek for "Messiah." You can further underscore the Jewishness of what you believe by explaining that by believing in Jesus, you came to believe in the God of Abraham, Isaac, and Jacob, the three patriarchs of the book of Genesis.

The unspoken objection. There is one underlying objection that almost all Jewish people have concerning placing one's faith in Jesus: that it is not a Jewish thing to do, that they will cease to be Jewish if they believe in Jesus, and that becoming a Christian means turning one's back on one's people, history, and heritage. In addition, many Jewish people fear the social consequences that they would experience should they come to faith in or even consider Christ.

Young Jews in a celebratory procession through the streets of the Old City, Jerusalem.

"Jewishness is a way of life." Whether or not a Jewish person adheres to some form of Judaism, his or her Jewishness is a way of life to be lived out in varying degrees. There are Jewish ways of thinking and doing that differ from Gentile ways. To a Jewish person, Gentiles can seem puritanical in dress and behavior, subdued in interpersonal communication, overly conservative in politics and lifestyle. Church services differ considerably from synagogue services, and church hymns are much different from the haunting chant of a cantor or the jazzy sound of an East European *klezmer* band. To a Jewish person, being a Christian means identifying with a way of life different from the Jewish one.

A Jewish friend needs to be encouraged that in following Jesus, he or she does not abandon Jewish identity. Perhaps your friend would be willing to meet with a Jewish believer in Jesus, or to read the story of a Jewish person who came to faith in Jesus (see the bibliography for testimony resources).

A Jewish gravestone, engraved with the Star of David.

Opposite: Statue commemorating some of those who perished during the Holocaust, Yad Vashem memorial, Jerusalem.

Jews presume a standing with God. Jews do not speak of "salvation," for there is nothing to be saved from. If there is a God, then Jewish people already have a relationship with Him. Jesus is superfluous for Jews.

In spite of the views expressed above, Jewish people are continuing to come to the Lord in record numbers. Many, moreover, have come to faith through the witness of a Gentile Christian.

The following sections can help you more effectively witness, both by showing what you might avoid and the positive things you can do.

Some Things to Avoid in Witnessing Situations

Avoid certain offensive words. The Gospel will always offend because of the message of the Cross, since none of us like being told we are sinful. However, there are other points at which Jewish people can take offense or exception. It is not necessary to be rigidly on guard, but one can avoid unnecessary negative emotional overtones by choosing certain words over others.

■ First, avoid Christian jargon in general. Some Christians speak in a language that carries little meaning for the unchurched: "the precious blood of our Lord Jesus Christ,"

"saved," "born again" all carry meaning for the Christian but not for the average secular or Jewish person.

■ Second, avoid certain terms and utilize others:

• "The Jews" or "you Jews" sounds anti-Semitic on the lips of a Gentile (though Jewish people will refer to "Jews" when speaking among themselves). It is better to say "the Jewish people." "A Jewish man" is better than "a Jew." "How do Jewish people observe Passover?" is a better question than "What do Jews do at Passover?" which has an alienating sound to it. Also, do not call a Jewish woman a "Jewess" but "a Jewish woman." And do not call the Jewish people "Hebrews." That term was in use among the Jewish people a hundred years ago but not any longer.

• "Jewish" is a word that should be used only to describe people, land, religion, or language. If you refer to "Jewish money" or "Jewish control of the media," you may well be harboring anti-Semitic attitudes.

• It is best to avoid the terms "missionaries" or "mission." They tend to connote rescue missions that help derelicts, or those who work overseas among primitive peoples, or even worse, those who are paid to "snatch Jewish souls."

• "The cross" symbolizes persecution for many Jews. It is better to speak about "the death of Jesus." "Convert" also implies leaving behind one's Jewishness. It is better to speak about "becoming a believer (or follower) of Jesus." But it is appropriate to explain that biblical conversion was spoken of by the prophets as meaning "turning back to God" rather than "changing one's religion" (see, for example, Isaiah 44:22; Jeremiah 4:1; 24:7; Joel 2:12).

• Some suggest replacing the name "Jesus" with the Hebrew equivalent of "Y'shua." While it is good to refer to "Y'shua"—and explain that such is His Hebrew name—no one will realize that you are referring to the historical person Jesus of Nazareth unless you also use "Jesus"! In today's climate,

Embroidered Star of David, a Jewish emblem.

the name Jesus does not provoke as negative a reaction as it once did. Also, it is preferable to speak of "the Messiah Jesus" rather than "Jesus Christ." Many Jews do not realize that "Christ" means "Messiah" and think that "Christ" was his last name!
•Finally, Jewish people enjoy telling Jewish jokes to one another, but a non-Jew should not do so. Many Jewish people will not know how to respond and will think you are ridiculing them. Similarly, do not criticize leaders in the Jewish community. Though no person in this world is above reproach in all things, let any justified criticisms come from Jewish people rather than from you.

Above all, however, remember that the Gospel can be inherently offensive! If someone takes exception to your witness, it may well be because he or she is taking exception to God.

Don't succumb to the fallacy of only showing love. Some Christians never voice the Gospel to Jewish friends because they fear a negative response. So they reason that they will "show love" to their friends and be a witness in that way. Of course, Christians should always show love to people. It is wrong, however, to imagine that you will "love someone into the Kingdom." Jewish people are already morally upstanding by general community standards. Most are "nice" people; many give to charitable causes. Simply living a life of love will not convey the saving Gospel. Rather, one must verbalize the Gospel, which can be done in the following way.

Some Things to Do in Witnessing Situations

Witness to friends who are Jewish. It is a good idea to witness primarily to Jewish people with whom you've established a friendship. You can ascertain if a friend is Jewish by the holidays he or she observes, or perhaps by whether he or she wears a

Star of David as jewelry, and often by the surname.

Then, it is important that you let the person know that you know he or she is Jewish. This is best done not by directly telling them, but in relationship-building ways such as sending Jewish holiday greeting cards at the appropriate time (see the chart on "Jewish Holidays"). Doing this not only clears the ground by letting the person know you recognize that he or she is Jewish but it is also a good way to continue to cultivate a friendship with someone Jewish.

Move to spiritual topics. Generally, we can be bolder in witnessing to a friend than to a stranger.

Often a holiday season is an excellent time to initiate a witnessing conversation. You might ask your Jewish friend to tell you something about what his or her Passover was like, or about *Hanukkah*.

Then you might try to initiate a conversation This should be done in a way that is natural for you. One way that works for some is by saying something surprising yet direct and then following it up with a question: "As a Christian, I'm discovering that our faith is basically Jewish. I guess you could say that I believe in the God of Abraham, Isaac, and Jacob. Why do you suppose it's mostly Gentiles who believe in Him even though Christianity is basically Jewish?" Let them respond and lead you into a conversation.

Jewish people frequently employ humor in discussing spiritual matters, so you could say something like, "We just had Easter which celebrates the resurrection of Jesus. Since we believe He rose from the dead and is still living, do you suppose we can say that He is the oldest Jewish person alive?"

If the chemistry of your relationship with a Jewish person is right, you can offer a challenge: "Let me ask you something. I believe in Jesus and you don't. And as Christians, we think we should be telling everyone about God and about Jesus. If you were I, how would you talk to (a basically nonreligious person like yourself, an Orthodox Jewish man like yourself, an atheist like yourself) about the Bible and Jesus?"

These are obviously not persuasive arguments, but remarks and questions designed to be an invitation. The person might respond by saying, "It would be impossible for me to believe in Jesus," or "I don't want to talk about that." Accept the answer, and

A Star of David necklace.

A Jewish prayer shawl, *dreidel,* **Hebrew Scriptures and** *matzo,* **or unleavened Passover bread.**

One of the parts that was added after the destruction of the Temple in A.D. 70 has to do with the three unleavened wafers (*matzo*) (see Rosen, *Christ in the Passover*). The three wafers are placed in a silk container called a *matzo tash,* which has three compartments, one for each wafer. Or, they are stacked on a plate with napkins separating them and covered with a cloth. The three wafers symbolize unity.

During the course of the ceremony, the host removes the middle wafer from the silk bag, breaks it in half, and puts one of the halves back in the *matzo tash.* He then wraps the other half in a napkin, puts it in another white silk bag, and hides it. This hidden wafer is called *aphikomen* ("after dish" or "that which comes last").[1] After the meal, the children make a game of looking for the *aphikomen* while the parents guide them. When found, the host breaks the wafer and distributes the pieces to the others, who eat the wafer with an attitude of reverence.

Ask your Jewish friend why the middle wafer is removed and not one of the others. Why is it broken? Also, why hide it and then bring it back into the ceremony later?

Could it be that this ceremony is more than what the contemporary *seder* depicts it to be, more than a game? Perhaps it conveys something that most Jewish people do not see. Remarkably, it graphically illustrates the Messiah, that He would have to die (breaking the wafer; Psalm 22; Isaiah 53; Daniel 9), be buried (hiding the wafer), and rise from the dead (bringing the wafer back; Job 19:25; Psalm 16:10; Rosen, 1978, 92).

While the Last Supper was indeed an observation of the Passover *seder,* Jesus was also implementing something new. Luke reports that Jesus "took bread, gave thanks and broke it, and gave it to them, saying, 'This is my body given for you; *do this in remembrance of me*'" (Luke 22:19, emphasis added). God had initially instituted the Passover *seder* to serve as an annual reminder of

if he or she is not willing to hear more, don't proceed. (If asked, however, it is appropriate to explain why it is that Christians consider it important to tell others about God.) On the other hand, you may encounter curiosity and a desire to hear more.

Use a Jewish frame of reference. If you receive a positive response, you can continue to talk about the Gospel in a Jewish frame of reference. For example, you can tell a Jewish friend how, when Jesus observed—a more Jewish expression than "celebrated" —the Last Supper, it was really a Passover *seder.* Although the ceremony has been expanded since the time of Jesus, the disciples and Jesus observed what was at that time the full order of service for Passover night (Luke 22:7–20).

how He had redeemed the people of Israel from their bitter slavery in Egypt. Jesus was now saying, though, that they should break the bread "in remembrance of me"! Jesus was indicating that while the Passover was intended to celebrate how God had won Israel's redemption from slavery to Egypt, so now it was to also signify the redemption from our slavery to sin that was about to be accomplished through His substitutionary death.

Or, as another way to put things in a Jewish frame of reference, when you speak about sin, you may find a more positive reception during the time of the High Holy Days (see chart of "Jewish Holidays"), when most Jewish people, even nonreligious ones, attend the synagogue and recite the prayers asking God for forgiveness. Although a Jewish person may try to brush off the idea of sin at other times of the year, most Jews are willing to give it a bit more thought at *Yom Kippur*, the Day of Atonement, when Jewish people ask God for forgiveness of any sins committed during the previous year.

Be Clear on Foundational Doctrines

The Gospel is based on the understanding that we are sinners in need of salvation that was accomplished through a savior. These three concepts—sin, salvation, and savior—are foreign to most Jewish people, however, and need to be properly conveyed (see also the "Three Branches" chart).

Sin: Jewish people think of sin in terms of individual deeds, not as a deep-seated characteristic of humankind. The label "sinner" is thought to apply only to notoriously decadent and evil people. You need to point out that all people sin (1 Kings 8:46), using the various biblical analogies. Even the great King David confessed his sin (see Psalm 51). Sin is falling short of the goal, like people knowing they should be showing love to their children but are never quite able to do it, or someone who aims to succeed in business but

doesn't quite get there. Sin is the spiritual equivalent of not meeting the goals God has set for us in relating to Him or others (see Romans 3:23). Sin is also like a disease from which we need to be healed. It is spiritual cancer. It is also spiritual pollution that destroys us like smog destroys the ozone layer. Ultimately, sin is going our own way in defiance of God. Sin separates us from knowing and serving God.

Salvation: Salvation is another foreign term to most Jewish people. A common objection is, "Jews don't believe in salvation." What is meant is that, "You Christians think we need to be saved from hell in the afterlife, but we Jews are concerned about how to live right here and now." A helpful entrée is to talk about "redemption" instead of "salvation." This is a term familiar to many from the Passover *seder*. You can explain that as God freed the Israelites from slavery in Egypt, so He wants to free us from the slavery to sin in our own lives (Matthew 20:28; Titus 2:14).

Savior: This is the third term not understood by Jewish people. It can be helpful to speak of a "redeemer"

A seder cup, used for wine during the Passover meal.

145

Jewish prayer shawls.

the Bible should be done only when your friend has indicated a willingness for you to be his or her "teacher" in this regard and for him or her to be your "student." Otherwise there is the sense that you are speaking from an "invisible pulpit" (Rosen, 1976, 55).

The Bible should be used to raise an issue or to speak to an issue. An example of the first approach—raising an issue—is going to the Bible to initiate a discussion of what sin is (Isaiah 53—the suffering servant who takes on the sins of his people; Psalm 51—King David's confession of sin; 1 Kings 8—King Solomon's prayer at the dedication of the temple). An example of the second approach—speaking to an issue—is going to the Bible in order to answer an objection.

In either case, it is good to begin with the Old Testament portion of the Bible, pointing to certain Messianic prophecies and then to their fulfillment in the New Testament (see the chart of "Selected Messianic Prophecies Fulfilled in Jesus").

Jesus often talked about how His life was the fulfillment of such prophecies (Matthew 5:17; 26:56; Luke 24:27, 44; John 5:37–40); and the apostles came to see it that way as well (John 2:17; Acts 3:18; Romans 16:25–26; Hebrews 1; 1 Peter 1:10–12).

Notice in particular the number of prophecies that come from Isaiah 53 (they appear in bold print in the chart). Then also, consider what God says through Isaiah:

> Therefore I told you these things [previous prophecies] long ago; before they happened I announced them to you so that you could not say, "My idols did them; my wooden image and metal god ordained them." *From now on I will tell you of new things, of hidden things unknown to you* (Isaiah 48:5–6, emphasis added).

instead of Savior and certainly to use the term "Messiah."

Putting it together: So rather than stating that "Jesus came to shed His blood to save us from our sins and be our savior," you can convey that "Jesus came to be our Messiah and Redeemer. His death was an atonement for our sins."

How to Convey Spiritual Truths by Using the Bible

Even though not many Jewish people accept the truth of the Old Testament, they do accord it respect. It is good to open the Bible with a Jewish friend and illustrate the Gospel not merely by your statements and stories, but directly by the Word of God.

If you are in your friend's home, use his or her Bible if he or she has one. It is not that common, though, for the Bible to be a household possession.

Like initiating a conversation, using

Do not be afraid to use the New Testament for more than just fulfillment of Messianic prophecy. You can also use the New Testament to show

the Jewishness of the Gospel. For example, Luke 2:21 talks about Jesus' *brit milah* (ceremony accompanying circumcision); Matthew 26 and Luke 22 show Jesus having a *seder*; John 10:22 shows Jesus in Jerusalem at *Hanukkah*, called here by its Greek name "Dedication."

the concord of spiritual teaching between Old and New Testaments. For example, on the matter of sin you can point to a passage such as Psalm 51 (and compare it with Romans 3:23 in the New Testament). On the idea of a New Covenant prophesied by God, show Jeremiah 31:31–34 (and compare Jesus' words in John 6:45).

how images from the Old Testament point to Christ, such as the blood of the Passover lamb being put on the sides and top of the doorframe—a foreshadowing of the Cross (Exodus 12:7); the rock that provided water in the wilderness—a foreshadowing of Jesus talking about himself giving "living water" so that those who drink of it would never thirst again (Exodus 17:6; John 4:10–14; 7:37–39; cf., 1 Corinthians 10:4); the people of Israel being healed when placing their gaze on the bronze snake at the top of the staff— a foreshadowing of how we are saved by placing our faith in the Messiah who was raised on the Cross (Numbers 21:8–9; John 3.14); God asking Abraham to sacrifice Isaac, his "only son"— a foreshadowing of how God sacrificed His only Son (Genesis 22.1–18; John 3:16); Jonah being swallowed by a large fish—a foreshadowing of Jesus' death and resurrection (Jonah 1:17; Matthew 12:40; Luke 11:30).

how that even Old Testament incidents not specifically mentioned in the New Testament can serve as analogies. For instance, the book of Esther talks about King Xerxes being persuaded to issue an edict that overruled his previous edict that had called for the death of the Jews. This incident can be used as an analogy to help a Jewish person understand how Jesus' atoning death and resurrection is the basis for God's new edict through which we can receive life in the face of certain death (Esther 8:5–8; John 3:16–18; Romans 6:23).

Referring to Old Testament incidents, such as the one from Esther and those in the previous paragraph, not only provides helpful analogies and images but also shows a Jewish person that you are familiar with and

Young Jews visit a memorial to some who died in the Holocaust, Yad Vashem, Jerusalem.

Selected Messianic Prophecies Fulfilled in Jesus

PROPHECY	FULFILLMENT
The Messiah will be from the seed of Abraham (Genesis 18:18); Isaac (21:12); Jacob (Numbers 24:17, 19); Judah (Genesis 49:10:); Jesse (Isaiah 11:1–2, 10); David (Jeremiah 23:5–6).	"Jesus ... the son of David, the son of Jesse, the son of Judah, the son of Jacob, the son of Isaac, the son of Abraham (Luke 3:31~33).
Born in Bethlehem (Micah 5:2; also John 7:42).	"So Joseph also went up from the town of Nazareth in Galilee to Judea, to Bethlehem the town of David" (Luke 2:4).
"He was despised and rejected by men" (**Isaiah 53:3**).	"Those who passed by [the Cross] hurled insults at him . . ." (Matthew 27:39–44).
"A man of sorrows" (**Isaiah 53:3**).	"Then [Jesus] said to them, 'My soul is over-whelmed with sorrow to the point of death'" (Matthew 26:38).
"Familiar with suffering" (**Isaiah 53:3**).	"He then began to teach them that the Son of Man must suffer many things" (Mark 9:31; also Luke 24:26).
"Be strong, do not fear, your God will come.... Then will the eyes of the blind be opened and the ears of the deaf unstopped. Then will the lame leap like a deer, and the mute tongue shout for joy" (Isaiah 35:4–6); "the LORD has anointed me to preach good news to the poor" (Isaiah 61:1).	"Go back and report to John what you hear and see: The blind receive sight, the lame walk, those who have leprosy are cured, the deaf hear, the dead are raised, and the good news is preached to the poor" (Matthew 11:4–5; also Luke 4:18).
"Surely he took up our infirmities and carried our sorrows" (**Isaiah 53:4**).	"[Jesus] drove out the spirits with a word and healed all the sick" (Matthew 8:16–17).
"They must not ... break any of [the Passover lamb's] bones" (Numbers 9:12); "He was pierced" (Isaiah 51:5); "They have pierced my hands and feet" (Psalm 22:16; also Zechariah 12:10).	"But when they came to Jesus and found that he was already dead, they did not break his legs. Instead, one of the soldiers pierced Jesus' side with a spear" (John 19:33–37).
"But he was pierced _for_ our transgressions, he was crushed _for_ our iniquities ... the LORD has laid on him the iniquity of us all" (**Isaiah 53:5–6**).	"The Son of Man [came] to give his life as a ransom _for_ many" (Matthew 20:28); "God made him who had no sin to be sin _for_ us" (2 Corinthians 5:21; also John 11:49–51; 1 Corinthians 15:3).
"He was oppressed and afflicted, yet he did not open his mouth ... as a sheep before her shearers is silent, so he did not open his mouth" (**Isaiah 53:7**).	"But Jesus remained silent" (Matthew 26:63); "When he was accused by the chief priests and the elders, he gave no answer" (Matthew 27:12).
"They divide my garments among them and cast lots for my clothing" (Psalm 22:18).	"[Jesus'] garment was seamless, woven in one piece. . . . 'Let's decide by lot who will get it'" (John 19:23–24).
"He had done no violence, nor was any deceit in his mouth" (**Isaiah 53:12**).	Judas: "'I have sinned,' he said, 'for I have betrayed innocent blood'" (Matthew 27:4; also Luke 23:41; 2 Corinthians 5:21).

PROPHECY	FULFILLMENT
He "was numbered with the transgressors" (**Isaiah 53:12**).	"Two robbers were crucified with him" (Matthew 27:38; also Luke 22:37).
"He was assigned a grave . . . with the rich in his death" (Isaiah 51:9).	"There came a rich man from Arimathea, named Joseph . . . Joseph took the body and placed it in his own new tomb" (Matthew 27:57–60).
"For he made intercession for the transgressors" (**Isaiah 53:12**).	"Father, forgive them, for they do not know what they are doing" (Luke 23:34).
"You will not abandon me to the grave, nor will you let your Holy One see decay" (Psalm 16:10); "Though the LORD makes his life a guilt offering, he will see his offspring and prolong his days. . . ." (**Isaiah 53:10-11**).	"Why do you look for the living among the dead? He is not here; he has risen!" (Luke 24:5–6; also Acts 2:31–32).
"The stone the builders rejected has become the capstone" (Psalm 118:22; Isaiah 8:14)	"But when the tenants saw the son, they said to each other, 'This is the heir. Come, let's kill him'" (Matthew 21:28–42).

(see Rosen, 1976, 58–60, and McDowell, ch. 9)

Jewish women pray at their separate section of the Western Wall, Jerusalem.

value the Old Testament Scriptures.

A helpful hint: Few Jewish people study the Old Testament very much. There is a good chance that you know the Old Testament better than does your Jewish friend. And in the event that a question comes up for which you don't know the answer, you can always say that you don't know but will look it up. Don't worry about losing credibility because you don't have the answers to everything.

RESPONDING TO HINDRANCES AND OBJECTIONS

Undoubtedly the time will come when a Jewish friend will put up objections to the Gospel. In many cases, objections are not thought out. Raising objections can therefore be a reflex action for your Jewish friend. He or she might also represent an "official line" rather than a personally held viewpoint.

Specific Objections

"Christians believe in three gods but Jews believe in one God." Even an atheist can raise this objection! What is meant may be no more than, "Our

religion teaches one God. So even though I do not believe in God, if I did, that is the kind of God I would believe in."

Jewish people understand the Trinity to somehow imply multiple gods. You can simply affirm that you believe that God is One, and point out that Jesus himself quoted the *Sh'ma* (the statement of God's oneness in Deuteronomy 6:4, quoted in Mark 12:29).

If your friend pursues the topic by saying, "I just don't see how God could be three in one—it doesn't make any sense," a light response will often answer the question better than an extended theological discourse. For example, you could try saying, "God is bigger than you and I and we'll never fully understand Him." This will deflect the conversation from becoming a fruitless discussion of an objection that is being raised more as a smokescreen than out of any real conviction.

"There's no proof that Jesus was the Messiah." This is typically a stereotyped response; the person may never have investigated any of the reasons for faith. Rather than initiate a long argument complete with all kinds

of evidence, you might start by asking, "What kind of proof would convince you?" That will raise more specific questions and objections in their mind.

"If Jesus is the Messiah, why isn't there peace on earth?" One answer is that we need to have peace in our hearts before there can be peace on earth. Suppose God suddenly declared all wars to cease but the people remained unchanged. In a short time the world would again be the way it is now.

Put the responsibility back on your friend by replying: "If you seek peace in your own heart first through Jesus, then you can do your part to help make the world a better place."

"How can you believe in God after all the persecution we've been through, not to mention the Holocaust? And it was Christians who did it!" People can misuse anything, even the Gospel. Tyrants misuse freedom and justice. That doesn't make freedom and justice any less important to seek after.

As for persecution, that goes all the way back to Pharaoh in Egypt, who obviously was not a Christian. There was persecution even then, and still the Jewish people believed in God.

"The New Testament is anti-Semitic." Ask which parts and which passages. Often a person will not be able to point to anything specific. Sometimes a Jewish person will have in mind certain harsh-sounding passages such as John 8:44 or 1 Thessalonians 2:14–16. You can point out that this was the manner of speaking of the prophets of Israel. Isaiah 1 furnishes a good example. Then you should point out that Jesus was not being anti-Semitic but was saddened at the sins of people (referring to all, not just to Jewish people). You can cite the passage at which Jesus weeps over Jerusalem, Matthew 23:37–39. Point out that you feel similarly about Gentiles who do not turn to God. All have sinned, and God's response to sin is the same for all people.

"Jews don't proselytize." This objection usually means, "I don't think people should push their beliefs on others. We Jews don't, and you Christians shouldn't either." You can

Tablets representing the stones inscribed with the Ten Commandments given to Moses on Mount Sinai.

point out that Isaiah said Israel was to be a light to the nations (Isaiah 42:6; 49:6).[2] Moreover, you can say that you don't believe in forcing religion on anyone either, but you have always found that discussion and persuasion are part of any friendship.

"I'm happy with my own religion." You can appropriately respond, "It's okay if you don't want to talk about spiritual things, but just remember that the goal of life is not to be happy but to know God. Sometimes what I believe makes me sad because it asks things of me that others might not do. We shouldn't believe in anything because it makes us happy, but because it's true. Ultimately, though, knowing the truth about God will bring us complete and lasting happiness and joy."

"If Jesus was the Messiah, why don't the rabbis believe in Him?" The answer is, because he wouldn't be allowed to be a rabbi much longer! With the kind of community responsibility that a rabbi has, not many rabbis will allow themselves the freedom to ask if Jesus might be the Messiah.

CONCLUSION

Above all, be encouraged that many Jewish believers in Jesus have come to faith through the loving witness of a Gentile Christian. God can and will use you as you seek to become more familiar with Jewish things and to open up the Gospel to your Jewish friends. The following resources can be a great help.

Endnotes:

1 Jewish law professor David Daube thinks the word means "The Coming One" and that the ceremony originally had a messianic implication with a view to the coming Messiah. This may well be the case rather than the traditional meaning of "after dish." See Daube, *He That Cometh* (London: Council for Christian-Jewish Understanding, 1966).

2 The "servant" here appears to apply first to Israel, and then to shade off into the Messiah. This issue does not need to be raised in conversation, as one traditional Jewish understanding applies the passages to the nation of Israel. However, the idea of the entire world being blessed through Israel is found as far back as Genesis 12:1–3.

BIBLIOGRAPHY AND RESOURCES

Fruchtenbaum, Arnold. *Jesus Was a Jew*. Tustin, Calif.: Ariel Ministries, 1974. Jewish apologetics written by a Jewish Christian.

Frydland, Rachmiel. *When Being Jewish Was a Crime*. Cincinnati: Messianic Jewish Outreach, 1978. A testimony.

Goldberg, Louis. *Our Jewish Friends*. Neptune, N.J.: Loizeaux Brothers, 1983. Helpful overview of Judaism and witnessing to Jewish people written by the former head of Jewish Studies at Moody Bible Institute.

Kac, Arthur. *The Messiahship of Jesus: Are Jews Changing Their Attitude Toward Jesus?* (revised edition). Grand Rapids, Mich.: Baker Book House, 1986. A compilation of positive statements about Jesus from Jewish people.

McDowell, Josh. *Evidence that Demands a Verdict*. San Bernardino, Calif.: Campus Crusade for Christ, 1972.

Questions and Answers from Jews for Jesus. San Francisco: Jews for Jesus, 1983. In-depth answers to typical objections.

Riggans, Walter. *Jesus Ben Joseph: An Introduction to Jesus the Jew*. Place not listed: MARC; Olive Press; Monarch Publications, 1993.

Rosen, Moishe. *Y'shua: The Jewish Way to Say Jesus*. Chicago: Moody Press, 1982. Overview of messianic prophecy.

Rosen, Moishe and Ceil Rosen. *Christ in the Passover*. Chicago: Moody Press, 1978.

Rosen, Moishe and Ceil Rosen. *Share the New Life with a Jew*. Chicago: Moody Bible Institute, 1976.

Rosen, Ruth, ed. *Testimonies*. San Francisco: Purple Pomegranate Productions, 1987.

Telchin, Stan. *Betrayed*. Lincoln, Va.: Chosen Books, 1981. A testimony. The 30-minute audio tape of Stan Telchin's testimony is available through "Life Story," Box 1417, Sumas, WA. 98295–1417.

The Y'shua Challenge: Answers for Those Who Say Jews Can't Believe in Jesus. San Francisco: Purple Pomegranate Productions, 1993.

JUDAISM, THE JEWISH PEOPLE, AND JEWISH HISTORY

Johnson, Paul. *History of the Jews*. New York: Harper & Row, 1987.

Kolatch, Alfred. *The First and Second Jewish Books of Why*. Middle Village, N.Y.: Jonathan David, 1981 and 1985. Explains specific customs.

Telushkin, Joseph. *Jewish Literacy: The Most Important Things to Know About the Jewish Religion, Its People, and Its History*. New York: William Morrow and Company, 1991. The essentials about Judaism and the Jewish people.

Wylen, Stephen. *Settings of Silver: An Introduction to Judaism*. New York and Mahwah, N.J.: Paulist Press, 1989.

ORGANIZATIONS

Chosen People
1300 Cross Beam Dr.
Charlotte, NC 28217
Phone: (704) 357-9000
FAX: (704) 357-6359

Friends of Israel
P.O. Box 908
Bellmawr, NJ 08099
Phone: (800) 2570-7843
E-mail: daniel__n__p@msn.com

Jews for Jesus
60 Haight St.
San Francisco, CA 94102-5895
Phone: (415) 864-2600
www.jews-for-jesus.org
E-mail: jfj@jews-for-jesus.org

Stan Kellner
P.O. Box 26415
Colorado Springs, CO 80936
A Messianic Jew who specializes in doing the "Christ in the Passover" ceremony (*seder*) and in teaching on the Jewish roots of the Christian faith.

Lausanne Consultation on Jewish Evangelism
North American Coordinator: Fred Klett
P.O. Box 133
Glenside, PA 19038
Phone: (215)576-7325
E-mail: FredCHAIM@aol.com

Marxism

Rick Rood

INTRODUCTION

Marxist ideology draws its inspiration from the writings of Karl Marx and Friedrich Engels. It stresses the need for a political and economic system that abolishes private property, and in which all material goods are held in common by all people. As we shall see, Marxism involves several areas of thought, including not only economics and politics but also ethics, history, human nature, and religion. It is a total "worldview."

Karl Marx.

It is not difficult to understand why Marxist thinking appeals to many people. We live in a world of economic extremes. The disparity between the rich and the poor is wide. Understandably, then, Marxism's promise of economic equality is attractive to many who desire to eliminate such extremes. Marxism also appeals to the idealistic and to those who are looking for hope and meaning in life but are disillusioned with other ideologies.

No one knows how many people in the world are committed to Marxism. But there can be no denying that it has had an unsurpassed influence on humankind during the twentieth century. Although it has suffered severe political and economic setbacks in recent years (particularly in the former Soviet Union and Eastern Europe), Marxism remains a viable and appealing ideology for many.

Even in American universities, Marxism wields tremendous influence. An article in *U.S. News and World Report,* January 25, 1982, stated that there were 10,000 Marxist professors on America's campuses. An article in the August 29, 1989, Denver *Post* stated that as many as 90% of faculty members at some midwestern universities are Marxists. The influence of these professors on the thinking of students in U.S. universities should not be underestimated.

HISTORY OF MARXISM

Early Roots

Throughout history there have been people who have proposed ideas similar to those of Karl Marx. In the 300s B.C., Plato proposed communal ownership of property by the ruling class in *The Republic*. During medieval times, many religious orders practiced the commonality of goods. Thomas More in his book *Utopia* (1516) proposed common ownership of property.

Several factors existing in the late 1700s and early 1800s provided the impetus for an increase in this type of thinking. One was the French Revolution, which emphasized the equality of all people. Another was the Romantic Movement, which fostered a high view of human nature and the perfectibility of people and society. A third was the Industrial Revolution, which thrived on a large unskilled labor force in the factories. Many of these laborers worked and lived under extremely difficult conditions.

In light of the influence of these factors, socialist thinking was found in many writers of the early 1800s. Among these were Henri de Saint-Simon, Charles Fourier, Etienne Cabet, Robert Owen (who founded New Harmony, Indiana), Louis Blanc, Pierre Proudhon, Prosper Enfanten, Victor Considerant, and Auguste Comte.

Karl Marx and Friedrich Engels

Karl Marx was born May 5, 1818, at Trier, Prussia, to Heinrich and Henriette Marx. Heinrich was a lawyer. Both were Jews, having descended from a long line of rabbis. In order to continue his law practice in a "Christian" environment, however, Heinrich converted to Lutheranism in 1816. Karl and his siblings were baptized in 1824.

During his years in school at Trier, Marx wrote a paper on John 15 concerning the importance of union with Christ. In it he said:

Union with Christ bestows inner exaltation, consolation in suffering, calm assurance, and a heart which is open to love of mankind, to all that is noble, to all that is great, not out of ambition, not

through the desire of fame, but only because of Christ (Geisler, 68).

His school records show that Marx was "of evangelical faith" and that his "moral behavior towards superiors and fellow pupils was good" (Mazlish, 45). Marx identified at least externally with the Christian faith.

In 1835, Marx went to the University of Bonn, and a year later to the University of Berlin. After completing his work in philosophy at the University of Berlin, his dissertation was finally accepted by the University of Jena, which granted Marx his Ph.D. in 1841.

By the time he had started his university education, he was an atheist. While there, he was influenced by Ludwig Feuerbach's critique of religion as a creation of man, as well as by Bruno Bauer and David Friedrich Strauss (the latter said Jesus never existed). As a student he identified with the "Young Hegelians," the liberal branch of the followers of Hegel.

Though Marx hoped to obtain a teaching position, his liberal political views forced him to pursue a career in journalism. In 1843, he married Jenny von Westphalen, who was from an aristocratic family in Trier. That same year they moved to Paris where Marx wrote briefly for a newspaper. There they came into contact with many radical thinkers. Among them was Friedrich Engels (son of a German industrialist), who would become Karl's lifelong friend and collaborator.

Between 1845 and 1848, the Marxes moved several times among various countries in Europe. In 1848, Marx and Engels published *The Communist Manifesto for the Communist League.* The League was composed mostly of intellectuals and professionals. The *Manifesto* was a summons to revolution. This established Marx and Engels as the leading theoreticians of the communist movement.

In 1849, Marx and Engels moved to England. Engels went to work for his father's factory in Manchester. The Marxes lived in London, where they spent most of the remainder of their lives in poverty. Marx's only regular income was as a foreign correspondent for the New York *Tribune.* Most of the rest of their income came from periodic gifts from Engels.

Marx devoted his life to studying at the British Museum and writing on a variety of themes, particularly economics. In 1858, he published *Outlines for a Critique of Political Economy.* In 1864, he emerged as leader of the First International Workingman's Association. In 1867, Marx published the first volume of *Capital,* which was largely a critique of capitalist economics. The second and third volumes were published by Engels (from Marx's notes) after his death. This would prove to be Marx's major life work.

Marx continued to write during his later years but suffered many serious health problems. He died March 14, 1883. Of his seven children (one died at childbirth), only two survived him (both of them later committed suicide) (Mazlish, 64).

Marx was relatively unknown outside revolutionary circles during his life. His works were not widely read until after his death. There were only six people at his funeral. The closing words of Engels' oration at his funeral, however, have proven true: "His name will endure through the ages, and so also will his work!" (Sowell, 186).

Marxism After Marx

Though Marx and Engels laid the foundation for the ideology that became known as Marxism, its development was shaped by a number of other writers in the late nineteenth and early twentieth centuries. In 1889, at the meeting of the Second International Workingman's Association in Paris, a conflict arose between Karl Kautsky and Eduard Bernstein. The latter believed that a gradual approach was better than the revolutionary doctrine propounded by Marx. He believed the political and economic system could be changed gradually. Those who followed Bernstein became known as "Revisionists." Modern "Eurocommunism" represented this line of thinking. Kautsky, on the other hand, defended the need for revolution to institute socialism. He became the leading theoretician of orthodox Marxism in the late nineteenth century.

No one influenced the future of the Marxist movement more than V. I. Lenin. He emerged in the early twentieth century as leader of the Bolshevik wing of the Social Democratic Party in Russia. It was because of his leadership that the communists came to power in Russia in 1917. He differed from Marx in at least the following respects.

Lenin and Trotsky.

Lenin and Stalin.

First, he believed that it was necessary for the Communist Party to take control of the revolution rather than expect the working class to instigate it on its own. He also believed that the party would need to take tight control of socialist society after the revolution.

Second, he believed that capitalism had not disintegrated, as Marx predicted, because of its imperialistic exploitation of the third world. Thus, he believed that a communist revolution would take place in a non-industrialized society like Russia rather than in industrialized countries like Great Britain or the U.S.

Since 1917, the communist movement has been more accurately defined as Marxism-Leninism. After Lenin died in 1924, Josef Stalin consolidated control over the Communist Party, and eventually became Head of State. He instituted the most brutal form of totalitarian rule. It is estimated that he was responsible for the liquidation of twenty million people (Hill, *Turbulent Times*, 70).

After World War II, communism spread to many other countries outside the Soviet Union, notably to China and Eastern Europe. The brutality of Stalinism gave rise in the 1950s to a more humanistic strain of Marxism, particularly in Czechoslovakia and Yugoslavia. The humanistic Marxists drew from Marx's earlier writings the idea that the goal of socialism was to liberate humankind from a state of "alienation," and to enable people to fulfill their potential. They sought a more democratic kind of socialism than did Stalin. In recent years, most communist societies have experienced severe economic crises which have led to the collapse of communist regimes.

THE MAJOR IDEAS OF MARXISM

1. Philosophical Materialism

Marxism is based on a materialistic perception of reality. That is, Marxists believe there is no supernatural or immaterial realm of reality. Reality is fundamentally material.

Not that Marxists deny the existence of the mind, or reduce thought to a physiological process, but they believe the mind is a product of the brain and does not survive death. Engels said,

The real unity of the world consists in its materiality.... But if the ... question is raised: what then are thought and consciousness, and whence they come, it becomes apparent that they are products of the human brain and that man himself is a product of nature (quoted in Noebel, 133).

Marxists thus deny the existence of a Creator and accept the Darwinian theory of evolution. They stress the importance of the scientific process in observing reality. They also emphasize the role of practical experience in testing ideas.

2. Dialectical Process

Closely associated with their materialism is the Marxist view that all reality is in the process of change and advancement through what they call the dialectic. Georg W. F. Hegel had developed the concept of the dialectic based on idealism (that is, that ideas were the driving force of reality). Marx and Engels adapted it to their materialism. They believed that all things are in a process of development, and that this development takes place through the interaction of opposing forces inherent in all things. These forces are called the "thesis" and "antithesis."

Through the conflict of these two forces emerges a new entity called the "synthesis." Marx and Engels believed that they saw this process at work in nature (for example, through the evolution of new species, or through the germination of a seed and its growth into a plant). They also believed it was at work in history, through the economic and social advancement of humanity. They saw this as an inevitable process of change, based on scientific social laws.

3. Economic Determinism

As a result of their materialist philosophy, Marxists hold to what is called economic determinism. Engels wrote in the preface to the 1888 edition of *The Communist Manifesto*,

In every historical epoch, the prevailing mode of the economic production and exchange, and the social organization necessarily following from it, form the basis upon which is built up, and from which alone can be explained, the political and intellectual history of that epoch (DeKoster, 11).

In other words, economics determines everything about a society, including government, the prevailing ideas, laws, and even religion. Economics, not ideas, is the determining factor in history. Even "human nature" is determined by the economic system.

Russia's Tsar Nicholas II shortly before his assassination by revolutionaries.

4. Class Struggle

Marx believed that the history of society was the history of class struggle. Ever since the means of production (factories, etc.) have been privately owned, society has been divided into competing classes. Engels wrote: "The whole history of mankind ... has been a history of class struggles, contests between exploiting and exploited, ruling and oppressed classes" (DeKoster, 11). One can easily see that economic and social change comes about as the result of the outworking of the dialectical process at work between the classes. The two opposing classes (representing the thesis and antithesis) conflict until a new social and economic order is created (the synthesis).

Marx taught that when a given stage in economic history reaches maturity, the next stage will emerge. It is necessary, however, that some form of revolution take place to bring about this change. Marx identified six stages of economic history.

First, there was *tribal communalism*. The tribal group owned all things in common.

Second, there was *slave labor*. Conquering groups enslaved their adversaries.

Third, there was *feudalism*. Powerful landowners granted protection and small portions of land to "peasants" who worked the land for them.

Fourth, there was *capitalism*. Under the capitalist system, the "bourgeois" owned the means of production, while the "proletariat" worked for wages.

Marx envisioned a fifth stage, *socialism*. After seizing the means of production from the bourgeois, the proletariat would institute a dictatorship through which it would cleanse society of all class distinctions based on private property.

The sixth and final stage of history would then appear—*Communism*. As class distinctions disappeared, the state itself would fade away. Peace and prosperity would prevail.

5. Critique of Capitalism

Marx agreed that the capitalist phase was necessary in order to amass the means of production and to develop them to their fullest potential. But he saw elements in capitalism that required its eventual overthrow. The most important was that he felt capitalism fostered exploitation of the proletariat by the bourgeois. He saw evidence of this exploitation particularly in what he called "surplus value." Adopting the commonly held "labor theory of value" (the idea that the value of a commodity is determined by the labor required to produce it), Marx observed that the capitalist did not pay the worker what his or her labor was worth, but withheld it for himself or herself. This difference between the value of the product and the wage paid to the worker Marx called "surplus value." He viewed the withholding of this "surplus value" as exploitation, and even theft.

The second element in capitalism of which Marx was critical was what he called "alienation." Marx believed that people derive meaning in life from their work and from the commodities they produce. In a real sense, people are what they make. When the capitalist extracts some of the value of the commodities a worker makes, the worker is alienated from his or her work ... from part of himself or herself (DeKoster, 32). He also felt that the worker was alienated from society in that his or her work in a capitalist economy was not a "community" effort, but merely an act for individual survival.

Marx predicted that capitalist society would eventually collapse. This would be due first to the strain of ever more intense economic crises. Second, it would be due to the "increasing misery of the proletariat." He believed that the bourgeois would become smaller and smaller, but richer and richer, and that the proletariat would become ever larger, but poorer and poorer. This "increasing misery" would drive the proletariat to revolt against the bourgeois and to take control of the means of production.

The young
Chinese Marxist
revolutionary
Mao Tse-tung.

6. The Final Stage of History

In contrast to those whom they termed "utopian socialists," Marx and Engels not only urged that society ought to be organized along socialist lines but said that socialism and communism were inevitable! Marx believed he had discovered the scientific laws of history, and that the dialectic insured that socialism would inevitably arrive. The arrival of socialism would not occur, however, until capitalist society had exhausted its potential for developing the means of production and for exploiting the proletariat. And when that occurred, the working class would revolt.

Marx anticipated that such working-class revolts would occur first in the most developed countries. Though he allowed for the possibility of a peaceful transition from capitalism to socialism, Marx believed a violent revolution was nearly inevitable. He did not conceive of capitalists surrendering their power without a fight.

Lenin differed with Marx on this point by suggesting that capitalism would begin to disintegrate at its weakest link—in a country like Russia.

After the revolution of the working class, Marx envisioned a period of socialism under the oversight of the "dictatorship of the proletariat." During this stage, society would be cleansed of its individualistic elements, a process which could take decades. Marx saw this as an era of increasing democracy, characterized by openness and equality. Under Lenin, and particularly under Stalin and later under Mao Tse-tung in China, it turned out to be anything but democratic and open!

Eventually, as society is purged of all its bourgeois elements, Marx foresaw the emergence of a purely communist society. In such a society all things would be held in common and there would be no need for a state. Human nature would be cleansed of any selfish tendencies, and peace and prosperity would prevail. This change was described by Leon Trotsky in 1924 in the following words:

> Man will become immeasurably stronger, wiser, and subtler; his body will become more harmonized, his movement more rhythmic, his voice more musical. The forms of life will become dynamically dramatic. The average human type will rise to the heights of an Aristotle, a Goethe, or a Marx. And above this ridge new peaks will rise (quoted in Lyon, 184).

Another communist thinker, Leonid Ilyichov, put it this way:

> A builder of communism is a fully developed person, combining a rich intellect, moral integrity, mature aesthetic tastes, and physical perfection ... people who have remade themselves ... (with) new attitudes to labor and to one's social obligations, (with) a new kind of discipline ... new moral principles ... self-discipline, and moral purity (Bockmuehl, 134).

Under communism, each person would contribute to society "according to his abilities," and would receive "in accordance with his needs." Marx and Engels even predicted the dissolution of the traditional family, the institution of a "legalized community of women," and the care of all children by society (Noebel, 463–464).

7. Marxist Ethics

As atheists, Marxists deny any morality based on God's character and commandments. They believe ethics are based on economics. Under capitalism, Marx taught that morality was simply a reflection of "bourgeois class interests."

For the Marxist, whatever advances communism is moral. Lenin stated: "Our morality is entirely subordinated to the interests of the class struggle of the proletariat" (Bales, 196). This means that lying, terror, and killing are moral if they advance the communist cause. It is no problem if millions of lives must be sacrificed now to promote the ultimate welfare of a future generation in a communist utopia.

8. Critique of Religion

Marx declared himself an atheist in the preface to his doctoral dissertation, endorsing the statement of David Hume, "In simple words, I hate the pack of gods" (Bales, 36). He embraced the idea of Feuerbach that God was simply the creation of people, who projected their own qualities onto an imaginary deity in whom they could find security. He shared the notion that only when people give up their belief in God will they be truly free.

Concerning the origin of religion, Engels said, "The first gods arose through the personification of natural forces ... out of the many ... gods there arose in the minds of men the idea of the one exclusive god" (Bales, 45).

It is well known that Marx viewed religion as the "opiate of the people." He believed that religion was simply a tool of the bourgeois to make the proletariat feel content with their lot by hoping for a better life in heaven.

Soviet revolutionaries on an improvized armed vehicle on the streets of Moscow, 1917.

Marx said, "The abolition of religion as the illusory happiness of the people is required for their real happiness" (Noebel, 70). Lenin said, "Every religious idea . . . is unutterable vileness . . . of the most dangerous kind" (Noebel, 73). In keeping with the notion of economic determinism, Marx believed that when the communist utopia arrived, people would no longer feel the need for religion. Religion would vanish, just as would the state.

As a result of these convictions about religion, Marxist states have always opposed religion. At times they have sought to actively destroy it. At other times they have sought to enlist the help of religious people in promoting their cause. They have always at least sought to control religion in their societies, believing that as the younger generation was educated in science, religion would fade away.

CHRISTIAN CRITIQUE OF MARXISM

Before offering some criticisms of Marxism, it must be acknowledged that some positive values can be ascribed to it. If it were otherwise, it would be hard to see why anyone would be attracted to it at all.

First, it must be said that Marxism does seek to do something about the oppressive conditions under which many people have worked and lived.

Second, it recognizes that there have been abuses under the capitalist system (Geisler, 67). The question, though, is whether the solution it offers is one that should be endorsed. Marxists often point to the improved living conditions in socialist societies like China and the former Soviet Union. One must ask, however, at what great cost in terms of human lives? Also, how much better would the conditions in such countries be if they had benefited from a democratic system?

Following is a list of brief responses to the major teachings of Marxism drawn from many of the sources in the bibliography.

Philosophical Materialism
■ Materialism ignores the evidence for humankind's immaterial and immortal nature.
■ It ignores the evidence that the universe had a beginning, and must have had a Creator.
■ It accepts uncritically the theory of evolution (contrary evidence notwithstanding).
■ It fails to explain how a material universe could be working toward a good purpose for humanity.

Economic Determinism
■ It overstates the role played by economics in society while nearly ignoring the role played by ideas.
■ If thought and ideas are the result of the economic system, how could the ideas of Marx and Engels have arisen in the midst of a capitalist system? And how could they change the system?

Dialectic Process
■ The observation of a few isolated instances in the past of this process does not warrant the conclusion that the dialectic is an "immutable law" of history and that the future is determined by it.
■ If the dialectic is a "law" of history, why did the revolution not occur in an industrialized country?

Class Conflict
■ Economic classes are not always the most determinative influence in society. Race and religion are often stronger.
■ Different economic classes often unite against a common external threat
■ Economic classes are not always cohesive. They are often fractured by other issues.

Critique of Capitalism
■ Capitalist societies did not "self-destruct" as Marx predicted, nor did the proletariat grow more miserable. The conditions of the working class actually improved, due in part to enlightened social legislation.
■ Marx overlooked the fact that there are many other things that go into the cost of commodities besides labor (for example, the factory and tools, materials, training, sales, etc.).
■ Marx overlooked the advantages of capitalism over socialism. For example, by encouraging competition, capitalism actually promotes cooperation. It encourages people to band together in ways that utilize their personal strengths. By allowing millions of people to make day-to-day economic decisions, it taps the knowledge of more than just a handful of central planners who try to manage an economy. It also channels selfish tendencies toward service, and rewards those who serve others best.

Socialism and Communism
■ In a society where each is to receive in accordance with his or her need, who is to determine each person's need? How do we know people won't be just as selfish under communism as they are under capitalism?
■ Instead of the state "withering away," why is it that in Marxist societies the state has continued to expand?
■ Rather than becoming a "classless society," Marxist societies have created a new "elite" class of rulers and managers who are constantly fighting for power.
■ Socialism collects too much power in the hands of a few with no "checks and balances."
■ Socialist societies have failed economically, except where they have reverted to a degree of free market practices.
■ If the bourgeois will not give up power without a fight, how do we know the dictatorship of the proletariat will not also resist its relinquishing of power?
■ The change in the economic system has failed to produce the "new man" who is devoid of selfish tendencies

and lives only for humanity. If the Russian revolution had brought about a change in human nature, why did Stalin have to purge the most dedicated communists in his Politburo in the 1930s?

Morality
■ If there is no transcendent standard for morality, how can we say people "ought" to promote communism?
■ The idea that "the end justifies the means" has led to horrendous abuses of power and to the total disregard for individual human rights.

Critique of Religion
■ Marx's atheism ignores the evidence for God's existence.
■ The idea that religion developed from polytheism to monotheism is faulty. Even the most "primitive" cultures have a belief in a supreme God.
■ Marxists are hard-pressed to explain why religion has persisted and even continued to grow in socialist societies if religion is simply a reflection of the economic system.
■ Marx's rejection of religion is based on its abuse, not on its true nature.
■ Marx's rejection of Christianity

ignores the historical evidence for its truthfulness.

Marxism's Most Basic Flaw
The fundamental flaw of Marxism is that it is built on a faulty view of human nature. Marxism teaches that aside from a few biological drives, there is no unchanging human nature. Human nature is determined by the prevailing economic system. Therefore, if the economic system is changed, human nature will change.

This doctrine is not only denied by Scripture, but it is also contradicted by the facts of history. Socialist societies have failed to produce any such change in human nature. This was acknowledged by Alexander Tsipko (consultant to the Communist Party Central Committee in the Soviet Union in 1988–89) in a 1989 article, in which he declared, "All our absurdities stem from our dogged refusal to see man as he really is. . . ." (Hill, *Turbulent Times*, 63). Even Lenin decried the lack of change in socialist people in 1919, when he said, "The workers are building the new society without having turned themselves into new men who would be free from the dirt of the old world. They

Children on an Israeli kibbutz. The fundamental flaw of Marxism is that it is built on a faulty view of human nature.

Contrast Between Marxism and Christianity

	MARXISM	CHRISTIANITY
GOD	Atheistic—there is no God. Matter is the fundamental reality.	Theistic—there is one Creator God. Reality consists of both matter and spirit.
THE NATURE OF HUMANITY	Humanity has evolved from animals. Humanity's nature is determined by economic forces.	Humanity was created by God. Humanity is unique from the rest of creation because we are made in the image of God.
ETHICS	There are no transcendent, moral absolutes. Whatever advances communism is right.	Moral absolutes are based on God's holy character and commandments.
THE PROBLEM	Humanity is alienated from the fruit of our labors because of the distinction between the laborer and the owner.	Humanity has rebelled against God, and we map the results of our sin through personal and social strife.
THE SOLUTION	Humanity can be "saved" from alienation by eliminating private property and class distinctions We can each become a "new man" through economic, political, and social means.	Humanity can be saved by trusting in Christ. We can each become a "new man" through the regenerating work of the Holy Spirit (2 Corinthians 5:17).
THE FOUNDATION FOR HOPE	Humanity's hope is to be found in political revolution.	Humanity's hope is to be found in the sacrificial death of Jesus Christ, who conquered death for us. Our hope will be fully realized when Jesus returns to rule over all the earth with justice.

are still in it up to their knees" (Bockmuehl, 129).

Since the fall of the communist regime, the people of Russia have begun to see the effects of the lack of a religious foundation in their culture. In 1992, Gorbachev said, "Ignoring religious experience has meant great losses for society" (Yancey, *Christianity Today*, 19). Having removed any basis for morality by denying the existence of God, communism has left the people without any reason for pursuing an unselfish ethic. For example, a poll conducted by *Pravda* in the early 1990s revealed that people in Russia would sooner spend money on liquor than support needy children. The poll revealed that "70% of Russian parents would not allow their children to have contact with a disabled child; 80% would not give money to help; some advocated infanticide" (Yancey, 75). Marx's theory has been disproved by history.

Is There a Biblical Socialism/Communism?

Many have suggested that there is support for socialism in the Bible. Appeal is often made to the passages in Acts 2:44–45; 4:32–35, which describe the early church as holding their possessions in common, and in 2 Corinthians 8:13–14, which encourage "equality" among Christians. These passages do encourage a spirit of sharing among Christians, and we should heed them. But a few things should be kept in mind.

First, the sharing was voluntary, not compulsory. Property was always deemed to be private until the owner chose to contribute it (see Acts 5:4).

Second, while believers are encouraged to share with those in need, they are never told to share with those who are able but unwilling to work for their own livelihood (2 Thessalonians 3:10–12).

It has also been emphasized that the testing of personal stewardship requires the possession of personal property. The aim of Marxism, however, is not a matter of the stewardship of one's personal property but the abolishment of personal property.

PRINCIPLES OF MINISTRY TO MARXISTS

■ Be prepared to acknowledge the abuses of many capitalists. People are greedy and selfish, and are not above using and abusing other people (see James 5:1–6).
■ Be prepared to acknowledge the abuses of religion. People have used religion to keep others "in their place" (for example, the endorsement of slavery and of racism by many Christians of former generations). But this does not mean the Bible supports such ideas.
■ Be prepared to acknowledge the positive qualities of some Marxists. Some are motivated by compassion for the oppressed.
■ Encourage, however, an objective evaluation of Marxism. Marx stressed the testing of ideas by practice. Do the facts support the theory? Has human nature changed due to a change in the economic system?
■ Encourage the examination of the evidence for the existence of God, the historicity of Christ, and the reliability of the Bible (see chapter on "How Can We Know the Bible Is the Word of God?").
■ Marxists usually think Christianity is "unscientific." Point out that there is no conflict between objective science and biblical faith. If they are troubled by the conflict between creation and evolution, expose them to good material regarding this subject (see chapter on Secularism).
■ Point to the practical effects of Christian faith in the lives of Christians, and to the changes Christians have effected in society. Christians have been responsible for the advancement of women, for the abolition of slavery, for the building of hospitals and orphanages, for the feeding of the hungry, for the training of workers, and for many other social projects.
■ Love them. Pray for them. Encourage them to study God's Word with you.

BIBLIOGRAPHY AND RESOURCES

Adeney, David. *China: The Church's Long March.* Ventura, Calif.: Regal Books, 1985.

Bales, James D. *Communism: Its Faith and Fallacies.* Grand Rapids, Mich.: Baker Book House, 1962.

Billingsley, Lloyd. *The Generation That Knew Not Josef—A Critique of Marxism and the Religious Left.* Portland, Ore.: Multnomah, 1985.

Bockmuehl, Klaus. *The Challenge of Marxism.* Colorado Springs, Colo.: Helmers and Howard, 1986.

Bourdeaux, Michael. *The Gospel's Triumph Over Communism.* Minneapolis: Bethany House, 1992.

Carson, Clarence B. *Basic Communism: Its Rise, Spread and Debacle in the Twentieth Century.* Wadley, Ala.: American Textbook Committee, 1990.

DeKoster, Lester. *Communism and Christian Faith.* Grand Rapids, Mich.: Wm. B. Eerdmans Publishing Co., 1962.

Geisler, Norman L. *Is Man the Measure?* Grand Rapids, Mich.: Baker Book House, 1983.

Hill, Kent R. *The Puzzle of the Soviet Church.* Portland, Ore.: Multnomah, 1989.

Hill, Kent R. *Turbulent Times for the Soviet Church—The Inside Story.* Portland, Ore.: Multnomah, 1991.

Hook, Sidney. *Marx and the Marxists —The Ambiguous Legacy.* Princeton, N.J.: D. Van Nostrand Co., Inc., 1955.

Hook, Sidney. *Marxism and Beyond.* Totowa, N.J.: Rowman and Littlefield, 1983.

Kline, George L. *Religious and Anti-Religious Thought in Russia.* Chicago: The University of Chicago Press, 1968.

Lyon, David. *Karl Marx: A Christian Assessment of His Life and Thought.* Downers Grove, Ill.: InterVarsity Press, 1979.

Marx, Karl. *Communist Manifesto.* Chicago: Henry Regnery Co., 1968.

Mazlish, Bruce. *The Meaning of Karl Marx.* New York, Oxford: Oxford University Press, 1984.

McClellan, David. *Karl Marx: His Life and Thought.* New York: Harper and Row, 1973.

McClellan, David. *Marxism After Marx.* New York: Harper and Row, 1979.

McClellan, David. *Marxism and Religion.* New York: Harper and Row, 1987.

Nash, Ronald H. *Poverty and Wealth: Why Socialism Doesn't Work.* Richardson, Tex.: Probe Books, 1986.

Noebel, David A. *Understanding the Times.* Manitou Springs, Colo.: Summit Press, 1991.

Sowell, Thomas. *Marxism: Philosophy and Economics.* New York: Wm. Morrow and Co., 1985.

Stevenson, Leslie. *Seven Theories of Human Nature.* New York: Oxford University Press, 1987.

Yancey, Philip. "Praying With the KGB." *Christianity Today.* Carol Stream, Ill.: Christianity Today, Inc., January 13, 1992.

Yancey, Philip. *Praying with the KGB.* Portland, Ore.: Multnomah, 1992.

ORGANIZATIONS

Institute for East-West Christian Studies
The Graham Center
Wheaton College
Wheaton, IL 60187-5593
Phone: (708) 752-5917

Keston College
Keston Research
33a Canal St.
Oxford, England OX2 6BQ

Slavic Gospel Association
6151 Commonwealth Dr.
Loves Park, IL 61111
Phone: (815) 282-8900

The New Age Movement

William Honsberger
and Dean C. Halverson

NUMBER OF ADHERENTS

The number of adherents to the New Age movement is difficult to ascertain, mostly because the movement is a set of beliefs, not an organization. There are indicators in the culture, however (see Roof). For example, a poll released by CNN in 1990 estimated that 35% of all Americans believed in reincarnation. If accurate, this means that roughly 35–40 million people in the U.S. believe in one of the central tenets of the New Age. It is also estimated that the percentage of New Age adherents in Europe and South America is slightly higher than in the U.S.

DEFINING THE "NEW AGE" AND THE "MOVEMENT"

The term "New Age" refers to the coming "Aquarian age," which is in the process of replacing the old, or Pisces, age. According to astrologers, every 2,000 years constitutes an "age." New Agers predict this Aquarian Age will be a time of utopia.

The "movement" is like a smorgasbord for spirituality. It allows the religious consumer to pick and choose from among a wide variety of groups, teachers, and practices. He or she is free to choose the "path" or "door" according to whatever suits his or her particular taste in spirituality.

The New Age movement is like a smorgasbord for spirituality, allowing the religious consumer to pick and choose from among a wide variety of groups, teachers, and practices.

Druids greet the summer solstice on Primrose Hill, London.

A New Age person might be a Hindu, Buddhist, Wiccan (witch), or an astrologer, channeler, or parapsychologist. His or her cause might be "deep ecology," animal rights, holistic healing, or UFOs. The surface belief, expression, or practice is not that important. What is important is that underneath all the groups and practices lies a unifying philosophy that binds the movement together.

THE HISTORY AND ROOTS OF THE NEW AGE MOVEMENT

The New Age movement has collected and absorbed the beliefs

and practices of a wide variety of historical movements (see Burrows, chap.1).

It receives its name—the New Age—from astrology, which predicts a coming age of peace and harmony.

Its basic beliefs come from Hinduism and Buddhism. These religions were passed to the U.S. directly through Swami Vivekananda, D. T. Suzuki, Paramahansa Yogananda, Yogi Bhajan, Swami Muktananda, Alan Watts, Maharishi Mahesh Yogi, and others. They were passed indirectly through the nineteenth-century Transcendentalism of Whitman, Thoreau, and Emerson.

The New Age's bent toward channeling—contacting the spirits—

came through the Fox sisters, who in 1848 heard rappings that they claimed were coming from a murdered peddler who had been buried beneath their home in Hydesville, New York (Burrows, 21). Such spiritualism also came through the teaching on contacting "Ascended Masters"—advanced spirit beings—given by Madame Helena Blavatsky (1831–1891), the co-founder (with Henry Olcott) of the Theosophical Society in 1875. It also came through Edgar Cayce, the "sleeping prophet" (1877–1945), and through Jane Roberts (1929–1984), who channeled a "spirit entity" named Seth.

The New Age approach to the power of the mind with respect to healing came through Phinehas P. Quimby, who helped spawn the Mind Science groups such as Christian Science (Mary Baker Eddy), Unity School of Christianity (Charles and Myrtle Fillmore), and the Church of Religious Science (Ernest Holmes).

Its concern for ecology was received through the Native American religions and through Rachel Carson's *Silent Spring* (1962).

The New Age movement is not only the result of the teachings, philosophies, and practices of previous movements, but it serves as the undergirding influence behind the teachings, practices, and contemporary trends in:

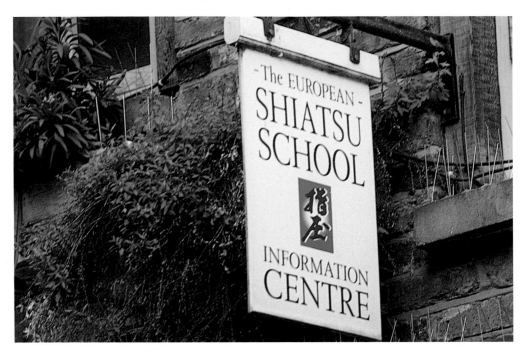

Shiatsu, Yoga, and acupuncture are all alternative therapies claimed by the New Age movement.

■ medicine (holistic health, Therapeutic Touch, Bernie Siegel, Deepak Chopra),
■ education (using guided imagery and meditation in the classroom, "values clarification"),
■ politics (globalism, Robert Muller of the United Nations, Planetary Citizens, Global Education Associates),
■ music (Stephen Halpern, Yanni),
■ science (Fritjof Capra's *The Tao of Physics*, the monistic/mystical interpretation of the new physics),
■ psychology (transpersonal psychology, the human potential movement),
■ ecology (the Green movement, "Deep ecology"),
■ business (Transformation Technologies, "Organizational Transformation," Lifespring, Forum, Anthony Robbins),
■ religion (*A Course in Miracles*, Marianne Williamson, Unity School of Christianity) (see Miller, chaps. 5–6, and Chandler).

Opposite: A Hindu statue. New Age thought draws from several Eastern religions.

More recently, though, the New Age has taken on a new look. It has gone from Shirley MacLaine's being a cover girl for the New Age on *Time* magazine in December 1987, to MacLaine's now resenting being called a New Ager. Her disassociating herself from the term "New Age" does not mean, however, that she has renounced her New Age beliefs. In fact, she once commented in an interview that she is not nearly as controversial as she used to be (Denver *Post*, March 24, 1994). This is true, though, not because she has changed, but because her ideas have become "mainstream." Most New Agers now prefer to say they are into "spirituality."

One of the rising trends in New Age spirituality is Wicca, the religion of witchcraft. It is closely related to goddess worship and neopaganism. All of these different groups hold to the divinity of nature and to the idea that spiritual power can be attained through the manipulation of these "natural forces." While Wicca originally attracted older adherents, it is quickly becoming a major attraction for young people. It promises power, mystery, self-gratification, and rebellion against Christianity.

Another recent development is the "marriage" between New Age

Some New Age believers trace mystical patterns back to the pyramids of Egypt.

thought and the UFO movement. Many channelers are channeling aliens from other galaxies and dimensions. These beings tell of an impending dark time for earth, which will only be survived by those who align themselves with the alien entities. These aliens are considered to be Ascended Masters, or *bodhisattvas* (see Buddhism), who have come to enlighten and rescue the earth from the evils of the old paradigm, especially Christian beliefs.

THE CORE BELIEFS OF THE NEW AGE MOVEMENT

The major unifying beliefs of the New Age movement include the following.

1. The Problem Is That of Perception

Humanity's most fundamental problem has to do with perception. To be more specific, all of humanity is suffering from a severe case of ignorance in that we have forgotten our true nature. We have forgotten that we are unconditionally connected to and emanated from God, which is Universal Mind.

During the "old age" of Pisces we relied on the dualistic way of thinking that says humankind is unique and separate from the rest of nature. Such a perspective must be changed, however, says the New Age movement. Barbara Marx Hubbard, a leading advocate of the New Age, calls the dualistic worldview the "fatal human flaw [which] is the illusion that we are separated from each other, from nature, and from the creative processes of nature herself" (Hubbard, 239).

Coming to a new way of thinking is seen as important by New Agers for two reasons. First, if it does not happen, then the world is in grave danger. Western, rational, linear, and separatistic thinking, it is claimed, has brought us science, which brought us technology, which brought us economic domination by a few, which has taken us to the brink of extinction through international strife, environmental disaster, and societal disharmony.

Second, the new paradigm is important in assisting in our search for spirituality. The materialistic and naturalistic worldviews, which predominate in Western culture, have hidden the sense of the sacred. Neither do New Agers consider it possible to find the sacred in the religions of the West. Adherents of the New Age believe, though, that a sense of spirituality and sacredness can be found in the alternative religions, which are most predominantly influenced by the religions of the East.

What we need, then, is a new consciousness, a new awareness, an enlightened way of thinking, a paradigm shift. As we incorporate the enlightened perspective of the New Age, we will find a power within by which to transform ourselves, and thereby the world.

2. The New Age View of God

The goal of the variety of New Age methods and beliefs is to come to the realization of the central truth of the New Age, which is that everything is fundamentally divine because

everything flows from the divine Oneness that is the existential Substance—the essential Reality—that is beneath all things.

When a New Ager speaks of God, he or she is not referring to the Judeo-Christian concept of God as a personal, holy Being who has existed before all things and is separate from all things. Instead, two key words describe the New Age movement's concept of God: *monism* and *pantheism*.

Illustration of a procession of the Hare Krishna sect.

New Age believers draw their ideas from a wide range of sources.

This eclectic mix of religious objects in a New Age shop window epitomizes the movement's beliefs.

Monism is the belief that God is One in the sense of being a oneness without duality or differentiation. There is no separation within God. It is "beyond" all such distinctions, including distinctions between persons and between good and evil. The New Age movement characterizes this oneness as a force or an energy. But, contrary to Naturalism, which says that matter (or physical energy) is all there is, the Ultimate Reality of the New Age is not a lifeless energy. Instead, it is a Cosmic Mind or Consciousness, often called the Universal Self.

All New Age practices are in some way based on getting in touch with or manipulating the fundamental force or energy or Mind of the universe. Depending on the practice, this fundamental force can be called by different terms, such as psychic energy, consciousness, color, mind, light, vibration, vital energy, life force, *ch'i*, *prana*, or an aura.

Considering that the New Age God is the divine energy that flows within and beneath all things, one can understand the significance of the second term that describes the New Age concept of Ultimate Reality— pantheism. Pantheism is the belief that "all is God" or "all is divine." What this means is that everything is inherently connected to and is an emanation from the divine Oneness.

3. The New Age View of Humanity

If God is an underlying life force or a vital energy from which all reality emanates, then it stands to reason that we, as humans, are unconditionally connected to it. If God is the Universal Self, then we are the particularizations of that Universal Self. We are like individual streams that flow from the infinite lake. Just as the water in the streams is the same in essence with the water in the lake, so our essence is at one with God.

Christianity teaches that humanity's problem is that we have rebelled against God and have thereby broken our relationship with Him. The New Age movement teaches, on the other hand, that there is nothing we can possibly do to sever the connection that exists between us and the divine Oneness. Our problem is that of ignorance, says the New Ager, not rebellion. We have forgotten who we are in our true selves, which is one with the Universal Self. The goal of yoga, meditation, and other mind-expanding techniques is to experience that Oneness. Such an experience will change our lives, for as we experience the Oneness—the inter-connectedness—with all things, then we will be transformed to view and to value everything as a manifestation of the divine.

4. The Power of the Mind

As the existence of a transcendent God who created all things is denied, which is what the New Age movement does, then the objectivity—the solidness, the otherness—of external reality is diminished. When that happens, then the role of the individual in shaping reality increases in importance. That is precisely where the New Age movement is coming from. Moreover, because the basic "stuff" of the universe is Mind, as we learn the appropriate techniques, our minds

will be able to exert tremendous power over "reality."

The New Age claims made about the power of the mind range from believing that positive thoughts or affirmations manifest themselves in physical health and fulfilled dreams to the idea that, through the act of observation, the consciousness of each individual "actualizes"—brings into reality—one of the many possible, but as yet unrealized, realities.

The New Age draws on Chinese religious concepts such as Feng Shui, as well as Western pagan practices such as witchcraft.

An array of New Age religious artefacts.

5. The Immediate Goal

Some New Agers believe that humanity's goal is the perfection of our ability to love. They believe there are a number of lessons that we need to learn in life before we can go on to the next stage. Reincarnation, which is the idea that our essential selves live from lifetime to lifetime, allows the possibility of learning those lessons. Before entering each lifetime, we choose the situation in which we are about to enter. For example, we might choose to be born to a family that is part of a racial minority, or choose to be born physically challenged, or choose to have AIDS, or choose to be raped. Each experience provides the opportunity for the person to perfect whatever characteristic he or she needs to develop and to learn whatever lesson he or she needs to learn.

Other New Agers come from a perspective that is closer to the original Hindu concept of reincarnation, which is based on karma. Karma, which simply means "action," is the moral law of cause and effect—"you reap what you sow." According to this view, the actions that are part of one's present life are the direct results of actions committed in earlier lives. If you are

murdered, you were probably a murderer in a previous life. If you are poor, you were probably rich in a previous life and so on.

The goal of enlightenment is to release ourselves from attachment to all action, whether good or bad. As we experience such a release, we will escape the cycles of being reincarnated lifetime after lifetime.

The New Ager gives a different slant on the concept of reincarnation from that of Hinduism. To the New Ager, reincarnation is the doctrine of the second (and third, and fourth, etc.) chance. New Agers are attracted to the doctrine of reincarnation because they see it as a form of justice and as a way to escape the distasteful Christian doctrine of a God who judges a person after one lifetime. Reincarnation in that sense sounds like good news. We are on a spiritual evolution to perfection.

To the Hindu, on the other hand, reincarnation is anything but good news. Instead, it is itself something to be escaped. The goal is not to go from lifetime to lifetime seeking perfection, but to be released from the suffering that we experience as we are caught on *samsara*—the wheel of life, death, and rebirth.

Aborigine didgeridoos. The Australian aborigines have animistic beliefs. New Age people are open to searching for spirituality in variety of beliefs and practices.

A highly decorated display from the Hare Krishna sect, a modern school of Vishnu Hinduism founded in New York City in the 1960's.

6. The Call for Assistance

New Agers encourage people to get in touch with their spirit guides who are able to assist them along their path of spiritual evolution and transformation. The various kinds of beings that can be contacted include Ascended Masters, disembodied spirits who lived in physical bodies at one time, UFOs, the spirits of animals, and angels.

The channeling of such beings fills the void that is left by the New Age movement's concept of Ultimate Reality, which is that of an impersonal Oneness that is without differentiation. Being so abstract, it is impossible for us as persons to relate to such a reality. How, after all, does a person warm up to a force? We need something that is more personal. We need that which is able to care for us and to give us guidance. Shirley MacLaine wrote, "When I go within I look for communication and guidance ... and in general have a friendly exchange with someone or something which I perceive to be more advanced than I perceive myself" (MacLaine, 70). Therefore, we fill the void left between us and this abstract form of Ultimate Reality with spirit beings

Magical items from a New Age store.

To support their stance against judging, New Agers often cite Jesus as having told us not to judge (Matthew 7:1–5). A clarifying statement, however, is, "Stop judging by mere appearances, and make a right judgment" (John 7:24).

Also, raise the issue of what the New Ager means by "loving and tolerant." By way of an illustration, imagine that you are standing on the shore of a river and that you notice that some rafters are about to take the wrong fork in a river. This fork will lead them to a 50-foot fall. You, however, still have a chance to warn them so they can be diverted from certain disaster. Would it be loving and tolerant of you to simply allow them to continue on their way because they have already expressed their firm belief to you that the river holds no danger and that all paths in the river lead to the same place? Obviously, no.

Of course, New Agers would object to such an analogy because they don't believe that any religious path leads to destruction. But we as Christians do. The issue should be which worldview is true, not which is more loving and tolerant.

2. *"Because the book of Genesis teaches that humanity is separate from and above nature, Christian beliefs are responsible for people exploiting the resources of the planet and causing harm to the environment."*

First, don't get defensive. Perhaps there have been and are those who have indeed misinterpreted the Bible for the purpose of exploiting the environment (Drane, 7). Such an interpretation of the Bible is wrong, however.

The Bible is abundantly clear that God cares for how we handle His creation. The command for humanity to "rule" and "subdue" (Genesis 1:26, 28) the earth is in the context of humanity being made in God's image. This is significant because, just as God demonstrated His dominion by

who can be channeled and who will guide us along our paths.

7. The Ultimate Goal

Since Ultimate Reality, according to the New Age movement, is a Oneness that is beyond all separation and differentiation, then the ultimate goal is for each person to relinquish all attachment and identification with his or her individual ego and to become identified with, or merged into, the Universal Self. Rather than portraying the dissolution of the individual self as being something negative, the New Age movement portrays the eventual merging of all persons into the One in a positive light. It is seen as an expansion of the individual minds into the Universal Mind.

COMMON NEW AGE ARGUMENTS AND OBJECTIONS

1. *"Christians are so judgmental. I want to be part of something that is loving and tolerant to all."*

The problem with this objection is that while the New Ager is accusing Christians of being judgmental, he or she is at the same time being judgmental of the Christian. One cannot judge others for judging without being inconsistent.

The New Age and Christianity Contrasted

	THE NEW AGE MOVEMENT	CHRISTIANITY
GOD IS . . .	Impersonal. Without moral distinctions. The life force that underlies nature; the existential Substance beneath all things.	Personal. Morally holy. Creator; distinct from His creation.
HUMANITY IS . . .	Divine, in that we are onto–logically extended (extended in our beings) from God's existential Substance. Unconditionally extended from the Oneness, but we are ignorant of our true, divine nature.	Made in God's image, but we are ontologically separate (separated in our beings) from the transcendent, infinite, and holy God. Spiritually separated from God because of our sin and rebellion against Him.
SALVATION IS . . .	Gaining a new perspective, in which we see the inter-connectedness of all things, including ourselves, with the divine Oneness.	Being justified before and reconciled to God through faith in the atoning work of Jesus Christ. Salvation is also being given new life, through the transforming power of the Holy Spirit.
LIFE AFTER DEATH IS . . .	Spiritual progression for the purpose of attaining enlightenment. Expanding one's consciousness into the Universal Mind.	Spent in either heaven or hell. Either eternal fellowship with the personal God, or eternal separation from Him.

bringing order from the chaos through the act of creation (Genesis 1:2), so, too, is humanity to demonstrate our dominion by bringing order out of the chaos of nature (see Genesis 2:15; Isaiah 45:18), which is the state to which nature would naturally go if left unattended. Moreover, just as it is unthinkable that God would exploit His creation, so, too, is it unthinkable that in the command to "rule" and "subdue" is there any sense that humanity is justified in exploiting the earth.

The Bible is also clear that God will judge those who mishandle His creation. For example, God said to the people of Israel, "And if you defile the land, it will vomit you out as it vomited out the nations that were before you" (Leviticus 18:28). Also, through Jeremiah He said to the Jews, "I brought you into a fertile land to eat its fruit and rich produce. But you came and defiled my land and made my inheritance detestable" (Jeremiah 2:7). Notice how in the Jeremiah passage God expresses His desire for us to preserve the land so it can be inherited by the next generation, and the next.

Consider, also, that God values His creation so much that He includes it in His plan of salvation, for the end purpose of the salvation that God has provided is not only to liberate humanity from sin but also to liberate the earth from its bondage to decay (Romans 8:21).

New Agers use various methods to attempt to look into the past and future.

Second, to say that Christianity is responsible for the exploitation of the environment is an irresponsible over-simplification, for our culture is not the result of solely Christian principles. Since the nineteenth century our culture has derived its principles more from Secular Humanism, which was built on the individualism and scientism of the Enlightenment, the Naturalism of the theory of evolution, and the consumerism of modernization. Our culture is also the result of urbanization, which has caused people to forget their connection with nature (Wilkinson, 4). Because of Secular Humanism, humankind has divorced itself from belief in a Creator and has thereby come to see itself as the measure of all things, which has contributed to the lack of restraint when it comes to exploiting the environment.

Third, it should be pointed out that cultures based on non-Christian worldviews, such as the former Soviet Union (Marxism) and India (Hinduism), have environmental records that are much worse than those that are supposedly based on the Christian worldview.

Fourth, as Christians, we would agree with the New Age contention that "separation" is the core problem with respect to ecology. The difference, however, is in how "separation" is defined. The New Ager defines "separation" in an *ontological* sense in that we see ourselves as separate from the divine force within all things. The Christian, on the other hand, defines "separation" in an *obedience* sense in that we have rebelled against the Creator, and have subsequently refused to be accountable to the One who made and cares for the creation.

While the subject of ecology is important, and while the Bible is clear that God is concerned about His creation, the more immediate issue is that of being made right with God. Being ecologically correct does not make a person right with God. (For further discussion of the New Age approach to ecology, see Miller, "A Summary Critique.")

3. *"Christians believe God will send people to hell because of their bad deeds. How can people believe that a God of love would punish anyone by sending him or her to hell? Reincarnation seems so much more just."*

First, we have condemned ourselves. We are the ones responsible for having separated ourselves from Him.

Humanity's situation is like that of the prodigal son (Luke 15:11–24) in that the son was the one who separated himself from the father and left for a distant land. The father did not banish his son to that distant land; he left of his own free will. In the same way, we are the ones who have alienated ourselves from God and are "enemies in minds [against God] because of evil behavior" (Colossians 1:21). As Jesus said, "God did not send his Son into the world to condemn the world, but to save the world through him.... This is the verdict: Light has come into the world, but men loved darkness instead of light because their deeds were evil" (John 3:17, 19).

But just as the father in that story longed to be in relationship with his son, so, too, is God reaching out to us in love through Jesus Christ, even as we are in the midst of rebelling against Him (Romans 5:8; 1 John 4:9–10).

Second, the Christian position is realistic when it comes to acknowledging the consequences of sin. Sin, after all, is not an abstract concept; it is lying, cheating, stealing from, and slandering each other— sometimes in subtle ways and sometimes in not so subtle ways. Whether subtle or not, such actions carry consequences in that they put a strain on our relationships, or they break those relationships altogether.

Moreover, the biblical teaching on sin is realistic in that it acknowledges how we are hurt not only when someone sins against us directly but also indirectly, such as when someone sins against a person we love. If a schoolteacher, for example, treats my child unfairly, I will be upset with that teacher. In the same way, since God loves all people, He is offended when we hurt each other.

Third, New Agers are saying that a God who loves would not condemn people to hell. Consider, though, the option that everyone has the right to be ushered into God's presence:

■ If God allows all people into His kingdom just the way they are morally, then that means He must

The Hare Krishna sect practice charitable activities such as food distribution for the needy.

BELL 50mm	BELL 40mm	HEART 40mm	HEART 2mm	OCTAGON 50mm	OCTAGON 40mm	OCTAGON 26mm	SPHERE 5mm	SPHERE 6mm	SPHERE 30mm	SPHERE 20mm	PENDULUM 50mm	PENDULUM 44mm	PENDULUM 20mm
£15.95	£9.95	£9.95	£4.95		£9.95	£3.95			£9.95	£5.95	£3.95	£4.95	£2.95

POWER BRACELETS

Lilith £40
Individually made & hand painted

Some New Age believers use crystals in their religious practices.

allow mass murderers like Hitler, Stalin, and Pol Pot and serial killers like Jeffrey Dahmer into His kingdom. Would God's kingdom still be heaven, or would it be hell?

■ If God allows all people into His kingdom just the way they are morally, then it means He has condoned their actions. Would not such acceptance reflect flaws in God's character? Would we want to associate with such a God?

■ If God is absolutely holy, and yet all people are ushered into His presence without any moral change having been effected, might it not be a greater punishment for sinners to be in the presence of an absolutely holy God than what hell would be?

■ If God allows all people into His kingdom, but only after He has changed them to make them loving people regardless of whether or not they wanted to be changed, then has He not made them into robots with no free will?

New Agers would respond that the above arguments are precisely why reincarnation makes sense, because it gives people the opportunities, over the course of numerous lifetimes, to

learn the lessons of love and to conform themselves to the character of a holy God. There are several problems with this perspective, though.

A. Such a perspective underestimates the seriousness of sin. The Bible says we are dead in our sins (Ephesians 2:1) and that sin makes us blind to the truths of God (Ephesians 4:18). Such images convey the fact that we need outside help to be transformed; for dead people cannot give themselves life, and blind people cannot give themselves sight.

The hope for help that the New Agers have to offer was graphically depicted by a comic strip in which a man is pictured with water all around him. He is obviously drowning and going down for the third time. Both hands are raised high in desperation, and he's yelling, "Self-help! Self-help!"

B. In the process of learning the lessons of love we will inevitably do other bad things. And that means we will have to come back to pay for those things. The cycle is never-ending and hopeless.

C. People do not remember their past lives. How is it just to say that we are paying for our past actions when we don't remember what those actions are?

D. In some cases (Buddhism, for example) there is no existential continuity from one life to another, and yet karma continues from one life to the next. So, someone, who has had absolutely no connection with the person in the previous lifetime, is now paying for someone else's karma. Is that just?

E. New Agers are violating the law of noncontradiction by both affirming and denying the same thing and in the same respect. Let us explain. New Agers say reincarnation is more just than the idea that God judges people after one lifetime. What such a statement does is judge a system on the basis of something that is at the same time being denied. How is that? Because reincarnation is based on the *impersonal principle* of the law of cause and effect—you reap what you sow. But justice is an attribute that is exhibited *only by persons.* Just as the existence of laws implies a lawgiver, so justice implies a judge.

Therefore, by making the statement that reincarnation is more just than a God who judges, New Agers are implicitly pointing to a standard of justice. But justice points to the existence of a judge who is personal, because justice is something practiced by persons, not by an impersonal principle or an impersonal Oneness. Reincarnation, however, is based on that which is impersonal. Therefore, the statement from the New Agers about reincarnation being more just both affirms and denies the existence of a personal God, thereby rendering the statement meaningless.

F. The real heart behind the New Ager's call for justice is not so much that of justice but a concern for compassion. Where, they wonder, is the compassion of a God who judges? Several responses could be given:

■ Are they just as concerned about compassion for the victim? Does it show compassion for the victim to allow his or her murderer to go free and to not be judged?

■ While they see reincarnation as the gospel of the second chance, in reality there is no possibility for compassion or for forgiveness in reincarnation. The consequences of a person's actions are inevitable; there is no escaping them.

■ Where is the compassion to be found in a system that calls for people to suffer through myriads of lifetimes for actions about which they have no recollection?

■ Only a personal God is able to show compassion; and He has done so by providing forgiveness through Jesus Christ. The issue is not whether God is compassionate and forgiving (indeed, He died in our place—John 15:13), but it is whether the New Ager is willing to accept the means of forgiveness that God has provided.

4. New Agers rebel against the idea that God would judge. It's ironic, then, that they so readily embrace a system whereby humanity is judged unconditionally. Consider this: The goal of reincarnation is for each individual to merge into the Oneness. Such a state is where no distinctions exist, no events occur, and where there is only an eternal Now. Such a

The mysterious Stonehenge, Wiltshire, England, focus of New Age speculation.

state sounds more like eternal death than eternal life. If we value the existence of the individual at all, then such an outcome is the ultimate form of judgment, and there is no escaping it. (For further discussion on the Christian response to reincarnation, see Albrecht, and Geisler, and Amano.)

5. *"Christians are so arrogant. What gives them the right to say their way is the only way?"*

New Agers are here accusing Christians of being arrogant because Christians believe in a way to God that is exclusive. In other words, arrogance is defined as holding a belief that is exclusive of other beliefs.

According to their own definition of arrogance, New Agers are then also arrogant. Their inclusiveness—their belief that all ways lead to God— *excludes the belief* that there is only

one way to God.

Also, present the following scenario in order to illustrate why there is only one way. Suppose you are entirely responsible for having broken fellowship with your father or mother. How many ways are there for you to restore that fellowship? One way— through confessing your guilt and requesting forgiveness.

Such a scenario puts the issue of how many ways there are to God in the proper perspective. The issue is that of a broken relationship, not that of being ignorant of our connection to an inner divinity.

This is why "reconciliation" is one of the words that describes what Jesus accomplished on the cross (2 Corinthians 5:18–21). Reconciliation is the restoration of a relationship where before there was enmity. Jesus is the means by which God offers forgiveness and reconciliation with us, so our relationship with Him could be restored.

SUGGESTIONS FOR EVANGELISM

1. Acknowledge Their Search for Spirituality.

There is a search for the sacred taking place in the United States, and part of that is the result of the naturalistic perspective of Secular Humanism having left people spiritually empty. The New Age movement represents one form of that search. There are obviously many fundamental points on which we as Christians disagree with New Age beliefs, but we can affirm the New Ager in his or her realization that there must be something more to reality than cold and lifeless matter.

Also, we as Christians must feel a certain conviction that many New Agers have left the Church after having once been a part of it. The reasons for their leaving are numerous and varied, and it is easy to oversimplify them. Nevertheless, many New Agers apparently did not sense

Candles are often used in New Age rituals—as in many other religions.

A woman consults a tarot card reader.

the presence of the kind of spirituality that has since attracted them to the New Age movement. And for that we Christians should take a close look at ourselves. Are we so caught up in "playing church" that we are failing to develop a warm and personal walk with Christ that would be noticed by and attractive to others? Have we lost an appreciation for signs of the sacred that can be found in the everyday things around us that would stimulate the thinking of the New Ager toward the truth of God? Are we so stuck in our Christian subculture that we are unaware of the spiritual insights that can be found in non-Christian, even New Age, authors? (see Acts 17:28).

2. Major on the Primary Issues.

New Agers will no doubt be involved in practices that we as Christians would not recommend, such as yoga, using crystals, acupuncture, astrology, tarot cards, channeling, or some forms of the martial arts. It is best not to make such practices an issue at the beginning of your relationship. Instead, key in on the worldview that stands behind such practices.

For example, I have a friend who practices yoga. It would not have helped our relationship if I had told him at the beginning that he should not be practicing yoga because it is spiritually detrimental. Such a frontal attack would have alienated him. I have talked with him, though, about how many of the things that he is looking for through yoga—personal fulfillment, self-improvement, spiritual experience—would better be found in a relationship with a personal God.

3. Be Aware of the Inherent Contradiction in the New Age God.

New Agers often refer to Ultimate Reality as Universal Mind, or Infinite Intelligence, or as being unconditionally loving.

What New Agers are doing through such terms is mixing two kinds of language for God—the impersonal (universal, infinite, unconditional) and the personal (mind, intelligence, love).

By mixing the two kinds of language, New Agers are trying to get the best of both worlds, while at the same time avoiding the negative parts of either. For instance, at least two positive implications come from the concept of God being an impersonal oneness. First, God can be unconditional in its acceptance (thus, removing judgment); and second, God is then a power that we can manipulate (thus, denying that we are obligated to obey God).

Although New Agers are attracted to the positive implications of God being an impersonal force, they also realize that such a concept of God means God is rather cold and uncaring. For example, it is written in one of the foundational books for the Unity School of Christianity (a Mind Science group),

> God as the underlying substance of all things, God as principle, is unchanging, and does remain forever uncognizant of and unmoved by the changing things of time and sense. It is true that God as principle does not feel pain, is not

moved by the cries of the children of men for help (*Foundations*, 143).

Also, New Age author Stuart Wilde similarly wrote, "The Force . . . does not even have an immediate awareness of the negativity [of our suffering and pain]" (Wilde, 10).

In light of the cold and uncaring nature of a God who is an impersonal Force, New Agers also speak of God as being personal in that they give Him personal attributes, such as love, intelligence, and goodness (although they never talk about Him as morally holy).

The problem with mixing the two ways of talking about God—the impersonal and the personal—is that they are incompatible and mutually exclusive. This is true for two reasons.

Mysterious wood carvings from Jamaica, in the Caribbean.

First, because an impersonal Force, which is without internal distinctions, is not capable of exhibiting personal attributes such as love, forgiveness, empathy, knowledge, intelligence, creativity, and moral holiness. All such attributes involve the ability to make distinctions—something an impersonal Force is incapable of doing.

Second, the two ways of talking about God are incompatible and mutually exclusive because relating to an impersonal Oneness is different from relating to a personal God. They involve very different issues. To be specific, if God is personal, then there are moral issues in relating to Him, just as there are moral issues involved in relating to any person. This is true of even the most cursory of relationships. Take, for example, relating to a grocery store clerk. If the grocery store clerk discovers that I have stashed candy in my pocket without the intention of paying for it, our relationship will be strained, to say the least. I have violated the assumed moral issues of respect, trust, and honesty.

In a marriage relationship, there is the moral issue of sexual fidelity. In a person's relationship with God, there are not only issues of honesty and respect but also issues of fidelity (since He is the only true God) and obedience (since His commands are not arbitrary, but are in accordance with the way He made us). None of these moral issues would be involved, however, if it were true that God is an impersonal Oneness.

The point is that all interpersonal relationships, including our relationship with God, involve moral issues.

A further point is that if those moral issues are violated, there are consequences that result with respect to the relationship. Another way to put it is to say that sin, which is rebellion against God, carries consequences; and those consequences are the breaking of the relationship between us and God, which is spiritual death (Romans 6:23). Such things would not be true if God were an impersonal Force.

We have seen, then, how the two kinds of language used to talk about God—the impersonal and the personal—are incompatible and

All interpersonal relationships, including our relationship with God, involve moral issues.

God is an Impersonal Oneness

The Good News: Sin is not an issue with God, and it can be dealt with on the level of the human mind.

The Bad News: Forgiveness is not possible because moral laws become like the laws of nature, which means it is inevitable that we will reap what we sow.

God is a Personal Being

The Bad News: Sin carries real consesequences and it causes us to be separated from God.

The Good News: Forgiveness is possible because the source of moral law is the Person of God himself, and persons are capable of forgiving.

New Age beliefs encompass all sort of objects from crystals to tea leaves.

mutually exclusive, thus committing an inherent contradiction.

4. Use the Good News/Bad News Principle.

We as Christians must understand that it is repugnant to a New Ager to think that our sin causes spiritual death. How, they say, can anyone believe something that is so negative, so unloving, so judgmental, so unaffirming of humanity's potential! If New Agers are anything, they are positive in their beliefs, to the point that they reject anything and everything that smacks of even a hint of negativity.

It is somewhat ironic, then, that while New Age teaching begins with good news, it ends with bad news. Christianity, on the other hand, begins with bad news, but ends with good news.

GOOD NEWS/BAD NEWS

We will apply this good news/bad news principle to several New Age beliefs.

"God Is Unconditionally Loving"

The New Age belief: God loves us unconditionally, for we are extended from the impersonal Oneness.

The good news: God is unconditionally loving toward all. No one will be judged.

The bad news: The kind of God from whom we can be unconditionally extended is not the kind of God who is able to love. Why not? Because love is inherently interpersonal—something that happens between persons. The idea of "unconditional love" in the context of the impersonal Oneness of the New Age God is more accurately understood to be "unconditional absorption," which means the individual disappears into the Oneness just as a drop of water merges into the vast ocean. If the individual is valued, such absorption is not life, and neither is it good news.

"There Are Many Paths to God"

The New Age belief: There are as many paths to God as there are paths to the top of a mountain.

The good news: No one will be judged for failing to choose the right path to God. We can each choose whichever path suits us best.

The bad news: The emphasis of the analogy of the mountain is that salvation is based on *the path* that *we must walk*. In other words, salvation is a gradual process that is based on human effort. Also, there is no assurance concerning what happens after death. Who knows how he or she is going to be reincarnated?

Salvation, in Christianity, is a gift to be received, not something to be earned through human effort. Moreover, because God has accomplished our salvation on our behalf, we can have assurance. In addition, there is the hope of the survival of the person and of being in eternal fellowship with God.

"There Are Many Meanings and Methods of Salvation"

Let us say another thing about the subject of salvation while we are on that subject. Ask a New Ager the following questions:

■ What is reincarnation (or enlightenment)?
■ What is the goal of reincarnation (or enlightenment)?

As you listen to him or her talk about reincarnation or enlightenment, which

Relief of the deity Anubis from an ancient Egyptian tomb. New Agers draw on Egyptian, Geeek, Nordic and other ancient belief systems.

New Age Movement	Christianity
Good News: There are many paths to God.	*Bad News:* There is only one way to God.
Bad News: Salvation is based on human effort.	*Good News:* Salvation is based on God's grace, and received by faith as a gift.
Bad News: No assurance of what will happen after death.	*Good News:* Assurance for believers that we will be found right with God, based on the already completed work of Jesus Christ.

Magic card sets for sale in a street market.

"Faith Produces Healing"

The New Age belief: Health is a matter of the mind. If we implant positive thoughts—affirmations—in our minds, then those thoughts will manifest themselves as health.

The good news: The results of such positive thinking are guaranteed. Notice, for example, the words that speak of guarantees in this quote from Shakti Gawain: "The more we bring our consciousness into alignment with our highest spiritual realization, the more our bodies will express our own individual perfection" (Gawain, 59). Barbara Marx Hubbard speaks of the guaranteed power of the mind when she confidently writes, "In consciousness we know that as we think it, so it becomes" (Hubbard, 239).

are their terms for "salvation," listen for the kinds of language described in the following chart, and be aware of how that language differs from the biblical way of salvation.

The bad news: Who is at fault if the healing does not take place or if we do not manifest health? We are at fault because we have not implanted enough positive thoughts, or perhaps

#	The New Age Way of Salvation	The Biblical Way of Salvation
1.	The *meaning* of salvation is for the individual to merge into the impersonal Oneness.	1 The *meaning of* salvation is for the individual to be reconciled with the Person of God.
2.	Salvation is *based* on human effort.	2. Salvation is *based* on God's grace.
3.	The language *of* salvation points to Jesus as our *example of* what a self-actualized person is like.	3. The language *of* salvation points to Jesus not only as our *example of* what a person living in submission to God is like, but it also speaks of Him as our *Substitute* for the death penalty that we deserve to pay because of our sin.
4.	The language of salvation points to a *standard of perfection* that must be met in order to achieve salvation (or enlightenment).	4. The language of salvation points to *humanity's sinfulness,* which means we cannot possibly merit salvation.
5.	Salvation is a *gradual process* whereby we strive to manifest our perfection.	5. Salvation is *an immediate gift* that can be received by faith in Jesus Christ.

New Age Movement	Christianity
The Meaning of Faith: Faith is trust in the healing powers of the mind, and it is founded on the idea that in our true selves we have perfect health.	*The Meaning of Faith:* Faith is trust in the power of God to heal, and trust in the wisdom of God as to whether or not to heal us.
The Results of Faith (the Good News): results of faith are guaranteed, because faith is based on predictable forces, such as the Mind and the perfect health that resides within our true selves.	*The Results of Faith (the Bad News):* The results of faith are not guaranteed in this lifetime, because faith is based on God's sovereign and loving will, not on ours.
The Meaning of Failure (the Bad News): The failure to he healed reveals a lack of adequate faith, or very possibly a spiritual defect within that is manifesting itself.	*The Meaning of Failure (the Good News):* The failure to be healed does not mean personal inadequacy, nor does it alter one's confidence in God's love, because He has guaranteed that He will heal us in His time, as evidenced by the resurrection of Jesus Christ.

our thoughts were not positive enough. Dr. Marcia Angell, editor of the *New England Journal of Medicine*, wrote that the "view of sickness as a personal failure [brought on by the belief that positive thoughts will produce health] is a particularly unfortunate form of blaming the victim. At a time when patients are already burdened by disease, they should not be further burdened by having to accept responsibility for the outcome" (Angell, 1571).

CONCLUSION

New Agers are on a search for spirituality. They fail to consider Christianity, however, because they have negative stereotypes of Christians. Just by showing concern for the New Ager, having a listening ear, and not automatically judging him or her, you will go a long way to breaking their stereotypes of Christians.

When talking with a New Ager, keep in mind the two major themes developed above: (1) God is personal, and (2) The good news/bad news principle. These two themes will help you discern the biblical response to a lot of issues that the New Ager will present to you. They will also help you bring the New Ager to the point of questioning his or her firmly held beliefs about God and how one gets to know Him.

BIBLIOGRAPHY AND RESOURCES

Books Cited in the Text

Albrecht, *Mark. Reincarnation: A Christian Appraisal.* Downers Grove, Ill.: InterVarsity Press, 1982.

Angell, Marcia. "Editorial: Psychosocial Correlates of Survival in Advanced Malignant Disease." *The New England Journal of Medicine.* June 13, 1985, Vol. 312, no. 24.

Burrows, Robert. "The Coming of the New Age." *The New Age Rage.* Karen Hoyt, ed. Old Tappan, N.J.: Fleming H. Revell Co., 1987.

Capra, Fritjof. *The Tao of Physics.* Boulder, Colo.: Shambhala, 1975.

Drane, John. "Defining a Biblical Theology of Creation." *Transformation.* Oxford, U.K.: Oxford Centre of Mission Studies, April/June 1993.

Foundations for Unity. Unity Village, Mo.: Unity, 1982, Series 2, Vol. 3.

Gawain, Shakti. *Creative Visualization.* New York: Bantam Books, 1985.

Geisler, Norman and J. Yutaka Amano. *The Reincarnation Sensation.* Wheaton, Ill.: Tyndale House Publishers, 1986.

Hubbard, Barbara Marx. *The Hunger of Eve.* Eastsound, Wash.: Island Pacific Northwest, 1989.

MacLaine, Shirley. *Going Within.* New York: Bantam Books, 1989.

Miller, Elliot. *A Crash Course on the New Age Movement.* Grand Rapids, Mich.: Baker Book House, 1989.

Miller, Elliot. "A Summary Critique: Toward a Transpersonal Ecology." *Christian Research Journal.* San Juan Capistrano, Calif.: Christian Research Institute, Spring, 1992.

Roof, Wade. *A Generation of Seekers: The Spiritual Journeys of the Baby Boom Generation.* New York: HarperCollins, 1993.

Wilde, Stuart. *The Force.* Taos, N.M.: White Dove International, 1984.

Wilkinson, Loren and Mary Ruth Wilkinson. "The Depth of the Danger." *Transformation.* Oxford, U.K.: Oxford Centre of Mission Studies, April/June 1993.

Books Critical of the New Age Movement

Alnor, William. *UFOs in the New Age.* Grand Rapids, Mich.: Baker Book House, 1992.

Ankerberg, John and John Weldon. *The Facts on Astrology.* Eugene, Ore.: Harvest House Publishers, 1988.

Ankerberg, John and Craig Branch. *Thieves of Innocence.* Eugene, Ore.: Harvest House Publishers, 1993.

Chandler, Russell. *Understanding the New Age.* Dallas: Word, 1991.

Clark, David and Norman Geisler. *Apologetics in the New Age.* Grand Rapids, Mich.: Baker Book House, 1990.

Ferguson, Duncan, ed. *New Age Spirituality: An Assessment.* Louisville, Ky.: Westminster/Knox Press, 1993.

Gray, William. *Thinking Critically About New Age Ideas.* Belmont, Calif.: Wadsworth Publishing, 1991.

Groothuis, Douglas. *Confronting the New Age.* Downers Grove, Ill.: InterVarsity Press, 1988.

Groothuis, Douglas. *Revealing the New Age Jesus.* Downers Grove, Ill.: InterVarsity Press, 1990.

Groothuis, Douglas. *Unmasking the New Age.* Downers Grove, Ill.: InterVarsity Press, 1986.

Halverson, Dean. *Crystal Clear: Understanding and Reaching New Agers.* Colorado Springs, Colo.: NavPress, 1990.

Mangalwadi, Vishal. *When the New Age Gets Old.* Chicago: Cornerstone Press, 1994.

Reisser, Paul, Teri Reisser, and John Weldon. *New Age Medicine.* Downers Grove, Ill.: InterVarsity Press, 1987.

Rhodes, Ron. *The Counterfeit Christ of the New Age Movement.* Grand Rapids, Mich.: Baker Book House, 1990.

Sneed, David and Sharon Sneed. *The Hidden Agenda: A Critical View of Alternative Medical Therapies.* Nashville: Thomas Nelson Publishers, 1991.

Strohmer, Charles. *What Your Horoscope Doesn't Tell You.* Wheaton, Ill.: Tyndale House Publishers, 1988.

Books Supportive of the New Age Movement

Adler, Margo. *Drawing Down the Moon.* Boston: Beacon Press, 1981.

Campbell, Joseph. *The Power of Myth.* New York: Doubleday Press, 1988.

Capra, Fritjof. *The Turning Point: Science, Society, and the Rising Culture.* Toronto: Bantam Books, 1982.

Castanada, Carlos. *The Teachings of Don Juan: A Yaqui Way of Knowledge.* New York: Ballantine Books, 1968.

Chopra, Deepak. *Quantum Healing: Exploring the Frontiers of Mind/Body Medicine.* New York: Bantam Books, 1989.

de Chardin, Pierre. *The Phenomenon of Man.* New York: Harper & Row, 1961.

D'Antonio, Michael. *Heaven on Earth: Dispatches from American's Spiritual Frontier.* New York: Crown Publishers, 1992.

Ferguson, Marilyn. *The Aquarian Conspiracy.* Los Angeles: J. P. Tarcher Press, 1980.

Fields, Rick, *et. al.*, eds. *Chop Wood, Carry Water.* Los Angeles: J. P. Tarcher, 1984.

Fox, Matthew. *The Coming of the Cosmic Christ.* San Francisco: Harper & Row, 1988.

Muller, Robert. *New Genesis: Shaping a Global Spirituality.* Garden City, N.Y.: Doubleday, 1982.

Russell, Peter. *The Global Brain.* Los Angeles: J. P. Tarcher, 1983.

Siegel, Bernie. *Love, Medicine, & Miracles.* New York: Harper & Row, 1986.

Spangler, David. *Revelation: The Birth of a New Age.* Elgin, Ill.: Lorian Press, 1976.

Williamson, Marianne. *A Return to Love.* New York: HarperCollins, 1992.

Zukav, Gary. *The Seat of the Soul.* New York: Simon and Schuster, 1989.

ORGANIZATIONS

Christian Research Institute
P.O. Box 500
San Juan Capistrano
CA 92693-0500
Phone: (714) 855-9926

Spiritual Counterfeits Project
P.O. Box 4308
Berkeley, CA 94704
Phone: (510) 540-0300

Secularism

Dean C. Halverson

SECULARISM AMONG THE NATIONS

If one combines the numbers for both the "atheists" and the "non-religious," the total number of secularists is around 20% of the world's population (Barrett, 25).

In the following countries, atheists or nonreligious individuals make up more than 10% of the population (Johnstone): Albania, Australia, China, Cuba, former Czechoslovakia, France, French Polynesia, Hungary, Italy, Japan, North Korea, Macao, Mongolia, Netherlands, New Zealand, Poland, Romania, Singapore, Sweden, the former U.S.S.R., United Kingdom, Uruguay, Vietnam, and former Yugoslavia.

It has been said that shopping malls are today's places of worship.

DEFINING THE TERMS

An "atheist" is one who says there is sufficient evidence to show that God does not exist. An "agnostic" is one who says there is insufficient evidence to know whether or not God exists. The "functional atheist" is one who is apathetic concerning God's existence. For the purposes of this profile, the term "secularist" will be used to include all three.

THE RISE OF SECULARISM

The Renaissance
(ca. A.D. 1400 to 1600)
In the early 1400s, Gutenberg invented the printing press with movable type. As a result, the writings of the past became much more accessible to the public. Such increased accessibility sparked two responses. One was a greater awareness of and obedience to God's Word, which led to the Reformation. The other was a pursuit of humanistic themes, which drew from the writings of Greek and Roman thinkers and served as the foundation for the Renaissance. The word "renaissance" means "rebirth," and that which was

reborn was humanity's sense of
independence and individualism.

Toward the end of the Renaissance,
the modern method of empirical
science began to develop. The key
players were Nicholas Copernicus
(1473–1543), Johannes Kepler
(1571–1630), and Galileo Galilei
(1564–1642). Although it may seem
ironic now, each of these men
believed in the Christian God. They
viewed science as one of the means
by which to study the handiwork of
an almighty Creator and to discern His
natural laws. Galileo considered God
to have written two "books": the
Bible and nature (Hummel, 106).

Contrary to popular belief, the cause
for the division between Christianity
and science originated not with the
church but with the university
professors who were threatened by
Galileo's revolutionary ideas. These
professors were steeped in the Greek
scientific method, which included
observation to a small extent, but it
explained the workings of nature
mostly through rational deduction
from first principles, or assumptions.

Based on such assumptions, an
entire view of the universe had been
developed, apart from actual
observations of the universe.
Consequently, the professors
embraced such misconceptions as the
sun having no imperfections, the
moon being a perfectly smooth sphere
that shone with its own light, and the
earth alone having a moon (since it
was believed that the earth was at the
center of the universe).

Galileo's recently invented telescope
quickly demonstrated the incorrectness
of such assumptions (Hummel,
91–94).

Not willing to be undermined by
Galileo, the professors decided to
make the controversy a religious one
rather than an academic one
(Hummel, 92). They argued that the
heliocentric (sun-centered) view
contradicted Scripture. For example,
Psalm 104:22 says, "The sun rises."
Therefore, the sun must revolve
around a stationary earth.

In the face of what at that time
appeared to be a genuine
contradiction between Scripture and
the heliocentric theory, the theologians
of the Roman Catholic Church had no
choice but to condemn Galileo's views,
since the conflict had challenged the
authority of the church.

As a result of this controversy

During the
Renaissance men
began to explore
the universe with
an enquiring
mind

between the church and Galileo, the schism between reason and faith had begun. There were now two apparently irreconcilable sources of truth: the church and science.

In the way that philosopher René Descartes (1596–1650) responded to a movement called Pyrrhonism he contributed to the trend of moving the source of truth away from the church. Pyrrhonism (named after the Greek skeptic Pyrrho, 365–275 B.C.) was a form of utter skepticism whereby everything was doubted. As a result, nothing could be known for certain. The significance of Descartes' *cogito ergo sum* ("I think, therefore I am") is that he had used the Pyrrhonists' own method of questioning everything in order to establish one unquestionable fact: The doubter could be certain of his own existence (Brown, 184). Descartes had no intention of being a religious reformer; nevertheless, his new method of approaching truth shook Christianity to its core. It was used to shift the foundation for certainty from God to man.

The Enlightenment
(ca. A.D 1600 to 1800)
The successes produced by science ushered in the Age of Enlightenment. During the Enlightenment, people began to elevate science to the level of being the ultimate test for truth.

The discoveries of the laws of science by men like Francis Bacon (1561–1626), Robert Boyle (1627–1692), and Isaac Newton (1642–1727) gave support to the analogy that the universe was like a machine. Such an analogy tended to dismiss the need for a God as Sustainer of the universe.

Other challenges to the Christian worldview came through philosophers Thomas Hobbes (1588–1679), David Hume (1711–1776), and Immanuel Kant (1724–1804). Hobbes drew out the implications of a materialistic philosophy in which matter was the ultimate stuff of the universe. Hume, in his *Enquiry Concerning Human Understanding,* presented arguments against the veracity of the miracle accounts in the Bible. And Kant encouraged people to assert the power of their own intellect and to throw off the shackles of ecclesiastical authority (Brown, 286–287).

Still, even with the onslaught of the Enlightenment, most people in the nineteenth century, including scientists, believed in the existence of a rational and personal Creator. The reason was that there was no alternative theory to that of creation that could adequately explain the existence of an orderly universe. That changed with Charles Darwin.

The Modern Age
(ca. 1800 to present)
In 1859, Charles Darwin (1809–1882) published *On the Origin of Species by Means of Natural Selection, or The Preservation of Favored Races in the Struggle for Life.* In it, Darwin theorized that life forms had resulted from natural, random processes and not from the design of an intelligent Creator.

As a result, the gap that had previously been filled with a religious faith in a Creator could now, through the theory of evolution, be filled with a purely scientific and naturalistic explanation. Many scientists became enthralled with the theory of evolution and began to apply it to every field of study, including history (Marx) and psychology (Freud).

The result of Darwinism was that, for many, the belief in God became an unnecessary hypothesis. If mankind was to find solutions for its problems and hope for its future, people must look to themselves, not to God.

THE BELIEFS OF SECULARISM

1. The Denial of God
The most fundamental tenet of secularism is the denial of the existence of the supernatural. Matter is all that exists.

According to secularism, belief in

God is nothing more than a projection of man's own thoughts and desires. God did not make man in His image; instead, man made God in his image.

2. The Denial of Miracles

After having denied God's existence, it is logical then to conclude that miracles—the result of God's intervention—are not possible. The miracles recorded in the Bible, secularists surmise, must have been the embellishments of the authors who were promoting their particular religious agenda (Geisler and Brooks, chap. 5; Geisler, 1992).

3. The Fact of Evolution

Secularists assert that the existence and complexity of the universe can be sufficiently explained through naturalistic principles as set forth in the theory of evolution. Personality and mind are also the products of the evolutionary process and are sufficiently explained through the interaction of chemical and biological elements. Thus, there is no "ghost in the machine."

4. The Potential of Humanity

Secularists see religion as being restrictive and escapist. Religion does nothing more than assuage the fears of an ignorant people. If humanity is to survive, secularists say, humankind must face problems squarely and find the answers within themselves, reason, and science. Secularism begins and ends with humanity. Humanity will be able to face the issues squarely only when freed from the shackles of religion.

5. The Centrality of Science

Secularists are confident that the scientific method of inquiry is the only reliable avenue by which to discover truth and knowledge. According to the secularistic point of view, there is an irreconcilable antagonism between reason and faith, science and religion, empirical observation and revealed authority. The two avenues to truth and knowledge are mutually exclusive.

6. The Stress on Relativity

Secularists deny that there is an absolute moral reference point beyond humanity, such as a holy God. They contend that humankind does not need an absolute moral standard beyond itself in order to have a sufficient foundation and motivation for moral behavior. Humanity is by nature good, and all that is needed to realize that innate goodness is education, not religious transformation.

7. The Finality of Death

At death, the individual ceases to exist in any cohesive or conscious form. As the signers of The Humanist Manifesto II wrote, "There is no credible evidence that life survives the death of the body" (Lamont, 293).

In 1859, Charles Darwin (1809–1882) published On the Origin of Species by Means of Natural Selection.

Humanists believe there is no credible evidence that life survives the death of the body.

A. The Origin of the Universe and of Life. The second law of thermodynamics says that while the total amount of energy remains constant (the first law) the availability of usable energy is constantly decreasing (the second law). Energy inevitably moves toward a state where it is increasingly unusable and inaccessible. The inevitable cooling of a cup of hot tea is an example of the constraints imposed by the second law.

What are the implications of the second law with respect to the origin of the universe? It means that the universe had a beginning. If the universe has always existed, then an infinite amount of time would have already passed before reaching this present moment. But it cannot be true that an infinite amount of time has passed to get to this point because, according to the second law, the universe, which contains a finite amount of energy, would then be in a state of equilibrium—a cold and lifeless state of absolute rest.

The question that obviously follows is: If the universe has not always existed, then who or what caused it to come into existence? We can appeal to science for the answer. Scientists understand that the universe was tuned at its inception to a precision of greater than sixty decimal places, which is a precision equal to the number ten multiplied by itself more than 60 times. Unless the universe had been that finely tuned, it would not have "worked." But all known natural processes are not tuned that finely, only to several decimal places. Only a First Cause with supreme intelligence could have produced such phenomenal accuracy.

Other questions include: What is life, and how did it originate? Could life have arisen from the gradual changes that resulted from the interaction between natural forces over billions of years?

To help answer such questions, try doing a simple experiment. Pour salt and pepper into a clear container that can be covered and keep the salt and pepper separate. Then shake it. What

SUGGESTIONS FOR EVANGELISM

1. What Kind of God Did the Person Reject?

Don't assume, for instance, that all secularistic international students have rejected the personal God of the Bible. Because they come from cultures influenced by various non-Christian religions, they might not have considered the possibility that a personal God who loves them exists. Ask questions to discern his or her concept of God.

2. Offer Evidence for God's Existence

In the following section some of the evidences for God's existence are listed. Notice how each new bit of evidence tells us a little more about the nature of God—from Cause, to Intelligent Cause, to Moral Being, to Fulfiller of our Longings.

Secularism and Christianity Contrasted

	SECULARISM	CHRISTIANITY
GOD	Matter, in one form or another, is all that has existed from eternity and all that will ever exist.	God alone is infinite and eternal. The material universe is finite and has not always existed. God created it out of nothing.
HUMANITY	Humanity is by nature monistic (a oneness) in that the person consists of only one substance: matter. Humanity represents the highest point of the gradual and random processes of evolution.	Humanity is by nature dualistic in that the person consists of two substances: body and spirit. Humanity, being made in the image of God, represents the highest point of God's creation.
HUMANITY'S PROBLEM	The problem is that humanity depends on the escapist promises of religion, rather than facing problems squarely and believing that humankind has the potential to create a world in which peace and justice will prevail.	The problem is that humanity has rebelled against a personal and holy God. As a result, we live for ourselves and place our hope in false gods, such as success, money, nature, science, education, etc.
THE SOLUTION	The solution is in extending the scientific method of rational inquiry into all aspects of life, while at the same time maintaining a sense of compassion for the individual.	The solution is in humanity being restored to a right relationship with a holy God through faith in Jesus Christ. While Christianity encourages the rational inquiry of science, it opposes scientism, which goes beyond the limits of science in that it claims that the scientific method is a sufficient avenue to all truth.
JESUS CHRIST	At most, Jesus was a good moral teacher. Because the biblical authors embellished the details of Jesus' life, though, we can be certain of very little concerning the historical details of His life.	Jesus was the very embodiment of God on earth. The Bible meets the qualifications for being authentic history. It records that Jesus lived, died for our sins, and rose from the dead.
AFTER DEATH	There is no survival of the person's consciousness after death.	There is personal survival after death, either to eternal life with God or to eternal separation from Him.

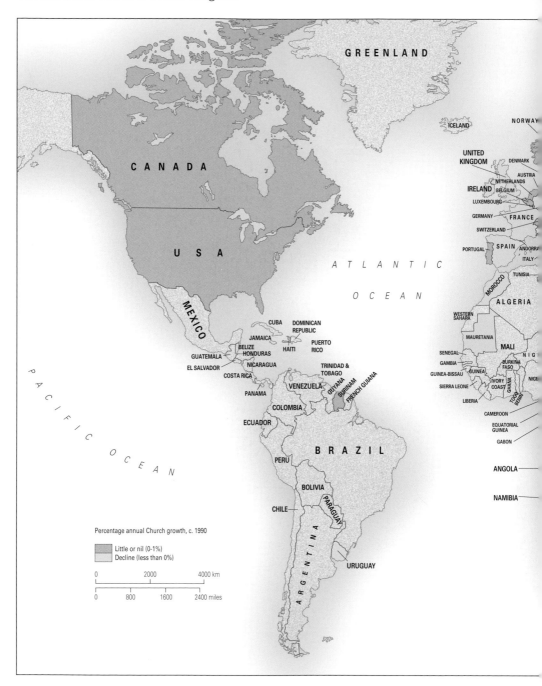

Percentage annual Church growth, c. 1990

Little or nil (0-1%)
Decline (less than 0%)

0   2000   4000 km

0   800   1600   2400 miles

happens? The salt and pepper become mixed. Now continue shaking the container to try to unmix the two. Do they become unmixed? What would be the best way to separate the salt from the pepper?

What does this experiment illustrate? First, that the random processes of nature destroy, not create, patterns. Second, that it would take an intellect (by physically separating the salt from the pepper) to restore the pattern (see

AREAS OF CHRISTIAN STAGNATION AND DECLINE

Gange, chap. 7).

Living cells are like the pattern of the salt and pepper being separated, except that the patterns in such cells are much more complex. They are not only complex but also viable in that not just any pattern will do; living cells must contain a particular pattern that will produce and sustain life. Such a pattern, moreover, contains a vast amount of information, such as is found in DNA. Life is not the mere repetitive pattern that is contained in crystals, which the random processes of nature can produce. Instead, life is like the pattern contained in a blueprint, which can be produced only by an intelligent being.

The question of origins concerns the issue of what is a sufficient source for the information—the coherent and viable patterns—contained within living cells? To say that the information contained in a complex living cell came from the random and gradual evolutionary processes of nature is to believe that one can separate the salt from the pepper by shaking the container—an outcome that, being unobserved, is a matter of faith and one that goes against the observed second law.

The best explanation for the source of information in living cells is not blind nature but a Supreme Intellect. After all, it is an everyday empirical fact that people, not random forces, are the source of meaningful and coherent patterns, such as books, cars, buildings, etc. Also, it is not mere coincidence that the theme of separation—the instilling of information—is found in the creation account of Genesis 1, where God brought order to the formless chaos by separating light from darkness; the waters above from the waters below; sea from land; time into days and years; life in the sea, in the air, and on the land (each after its own kind); man from dust; and woman from man.

B. The Presence of Design. The argument from design is built on the premise that design indicates the work of an intelligent designer (see Psalm 19:1, Romans 1:20). The classic example is that of a watch. Obviously, the intricate inner workings of a watch could not have come about as the result of random chance, but only by the thoughtful planning of an intelligent designer (see Olsen, 26–27, and Denton, chap. 14). The same is true of the relationship between the creation and the Creator (for example, the intricacies of the human eye).

C. The Stirring of the Conscience. Our consciences and feelings of guilt give evidence to our moral nature. Such moral feelings are like currency—they are worthless unless backed up by something of value outside themselves. They also indicate that the best explanation for why we have moral sensibilities is that our Source must be both moral and personal, for impersonal natural forces do not have moral sensibilities. In other words, since there is a moral law binding on all of us, there must be a Moral Lawgiver (see Geisler and Brooks, chap. 13).

D. The Longing for Something Beyond. While secularists might say publicly that they accept death as being the final end, there is nevertheless that private doubt that lingers. For example, Corliss Lamont, who was voted Humanist of the Year in 1977, wrote, "Even I, disbeliever that I am, would frankly be more than glad to awake some day to a worthwhile eternal life" (Lamont, 98). Atheist philosopher Bertrand Russell expressed some hesitation concerning the idea that this life is all there is: "It is odd, isn't it? I care passionately for this world and many things and people in it, and yet . . . what is it all? There must be something more important, one feels, though I don't believe there is" (Heck, 224).

What would the source be of our yearning for an existence beyond? Perhaps the universe has played a cosmic joke on us. Or perhaps our yearning is a mistake of evolution. What if it's not a joke or a mistake but a pointer to that which is real and true?

RESPONDING TO HINDRANCES AND OBJECTIONS

1. The Problem of Evil
The problem of evil is that if there is an all-powerful and all-good God, then He wouldn't allow evil. But evil does happen, so God is either not all-

Contradictions and Problems within the Secularistic Worldview

SECULAR ASSERTION	CONTRADICTION OR PROBLEM
"There is no absolute truth."	Such a statement itself claims to be an absolute truth.
"Life is meaningless."	The person who makes such a statement contradicts himself or herself because he or she is claiming to make a meaningful statement (Zacharias, 73). Why bother making a statement that has meaning if life is meaningless?
"Science is the only avenue to truth."	Such a statement cannot itself be proven to be true by its own avenue to truth—the scientific method.
"All morality is relative."	How can we tell if a person who makes such a statement is telling the truth, since he or she might consider it convenient to lie? Plus, such a person often does not hesitate to make moral judgments concerning social issues, or concerning his or her view of God (for example, Why did God permit evil?).
"Each individual determines his or her own purpose in life. There is no ultimate purpose."	If there's no ultimacy to any purpose, then even the individual purposes are meaningless. Also, how does anyone know there is no ultimate meaning unless he or she has an ultimate perspective?
"The theory of evolution, which is *lauded as a natural law,* contends that complexity (life) arises out of simplicity (nonlife) without the aid of intelligence."	But the law of entropy, which is *an indisputable law of nature,* says that complex things disintegrate to a state of simplicity (see Noebel, 330–333).
"Humanity is, by nature, good!"	Such a statement lacks meaning since there is no moral reference point in secularism by which to gauge goodness. Also, if humanity is indeed by nature good, then why doesn't goodness come more naturally to people?
"What is needed today is rational and logical thinking."	How can our thoughts be trusted to reflect reality if they are nothing more than the product of chemical and biological elements?

powerful or not all-good.

One may respond to this objection by pointing out, first, that the problem of evil actually assumes the existence of an absolute standard of goodness. Such a standard can be based only in a holy God, the very thing that the argument is trying to deny (see Geisler and Brooks, chap. 4; Zacharias, 174–178).

Second, identify the source of evil (see Kreeft, 49–56). We are talking about moral evil, not natural disasters or physical diseases. With respect to moral evil, we are persons, and persons have the ability to choose between good and evil. Evil is the result of persons having chosen wrongly. God cannot be held responsible for the way His creatures have chosen to go against Him, since their ability to choose is real.

Could God have made a world where the people were programmed to choose to do only that which is good? Yes, but such creatures would have been automatons, not persons, and they would not have had the ability to make real choices.

Third, when a person cites the problem of evil as an objection, he or she is assuming that God has not dealt with evil. The Bible declares, however, that God has dealt with evil through the substitutionary atonement of Jesus Christ. The real issue with those who cite the problem of evil is that God has not dealt with it in a way that they expected it to be dealt with or in a way that alleviated evil as soon as they desired it to be so.

We can know for certain that even though evil is not now entirely defeated it eventually will be. We know this because of the historically verifiable resurrection of Jesus Christ, whereby God conquered death—the consequence of evil and sin.

2. "How Can a Just God Judge Those Who Have Never Heard of Jesus?"

This objection raises the issue of justice. So, before responding to the objection directly, ask your friend to consider something: What is the source of your sense of justice?

Some might answer that each individual is his or her own source. Others might say that the moral foundation for our sense of justice is to be found in social consensus.

The problem with such answers is that they derive the sense of "ought" from that which "is." But that which "is" is an insufficient basis for our sense of "ought." Just because most people have told a lie does not negate our sense that lying is morally wrong. If we base our sense of justice on nothing higher than ourselves or social consensus, then we will be mired in moral relativity. But "relative justice" is a contradiction in terms.

In order for one's sense of justice to have meaning, it must be based on a firm moral standard. What we observe is that moral sensibilities are properties of personal beings, not natural forces. But what kind of being would be (1) personal, (2) beyond humanity, and (3) have moral sensibilities? The answer: God!

Therefore, the sense of justice raised in the objection actually affirms the existence of the very thing that is being questioned, for only a personal, transcendent, holy God is a sufficient moral basis for our sense of justice. In brief, then, things can't be ultimately unjust unless there is an ultimate Justice (God).

But will God indeed judge those who have never heard of Jesus? No and yes. No, in the sense that He will not judge us on the basis of revelation that we have not received. Yes, He will judge us on the basis of how we respond to the knowledge that we have received (Romans 2:12).

Moreover, God has given everyone an awareness of who He is through that which is called "general revelation." This includes the disclosure of God through creation and conscience (Lewis & Demarest, chap. 2; Romans 1:19–20; 2:14–15; see also Psalm 8:1, 3; 19:1–4; Isaiah 40:12–14, 26; Acts 14:15–17; 17:24–25).

3. "The Bible Is Not Worth Serious Consideration."

Secularists dismiss the Bible, contending that it is filled with myths, contradictions, and scientific inaccuracies. Because of space limitation, only a few responses to this objection will be summarized (see the chapter on "How Can We Know the Bible Is the Word of God?"; Boice, chap. 5; and Geisler, *Critics*, chap. 1).

First, ask if your friend has read the Bible. If not, encourage him or her to read it before you take the question seriously. It is very possible that an attitude toward the Bible was received through the influence of someone else and not through firsthand experience.

Second, if your friend claims to be educated and knowledgeable about things, he or she should become familiar with the Bible. Why? Because it is the one book that has had a major influence on the cultures of the world. According to the *Guinness Book of World Records*, the Bible is the number one best seller of all time (MacFarlan, 383). It has also had significant influence on Western literature. One source on literature says, "Great authors commonly show a familiarity with the Bible, and few great English and American writers of the seventeenth, eighteenth, nineteenth, and twentieth centuries can be read with satisfaction by one [who is] ignorant of biblical literature" (Holman, 61–62).

Third, the Bible should be given serious consideration because it is historically accurate (see Bruce; Geisler and Brooks, chap. 9; Kitchen; Wilson; and Yamauchi).

Fourth, the secularist should give the Bible serious consideration because it is unique among religious scriptures. It is unique in that it speaks of a God who is absolute in His holiness and who judges sinners. In light of that fact, consider this: Would bad men write the kind of fierce judgments spoken of in the Bible against their own sin, and thereby convict

The Bible is the number one best-seller of all time.

themselves? Or, on the other hand, would good men put "Thus saith the Lord" on something they had devised themselves? Isn't it more likely that it came from God? (Boice, 57–58).

Other approaches to this objection include these facts:

■ The Bible's amazing unity, considering it consists of 66 books that were written over a fifteen-hundred-year period (see McDowell, 18).
■ The biblical authors' being led to avoid scientific misconceptions about the body, the heavens, and the earth, which were popular in the cultures and religions of the time (see Barfield; Montgomery, part 3).
■ The fulfillment of prophecy (see McDowell, chap. 9; Montgomery, part 4, chaps. 3–4).

4. "Evolution Sufficiently Explains the Origin of the Universe and the Diversity of the Species."

Admittedly, most of us don't have the expertise to present the evidence against evolution with any sense of scientific sophistication. How, then, should we respond to the objections raised by those who believe in the theory of evolution?

A. Keep It Simple. Keep the meaning of creation basic. Your definition of creation should include nothing more than the belief that an intelligent Creator is necessary to explain the origin of the universe. Anything more will divert the discussion away from the core issue.

B. Evolution, Like Creationism, Is Also Based on Faith and Inference.
Evolution is based on faith just as much as creationism is.

Be aware that evolutionists move from the observable to the theoretical in a way that is not warranted by the evidence. They observe, for example, that minor changes occur within species (microevolution), but they extrapolate from those observations the theory that such changes eventually add up to the formation of entirely new species (macroevolution).

While microevolution is empirically verifiable, the extrapolation to macroevolution is only a theory that has never been observed and that is a matter of faith (Johnson, 1991, 115).

C. Belief in Creation Is a Reasonable Inference. Creationism is a reasonable alternative to evolution. After all, one of the principles of science is that every effect has a sufficient cause. Creationism posits a sufficient cause for our existence as persons: a personal God who is morally holy, intelligent, and self-existent.

Evolution, on the other hand, posits what appears to be an insufficient cause in that the complex (human life) comes out of the simple (nonlife). In other words, the theory of evolution says that the universe arose from nothing without a cause. Is that reasonable?

Creationism is reasonable, moreover, because it is able to make a distinction between *operation science*, which has to do with the principles that govern the continued operation of the universe, and *origin science*, which has to do with the principles that caused the universe to begin. By saying that science can make statements about the origin of the universe, evolutionists are assuming that the very same laws involved in the operation of the universe are adequate to explain the origin of the universe. Such an assumption is similar to saying that the very same laws that explain how a car functions are sufficient to explain how the car was designed and built. They aren't, because the origin of the car needed the guidance of intelligent beings (Geisler, 1983, 137–138).

If you want to garner further evidence against evolution, the following are fruitful lines of argumentation (see Noebel, chap. 14):

■ The fossil record: the sudden appearance of complex life forms and the lack of transitional forms.
■ The problem of life coming from nonlife (see Gange, chap. 9; Thaxton).

■ The problem of complexity arising out of simplicity without the aid of intelligent intervention.
■ The immense amount of information encoded into the DNA, which would indicate an intelligent source rather than that of random chance (see Gange),
■ The lack of mutations that are beneficial to an organism's survival.
■ The limits to the amount of change possible within a species.

For books that address the theory of evolution from a scientific perspective, the following three are recommended: *Evolution: A Theory in Crisis* by Michael Denton; *Darwin on Trial* by Phillip Johnson; and *Of Pandas and People* by Percival Davis and Dean Kenyon.

RECOMMENDED RESOURCES

For books that address in one volume most of the common objections raised by secularists, see Geisler and Brooks; Kreeft; and Moreland (1987).

For books that could be given to a secularist and that argue from the scientific evidence for the existence of an intelligent Creator, see Gange and Ross.

For a book written from the Christian perspective that contrasts in most every discipline (theology, philosophy, ethics, biology, psychology, etc.) the biblical Christian worldview with the worldviews of Secular Humanism and Marxism/Leninism, see Noebel.

BIBLIOGRAPHY AND RESOURCES

Aldrich, Joseph C. *Life-Style Evangelism*. Portland, Ore.: Multnomah Press, 1981.
Barfield, Kenny. *Why the Bible Is Number 1: The World's Sacred Writings in the Light of Science*. Grand Rapids, Mich.: Baker, 1988.
Barrett, David. "Annual Statistical Table on Global Mission: 1994." *International Bulletin of Missionary Research*. Gerald Anderson, ed. New Haven, Conn.: Overseas Ministries Study Center, January 1994.
Boice, James M. *Foundations of the Christian Faith*. Downers Grove, Ill.: InterVarsity Press, 1986.
Brown, Colin. *Christianity & Western Thought: A History of Philosophers, Ideas & Movements*, Vol. 1. Downers Grove, Ill.: InterVarsity Press, 1990.
Bruce, F. F. *The New Testament Documents: Are They Reliable?* Downers Grove, Ill.: InterVarsity Press, 1978.
Davis, Percival and Dean Kenyon. *Of Pandas and People: The Central Question of Biological Origins*. Dallas: Haughton Publishing, 1989.
Denton, Michael. *Evolution: A Theory in Crisis: New Developments in Science Are Challenging Orthodox Darwinism*. Bethesda, Md.: Adler & Adler, 1985.
Gange, Robert. *Origins and Destiny: A Scientist Examines God's Handiwork*. Dallas: Word Publishing, 1986.
Geisler, Norman. *Is Man the Measure?* Grand Rapids, Mich.: Baker Book House, 1983.
Geisler, Norman. *Miracles and the Modern Mind*. Grand Rapids, Mich.: Baker Book House, 1992.
Geisler, Norman and Ron Brooks. *When Skeptics Ask: A Handbook on Christian Evidences*. Wheaton, Ill.: Victor Books, 1990.
Geisler, Norman and Thomas Howe. *When Critics Ask: A Popular Handbook on Biblical Difficulties*. Wheaton, Ill.: Victor Books, 1992.
Hayward, Alan. *Creation and Evolution: Rethinking the Evidence from Science and the Bible*. Minneapolis: Bethany House Publishers, 1995.
Heck, Joel, ed. *The Art of Sharing Your Faith*. Tarrytown, N.Y.: Fleming H. Revell Company, 1991.

Holman, C. Hugh. *A Handbook to Literature,* 3rd ed. Indianapolis: Odyssey Press, 1975.

Hummel, Charles. *The Galileo Connection: Resolving Conflicts Between Science & the Bible.* Downers Grove, Ill.: InterVarsity Press, 1986.

Hunter, George, III. *How to Reach Secular People.* Nashville: Abingdon, 1992.

Johnson, Phillip. *Darwin on Trial.* Washington, D.C.: Regnery Gateway, 1991.

Johnson, Phillip. *Reason in the Balance: The Case Against Naturalism in Science, Law & Education.* Downers Grove, Ill.: InterVarsity Press, 1995.

Johnstone, Patrick. *Operation World.* Pasadena, Calif.: William Carey Library, 1986.

Kitchen, K. A. *The Bible in Its World: The Bible & Archaeology Today.* Downers Grove, Ill.: InterVarsity Press, 1977.

Knechtle, Cliff. *Give Me an Answer That Satisfies My Heart and My Mind.* Downers Grove, Ill.: InterVarsity Press, 1986.

Kreeft, Peter. *Yes or No: Straight Answers to Tough Questions About Christianity.* San Francisco: Ignatius Press, 1991.

Kurtz, Paul. *In Defense of Secular Humanism.* Buffalo, N.Y.: Prometheus Books, 1983.

Lamont, Corliss. *The Philosophy of Humanism.* New York: Continuum, 1988.

Lewis, C. S. *Miracles.* New York: Macmillan, 1960.

Lewis, Gordon and Bruce Demarest. *Integrative Theology,* Vol. 1. Grand Rapids, Mich.: Zondervan Publishing House, 1987.

Lochhaas, Philip. *How to Respond to Secular Humanism.* St. Louis: Concordia Publishing House, 1990.

MacFarlan, Donald, ed. *Guinness Book of World Records.* New York: Bantam Books, 1991.

McDowell, Josh. *Evidence That Demands a Verdict.* San Bernardino, Calif.: Campus Crusade for Christ, 1972.

Montgomery, John, ed. *Evidence for Faith: Deciding the God Question.* Dallas: Word Publishing, 1991.

Moreland, J. P. *Christianity and the Nature of Science.* Grand Rapids, Mich.: Baker Book House, 1989.

Moreland, J. P. *Scaling the Secular City: A Defense of Christianity.* Grand Rapids, Mich.: Zondervan, 1987.

Nash, Ronald. *Faith & Reason: Searching for a Rational Faith.* Grand Rapids, Mich.: Zondervan, 1988.

Noebel, David. *Understanding the Times.* Manitou Springs, Colo.: Summit Press, 1991.

Olsen, Viggo. *The Agnostic Who Dared to Search.* Chicago: Moody Press, 1990.

Ross, Hugh. *The Creator and the Cosmos.* Colorado Springs, Colo.: NavPress, 1993.

Ross, Hugh. *The Fingerprint of God.* Orange, Calif.: Promise Publishing Co., 1989.

Russell, Bertrand. *Why I Am Not a Christian.* New York: Simon & Schuster, 1957.

Thaxton, Charles, Walter Bradley, and Roger Olsen. *The Mystery of Life's Origin: Reassessing Current Theories.* New York: Philosophical Library, 1984.

Wilson, Clifford. *Rocks, Relics, and Biblical Reliability.* Grand Rapids, Mich.: Zondervan Publishing House, 1977.

Yamauchi, Edwin. "Archaeology and the New Testament." *The Expositor's Bible Commentary,* Vol. 1. Frank E. Gaebelein, ed. Grand Rapids, Mich.: Zondervan, 1979.

Zacharias, Ravi. *Can Man Live Without God?* Dallas: Word Publishing, 1994.

Zacharias, Ravi. *A Shattered Visage: The Real Face of Atheism.* Brentwood, Tenn.: Wolgemuth & Hyatt, 1990.

ORGANIZATIONS

Genesis Foundation (directed by Dr. Robert Gange)
P.O. Box 304
Princeton, NJ 08542
Phone: (908) 704-0499

Reasons to Believe (directed by Dr. Hugh Ross)
P.O. Box 5978
Pasadena, CA 91117
Phone: (818) 335-1480

Probe Ministries, Int'l
P.O. Box 801046
Dallas, TX 75204
Phone: (800) 899-7762

Ravi Zacharias Int'l Ministries, Inc.
4725 Peachtree Corners Cir., Ste. 250
Norcross, GA 30092-2553
Phone: (770) 449-6766

Shinto

David Clark

HISTORICAL ROOTS

To Westerners, Japan remains an enigma. This is nowhere more true than in its religions. Japan's traditional faith, Shinto (or *kami no michi*)—"the way of the gods"—is rooted in Japan's national history and is intricately intertwined with its culture.

Early Formative Period
(Pre-History–A.D. 790)
Early Shinto (before A.D. 538–552)· The phrase "early Shinto" describes the religious life that flourished in Japan before Buddhism arrived in that country in the sixth century after Christ. The main written sources describing early Shinto are documents called *Kojiki* and *Nihongi* (chronicles of early myths recorded after 712 by members of the imperial court) and the Engishiki (descriptions of early prayers and rituals).

Because the myths of the *Kojiki* and the *Nihongi* were written so much later than the actual period they purport to describe, there is some question as to how accurately they describe the beliefs and practices of early Shinto. Nevertheless, It can be known that the traditions of early Shinto centered around agricultural festivals, clan or family loyalty, and reverence for life. Also, local shamans, as religious functionaries, spoke for

A fierce Shinto mask from Japan.

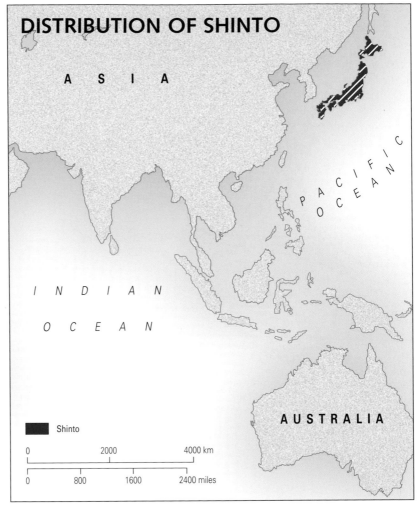

DISTRIBUTION OF SHINTO

ASIA

PACIFIC OCEAN

INDIAN

OCEAN

AUSTRALIA

■ Shinto

| 0 | 2000 | 4000 km |

| 0 | 800 | 1600 | 2400 miles |

the *kami* (gods) and combated evil spirits. They used *Kagura,* traditional Shinto sacred dance and music performed by young maidens (*miko*), to call forth the *kami*. Indeed, much of the traditional art, literature, and music of Japan may be connected to these shamanistic practices.

Many specific customs of the common folk in this period are now shrouded in some mystery. But one distinction clearly emerges from that ancient tradition, and that is that there are two major patterns of kami in Shinto: the *hitogami* and *ujigami*.

The *hitogami* are members of the class of *kami* (or *gami*, gods) associated with sacred persons like

shamans, sages, or saints. The hitogami system is strongly individualistic, and it reverences the important, sometimes idiosyncratic religious figures of Shinto history.

The *ujigami*, however, are a class of *kami* associated with families, clans, or a related local region. It is *ujigami*, not *hitogami*, that a Japanese family would reverence when participating as part of filial duty in ancestor veneration.

Early Interaction with Buddhism (552–710): Between 538 and 552, new religions came to Japan from China and Korea. The arrival of Buddhism, Confucianism, and Taoism

This Japanese temple is dominated by the unmistakable profile of Mount Fuji.

initiated new dynamics of religious interaction. In early Shinto, each community probably worshiped its local deity according to provincial custom. But under the influence of other faiths, the adherents of Shinto gradually organized their deities into a pantheon and coordinated a system of shrines.

Although neither Confucianism nor Taoism gathered a distinct religious following in Japan, great conflicts erupted over whether or not to accept Buddhism. These debates led to clan warfare and ultimately to the assassination of the emperor in 592. The winning clan leader placed on the throne his Buddhist niece, and she in turn chose as her regent the very influential Shotoku (573–621). Shotoku made Buddhism the national religion and used it as part of his campaign to consolidate the state and to create a more mature Japanese culture.

Despite Buddhism's importance in the imperial court, powerful clans still supported Shinto. Several emperors in the late 600s updated the Shinto rites and gave them parallel status with Buddhism. In this period, strong ritual connections emerged between the imperial court and the Grand Shrine of Ise. The Grand Shrine of Ise is dedicated to two goddesses, one of whom is the all-important Sun Goddess, Amaterasu.

The Writing of the Kojiki (712):

It was as part of this revival of Shinto in the imperial court that the emperor commissioned the writing of the *Kojiki*. The creation myths in the *Kojiki* present a cosmology of various gods. Seven generations of the *kami* culminate in the marriage of Izanagi (a male *kami*) and Izanami (a female *kami*). These two go down to an ocean, thrust a spear into the waves, and pull it out. At every place where a drop of brine falls from the spear, a Japanese island appears. Izanagi and Izanami then descend onto the islands and produce other *kami*. After several generations, Amaterasu, the Sun Goddess, appears. Amaterasu, in turn, becomes the great grandmother of Jimmu, the first emperor.

The universe portrayed in these sources no doubt reflects the basic outline of the early Shinto worldview. It includes the High Plain of Heaven

Buddhist bodhisattva painting. Shinto played a role in legitimizing Buddhism in Japan.

where the *kami* live, the human world, and a polluted shadow world below (*yomi*). The *kami* are gods or spiritual powers who can help or hinder human beings.

The emphasis on ritual purity runs deep in Japan. Shinto shrines are set apart; anything polluted by blood, disease, or death is prohibited. All who enter the grounds first cleanse themselves with water. More elaborate acts of ritual purification (such as standing motionless for several hours under a freezing waterfall) remove both inward and outward defilement and permit the *kami* to be present in helpful ways. These purification rites are called *harai*. (*Harai* also describes the state of ritual purity.) To experience the *kami*, sanctuaries of cleanliness, which are free from the contamination of the world, are most important. This waiting for the coming of the *kami* is still an important aspect of Shinto practice (Ellwood and Pilgrim, 106).

Buddhism's Rise in the Nara Period (710–784): Toward the end of the formative period, Buddhists developed a system of temples centering around Nara (southwest of Tokyo). Buddhists founded six philosophical schools and continued their interaction and competition with Shinto. But Buddhism never totally eclipsed the less glamorous Shinto faith. In fact, Shinto played a role in legitimating Buddhism. Indeed, by the end of this period, the Japanese people had laid the foundations of syncretizing the two religions.

Period of Development (A.D. 790–1600)

Heian Period (794–1185): As the Japanese moved their capital from Nara to Kyoto (784–794), the culture was moving toward feudalism. The imperial court was developing a highly stylized aesthetic cultural life. The Japanese consider the period after the move to Kyoto as the epitome of classical Japanese culture. The upper classes valued and aspired to *miyabi*, an elusive sense of courtly elegance and refined aesthetic taste.

Building on earlier foundations for cooperation, the Buddhists of this era developed an important concept, *honji suijaku*. This doctrine, translated as "true nature, trace manifestation,"

permitted the Buddhists to unify their gods, buddhas, and *bodhisattvas* (humans who attain buddhahood) with Shinto deities. The Buddhists considered the Shinto *kami* to be guardians, pupils, or expressions of Buddhist gods. In other words, the Shinto *kami* became "manifest traces" of true Buddhist realities.

Kamakura Period (1185–1333):
As the Heian period wore on, the emperors increasingly sought more power. So did many restless feudal lords. These warlords had real power because they represented the famous samurai warrior class. The samurai developed a distinctive lifestyle, *bushido*, which combined several religious traditions into an ethic of self-discipline, loyalty, courage, and honor. In 1185, members of the increasingly powerful samurai class defeated the old order and established a new capital in Kamakura.

Shinto in this era experienced something of a revival. In the late 1200s, devotees of the Yui-ichi school

of Shinto sought to reestablish the superiority and independence of Shinto. Now, with renewed self-confidence, the Yui-ichi school aspired to a purified Shinto, free of Buddhist and other influences. This pure Shinto included not only the shrine system with its various local activities but also the very important sense of national unity and identity derived from convictions about the divine origin of the imperial line and the spiritual uniqueness of Japan in the world.

To support the revival, the Yui-ichi school adapted *honji suijaku*, the "true nature, trace manifestation" doctrine. Now, the adherents of Shinto interpreted various Buddhist deities as manifest traces of the Shinto gods.

Period of Consolidation and Renewal (1600–present)

Tokugawa Period (1600–1867): Increasing political conflict and chaos after the Kamakura period gradually ended when a group of very

A rock garden designed for meditation in Japan.

determined feudal lords set out to unify and stabilize the country. The most revered of these is Tokugawa Ieyasu (1542–1616). While his predecessors had made considerable progress, it was Tokugawa who finally established a new shogunate with the seat of power in the new city of Edo (now Tokyo). These men not only conquered their rival feudal lords, but they also took control of the important Buddhist headquarters at Nara and of the imperial line itself.

For two and a half centuries, the Tokugawa government brought relative peace to Japan. The government became very protective of its own power, intrusive in the lives of the people, and resistant to international influence. As part of this policy, the Tokugawa shoguns banned Christianity but made Buddhism a branch of the state. The Tokugawa governors also revived Confucianism, an active faith of moral obligation or duty.

Meanwhile, Shinto continued to evolve toward nationalism. A renewed interest in Japan's classical literature permeated Shinto in this period. Advocates of Shinto sought to retrieve the historic Japanese spirit, to indoctrinate the people with this spirit, and to purge Japanese life of foreign influence. Several Shinto themes of the past—the divine origin of the imperial line and the sacredness of the national tradition—blossomed during the later Tokugawa period. This national ethos fostered a distrust and even hostility toward foreign ideas, including even those of China. The adaptation of Shinto themes to these nationalistic concerns created a kind of Shinto civil religion. The full fruit of this nationalism ripened in the twentieth century and culminated in World War II.

Meiji Period and the Modern Era (1868–1945): In 1868, various pressures, both from within Japan and from foreign nations, conspired to topple the Tokugawa regime. Soon the whole feudal system collapsed. A group of younger samurai class members restored the emperor to the throne in the famous Meiji restoration. Their banner cry was "return to antiquity," although ironically they quickly moved to bring Japan into the modern world. In 1889, the Japanese established a parliament system while retaining the emperor as a symbol. Japan turned its energies to becoming a powerful economic force influenced by Western-style democratic principles (although actual power continued in the hands of a small group of non-elected officials).

The government in the Meiji era lifted the ban on Christianity (as part of its movement into the modern world), disestablished Buddhism, and established Shinto as the state religion (as part of its restoration of the imperial line). In the late nineteenth century, missionaries reintroduced Roman Catholicism and introduced Protestantism for the first time. The Japanese made incredible economic and political strides, changing from a feudal state to a modern leader among the nations.

In the years leading up to World War II, Shinto played an increasingly prominent role in Japan's national life. The Constitution of 1889 officially declared a "nonreligious" Shinto. This set of values and ideals—it is hard to call this form of Shinto a religion—served to affirm the imperial way and to glorify the natural structure. To this nonreligious use of Shinto, the government wedded Confucian ideals such as loyalty and filial piety as well as samurai values like self-discipline. This reinforced the national consciousness of sacred superiority. The nationalists used these notions of sacred nationalism and a stated desire to bring the "whole world under one roof" to support Japan's involvement in World War II.

It is difficult to interpret the prewar era of development in Shinto. Some have called this nonreligious use of Shinto "state Shinto." But this fails to appreciate that different persons who participated in this civil religion saw it in different ways. Government administrators may have used Shinto for propaganda purposes, but the common folk approached the practice of Shinto in much the same way as they had for centuries.

Some scholars say that the nationalistic and militaristic use of Shinto is in fact the creation of a separate Shinto cult. One calls it the Kokutai cult (Woodard, 11). The nationalistic use of Shinto by the government between 1868 and 1945 was to some degree an overlay over the traditional religious life of those in the provinces.

At the end of World War II, the United Nations imposed a new Constitution on Japan. During the military occupation (1945–1952), the government (as reshaped by occupation authorities) required genuine religious freedom. Shinto was disestablished, and Emperor Hirohito officially disclaimed his divine status. In this context of total social breakdown and unprecedented freedom, many traditional religions struggled gradually to reorganize while many new faiths exploited their new opportunities.

Despite all that is new and foreign in Japan, that which is ancient and fundamentally Japanese still permeates the consciousness of the nation. In many areas, Japan maintains a remarkable tension between accepting new influences and retaining its ancient character. This is nowhere so true as in religion.

THE SHINTO WAY OF LIFE

1. The Spirit of Shinto

A. The Social Web. Shinto embraces the moral values of loyalty and duty to the family, clan, or group. Many aspects of Japanese culture illustrate this theme. For example, the word for human person is *ningen* (literally, "between people"). To be human is to be together with other persons. Japanese society emphasizes community over individuality. The Japanese language includes

conventions for speaking to those above, at, or below one's social standing. Verbal communication thereby reinforces a hierarchically structured system of human relationships in which everyone participates. The correct use of Japanese language links a person to the social web.

Reinforcing the principle of duty is the feudal notion of *ōn*, "indebtedness." Though some Japanese will deny that this concept is relevant to the modern context, the principle of indebtedness still exerts powerful influence on Japanese social relationships. *Ōn* arises when one receives something of value from another person. If, for example, one person saves another's life, this act establishes a special relationship between the two

At the end of World War II, Shinto was disestablished in Japan, and Emperor Hirohito officially disclaimed his divine status.

individuals, and the one who receives the benefit is placed in the debt of the other.

The feudal origins of ōn relate to a gift of land made by a lord to a vassal. In return, the vassal gave loyalty to the lord, thus establishing a mutual relationship of obligation.

The parent/child relationship is also key. Children are to care for their parents in old age and to venerate them after they are dead.[1]

These two examples—lord/vassal, parent/child—show two important features of this system of indebtedness: the relationship often develops between a superior and an inferior and the relationship is between particular people, not just loyalty to an abstract moral principle.

Related to ōn is giri, a social obligation requiring Japanese to act according to strict social norms toward those with whom a relationship has developed. Giri is a broader concept than ōn in that giri applies not only in hierarchical relationships (say, emperor to subject) but also to relationships with peers (say, between friends). One interesting expression of giri is gift giving, a regular occurrence in Japanese society. So many gifts are given, in fact, that wedding gifts are recycled.

As a high school boy, for example, I was surprised to receive from a neighbor a lacquer plate engraved with a bride and groom's name and wedding date. This bewildering experience raised my consciousness about the gift-giving network of duty and relationships.

B. Aesthetic Sensitivity. In addition to group loyalty, the Japanese highly value aesthetic sensitivity and refinement. This aesthetic sensitivity is directly relevant to the Japanese understanding of religious faith. The Japanese value "poetic realities"—"realities of immediate experience and feeling that resist any description" (Ellwood and Pilgrim, 105). For instance, Shinto speaks of naka ima (literally, the middle of now), the emphasis on living in the purity of the present moment.

By contrast, Western Christians often assume that right doctrine is centrally important to any religious faith. To the Japanese mind, this may not be so. From the Western perspective, the Japanese tendency toward vagueness and imprecision in religious expression is surprising, confusing, and even irritating. The Japanese way has its own rationale, however. Anyone who would understand the logic should enter into it and seek to appreciate it aesthetically.

The Japanese are known as an extraordinarily gracious people. At the interpersonal level, Westerners are struck by the extreme deference that Japanese people often show. Yet while this courtesy is remarkable, Westerners should not misread it. In business negotiations, for instance, the Japanese can be uncommonly tough opponents. A certain external agreeableness can shield from Western view the deep loyalties that the Japanese have for all things Japanese.

C. Emotional Depth and Purity of Heart. Another important feature of the Shinto view of life is its emotional depth and purity. We find this not only in the interest in ritual purification (harai) but also in the emphasis on a pure kokoro (heart). One cannot express Shinto morality in lists of rules. Shinto is more concerned to preserve or restore a ritual purity of an unclouded mind and an undefiled soul. These form the ground for proper action.

---

1. Should this act be called "ancestor veneration" or "ancestor worship"? It amounts to worship for a few devout Shinto believers, but it is a quasi-religious reverencing for the majority of secularized Japanese people whose Shinto experience is only a veneer. In both cases, however, it is a hindrance to the Gospel. Moreover, it is so entangled in Shinto customs, rituals, and idioms that Christians should not participate in it.

Truth (*makoto*) in this context is something lived out in *kokoro*. Truth is not propositional; truth does not refer to correct descriptions of actual states of affairs. Truth is, instead, experienced. Japanese expect that communicating *makoto* requires not explicit statements, but refined, allusive speech. This is most difficult for foreigners to master.

Shinto scholar Motoori Norinaga (1730–1801) captures this feature of Shinto. His concept is *magokoro*, "sincere heart," an ideal that combines both *kokoro* and *makoto*. *Magokoro* is the very essence of the gods and of whatever is divine within humans as well. The ideal is not a concept to be thought, however, but a quality to be experienced. Again, this sense of the quality of experience (over against an interest in precise theological statements) makes the Japanese religious experience quite different from that of Western forms of Protestant Christian experience.

2. The Practice of Shinto

The actual lived experience of Shinto is quite varied, but mostly it centers around the Shinto shrine. (Shinto places of worship are called "shrines"; Buddhist places are termed "temples.") The sacred grounds of a Shinto shrine are marked off by *torii*, large sacred gates shaped something like the Greek letter π, only with two horizontal bars. Along the path from the *torii* to the main building, one always finds a laver for purification.

The main shrine building houses several areas. In the most sacred place is the *shintai*, an object such as a mirror, jewel, or sword that embodies the *kami*. The *shintai* is not itself the direct object of veneration. The faithful worship the deity that indwells the *shintai*.

A worshiper will approach the main building, stopping to cleanse with water. She will present offerings by throwing a coin in a collection box or by lighting incense. In front of the main shrine building, she faces the altar area, bows her head, claps twice to summon the *kami*, and holds her hands together in front of her face. In this stance, she offers prayers to the *kami*. For more devout followers, worship involves attention to ritual

The sacred grounds of a Shinto shrine are marked off by torii, large sacred gates with two horizontal bars.

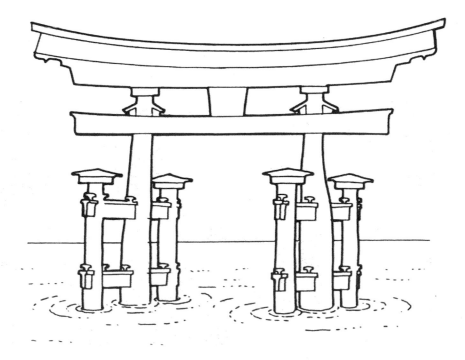

The Nature of the Gods (Kami) Contrasted with God

SHINTO	CHRISTIANITY
There are many gods (kami).	There is one triune God.
The kami are procreated by other gods.	God created all things and persons.
The kami indwell material objects and the natural world.	God transcends the world in His being.
The kami may be either helpful or hurtful.	God is loving and absolutely good.
The kami are the gods of Japan.	God is the Creator and Lord of all people.

purification and quiet waiting in expectation for the kami to come and commune with the believer. In many homes, a small family altar (kamidana) provides a place where ancestors are reverenced.

Worship, however, is not confined to overtly religious acts. Ellwood and Pilgrim capture the importance of worship this way:

> In general, the notion of right practice seeking purification and celebrating the vital forces of life permeates the Japanese religious sensibility and the whole of Japanese life. From the ancient mythic accounts of the actions of the original kami in creating the world to the ritual invocation of kami to bless a new oil tanker [or a new traffic light], from the most sacred ceremonies of the great Shinto shrines to a sense of proper social order and etiquette, the concern for right practice, purification, and life-celebration is evident. This religious awareness and form is deeply ingrained in the Japanese tradition (Ellwood and Pilgrim, 6–7).

Community celebrations center around annual matsuri. Broadly, matsuri means all Shinto ritual, including the ritualization of life itself. More specifically, however, the matsuri is a local Shinto festival that celebrates a local kami and invokes its presence.

SHINTO RESISTANCE TO CHRISTIANITY

Although the new constitution stripped back the nationalism of the pre-war era, traditional Shinto continues as an aspect of contemporary Japanese life. Only about 1.5 million of the 120 million Japanese declare themselves Christians. But 112 million adhere to Shinto. Many Japanese see themselves as followers of several religions, for 93 million are also Buddhists!

Despite these numbers, however, 65% to 75% of Japanese claim to follow no personal religion. For the most part, religious allegiance is nominal. To be Shinto, in the mind of many Japanese people, is simply to be Japanese (Reader, Andreasen, Stefansson, 33).

A major factor in the Japanese resistance to Christianity is its demand for exclusive religious allegiance. In a culture where Buddhism and Shinto have developed a "division of labor" (i.e., different tasks for different religions), this requirement for an either/or choice seems odd. For many Japanese, religions do not offer a personal faith; they provide ceremonial services. Traditionally, Buddhism conducts funerals, but Shinto performs weddings. Today, it is quite popular in Japan to have a

"Christian" wedding. But this means only that the dress, format, and setting are Western and churchlike.

Ironically, of course, the Japanese are quite exclusive culturally. But religiously, they are syncretistic, and thus for Christianity to compel an exclusive commitment to its own teachings and to its God alone seems difficult.

Christian teaching did make significant inroads during the Christian century (1549–1649). St. Francis Xavier (1506–1552) first introduced Roman Catholicism to Japan and met with initial success. According to estimates, perhaps 10% of the population was Christian during that era.

Yet Christianity could not make the religious compromise that Buddhism made. Although Buddhism is as much a foreign religion as Christianity, its accommodation of Shinto (for instance, through *honji suijaku*) meant that Buddhism was thoroughly "Japanized." As an uncompromisingly monotheistic religion, Christianity could never consent to such a process. A century after Xavier, during the Tokugawa era, terrible persecution fueled by anti-foreign and anti-Western passions wiped out the Christian movement. Christianity did not return to Japan for over two hundred years.

In the novel *Shogun*, one person is forced to decide whether to remain a Christian. She says, "I have been a Christian for a hundred years. I have been Japanese for a thousand." This captures, in the Japanese spirit, the sense of many Japanese that adherence to the foreign religion about Jesus means somehow to betray something fundamentally Japanese. Therefore, the Japanese people have not chosen Christianity in large numbers.

Both the Japanese resistance to Christianity and Japan's allegiance to the new god of materialism are connected to the fact that Shinto *kami* are very immanent. Historically, in views where the gods indwell nature, it becomes difficult to

St. Francis Xavier (1506–1552) introduced Catholicism to Japan and met with initial success.

distinguish the gods from nature. If one begins by saying that god refers to the life force immanent within nature, one ends up after a time only with nature. Thus the real religion of many Japanese, rightly proud of their economic achievements and power, is actually irreligious and secular.

Shinto is a deep tap root that sustains certain basic cultural customs or social patterns. It is also a bark that overlays a basically secular life orientation. But the real heart of the plant for many is participation in the business of business. The strongest personal religion is secular materialism.

The Human Relationships to the Gods (Kami) or God

SHINTO	CHRISTIANITY
The *kami* are offended by ritual or ceremonial pollution related to blood or death.	God is alienated by the moral rebellion expressed by the self-centeredness or disobedience of His creatures.
The *kami* might commune with those who are ritually purified and who wait for their presence.	God promises to be present to anyone who calls upon Him for forgiveness.
Shinto believers can fulfill their duty while following their own life agenda.	Christians follow God when they fulfill God's agenda and will.
Shinto believers gain the good graces of the *kami* by following the principles of purification.	Christians enjoy a relationship with God through trustful reliance (faith) on God.
Enjoying the good graces of the *kami* depends on human efforts.	A relationship with God is a gift (grace) that no one can deserve.

RESPONDING TO PEOPLE INFLUENCED BY SHINTO

1. Understand That Every Japanese Is Deeply Infused with Shinto.

Anyone who encounters Japanese culture experiences the universe of Shinto. Shinto is, in a sense, the very national air breathed by all Japanese. Thus, it is quite different from Christianity, where dedicated followers of Jesus may try quite deliberately to live out their faith every day. Shinto is more background belief and practice than is the lifestyle of a faithful Christian. Yet it is not for that reason any less powerful as an influence. Indeed, it may be for this reason all the more powerful.

2. Acknowledge the Striking Beauty of Japanese Culture.

Often, the aspects of Japanese culture that Americans and Europeans first come to know seem very strange: the *sumo* (huge wrestlers wearing very little clothing), *sushi* (raw fish and other sea creatures popularly eaten), and the *furo* (bathing with friends at the neighborhood bath house).

Yet, without question, Japanese culture is extraordinary. Beautiful national shrines are exquisite. The tea ceremony conducted by a skilled practitioner captures all the stylized beauty of the ancient traditions. Immaculate Japanese gardens skillfully create a sense of utter serenity and calm. The list goes on. A willingness to appreciate and enjoy such beauty is a priceless quality for anyone who would influence a Shinto person toward Christ.

3. Enlist the Aid of the Japanese Church.

Just as the Western church mirrors its setting, the Japanese church reflects its culture. A church in Japan is to Western eyes very hierarchical. The pastor holds the power in the group, and the elders exert authority over those who are younger. There is something very Japanese about this arrangement even if it seems unattractive to Westerners. A major advantage is that the church is a social group to which a Japanese person can belong. Without that belonging, commitment to Christ cuts a Japanese person off from a social network.

Contact your local ISI team member

or one of the groups listed under "Organizations" for a group to which your friend can belong.

4. Recognize That the Japanese Speak About Difficult Topics Very Carefully.

A Japanese person is deliberately subtle in his or her mode of speaking, especially when discussing matters with those who are above him or her on the social ladder. In Japan, it is not considered good form to be blunt, and most Japanese will hint delicately at important but unpleasant facts rather than say them right out loud. Ambiguity is, in fact, a sign of respect. Wordless agreements and unspoken understandings fill Japanese language.

A young Japanese man once came to me for help because he felt he was being treated unfairly. He never said, "Would you ask Mr. Smith to give me more time to complete some work?" Rather, he told me that he greatly respected an unnamed person, that he enjoyed working for him very much, that due to certain problems he was not able to finish a particular project, which he then delicately described. Next he said that he wanted to do well and that he really needed just a little more time. I was left to infer that I should intercede on his behalf. Fortunately, the employer relented before I intervened. But the experience illustrates the subtle modes of Japanese communication. Blunt Westerners would do well to recognize this feature of Japanese life.

5. Focus on Clarifying Religious Terms.

Although the Japanese value ambiguous ways of communication, a Christian sharing his or her faith must move with sensitivity toward clarifying key Christian terms.

The word *kami*, for instance, is notoriously vague. My father once spoke with four Japanese persons about God. Sensing their confusion, he asked them what the word *kami* implied to them. One proposed that

In Japan, it is not considered good form to be blunt.

kami is like a cloud floating along the ground, something like a ghost. The next said kami is pachi pachi (the sound of two hand claps at the shrine). The third suggested that kami is in the human heart. The last said she thinks of an old man with a beard who zaps bad people and puts them up in a tree. He takes money from the rich and gives it to the poor. Their answers helped my father realize that the Japanese view the kami as Merlin the magician, Robin Hood, and Santa Claus, all rolled into one.

The communication of Christian meanings is impossible without carefully defined Christian terms. To some degree this is circular. One cannot express Christian meanings without Christian words; one cannot define Christian terms without an understanding of Christian truth. Nevertheless, communicating the Gospel should begin with the biggest truth there is—God's existence and nature. God is the Creator who is fundamentally different from the creation. He is not any kami (a god), but sozosha (Creator) or sozo no kami (Creator God).

6. Use the Mars Hill Discourse.

Paul's sermon to the philosophers of Athens (Acts 17:22–31) clarifies God's nature. A Christian may express without reservation that the "God who made the world and everything in it is the Lord of heaven and earth and does not live in temples built by hands" (v. 24). This contrasts with the kami who are created and who indwell the shintai.

"He himself gives all men life and breath and everything else" (v. 25). God is the Creator of all—including spiritual beings, emperors, and ancestors.

"From one man he made every nation of men" (v. 26). The human family is one in its origin and in its need for a Savior.

Paul's words to his pagan audience address many of the monotheistic Christian teachings that a Japanese person, steeped in Shinto polytheism, tends to misunderstand.

7. Use the Harai (Purification) Concept.

The Japanese believe that those who wish to come into the presence of the kami must be pure. Harai, the act or state of purification to remove defilement, is therefore very important.

The need for harai parallels the biblical idea that moral righteousness is a prerequisite for entering God's presence. A skillful Christian can use this analogy as the basis for communicating a central Christian claim. As kami indwell shrines that are sanctuaries of purity, so God remains morally pure. As ritual pollution separates humans from kami, so moral pollution keeps humans from God. Thus, the Christian teaching that we must be changed before we are allowed to be in God's presence finds some echoes in Japanese thinking.

Despite initial similarities, Christians must explain several important distinctions in order not to distort the Gospel. The Japanese notion of pollution is ritual, not moral. The biblical teaching is that the cause of our pollution and consequent distance from God is our disloyalty to God. We humans express this infidelity when we treasure our own goals and values over God's. When we are consumed with our own interests and desires, we cannot come into God's presence. Only as we experience God's gift of forgiveness for this disloyalty do we become pure. Our need, therefore, is to give up our devotion to the kingdom of Self and allow God to make us faithful followers of the kingdom of God. We do not need ritual purification, but new life based on a relationship to a new King (2 Corinthians 5:17–18).

8. Counteract the Tendency Toward Syncretism.

On a peninsula on the eastern shore of Tokyo harbor stands a large female deity called Kwannon. I once climbed up inside the statue as people ascend the Statue of Liberty. The circular staircase winds up perhaps fifteen steps and stops at a landing before

The reconstructed Stoa, Athens, Greece, probable location of Paul's sermon on the Unknown God.

the steps begin again. At each landing a little alcove contains the statue of a religious figure. Among the many buddhas and *kami* stood statues of Jesus and Mary.

Following the *honji suijaku* principle, Japanese thinking has long identified the gods of various religions or vaguely accepted them all as legitimate deities in a hierarchically structured pantheon. It is all too easy to add the Christian God to the mix as yet another deity. Clarifying the nature of God must include identifying God as the only true God. Again, God is not just *kami*, but *sozosha*.

9. Declare That God Is Not Servant, but Lord.

I once viewed a National Geographic special program on Chinese native religions. One village elder explained the beliefs of his village. They worshiped a god, he said, because the god brought good weather and bumper crops. As long as the farming was good, they worshiped this god. If famine should come, however, the villagers would not hesitate to discard that god and find another. They needed a god who could guarantee rain.

This mentality is not far from the religious practice of many people—including some Christians (see animism chapter). We are tempted to love God for His gifts instead of loving the Giver of the gifts. But the point of worshiping God is not to gain certain advantages. We cannot use God to further our agenda. The irony of the Gospel is that as we truly forget our petty plans and commit our ways to God and His kingdom, we find the fulfillment we thought our plans would produce. We think satisfaction comes in fulfilling our interests, when only if we are planted like a grain of wheat and die do we find life.

10. Share That the Creator God Fulfills the Human Longing for Meaning.

The Japanese people enjoy the security of highly developed social networks and the joy of a brilliant culture history. But there is more to human existence than these. The Japanese word *ikigai* ("purpose in life") captures this idea. Few Japanese have found *ikigai*, however, even though failing to find it is a great loss.

The Christian faith declares that through God as revealed in Jesus, *ikigai* is found. When human longings for significance are so great that economic miracles, social networks, brilliant culture, and national honor do not satisfy, God's presence does.

SUMMARY

Japan today is a leading participant in the worlds of global trade, scientific and technological research, and international politics. Yet despite the post-World War II economic miracle, the Japanese are a people quite unlike Westerners. Though they receive much from many cultures, they successfully domesticate those borrowings into their own ethos.

A Christian who encounters a Shinto person should recognize that very ancient and powerful traditions shape this person's life. The Japanese sense of decorum, politeness, and apparent cooperation can mask the deep currents of national loyalties and cultural values that flow through the soul of every Japanese person. Yet the Japanese culture, for all its beauty, does not meet the most basic aspirations of the human heart. These are longings planted by God who has put "eternity in our hearts" (Ecclesiastes 3:11).

An admirer of Shinto will come to Christ only when economic success, cultural achievements, and community relationships are understood for what they are: expressions of a desire for significance in life, but that act as false substitutes for a truly fulfilling relationship with the Creator God. Followers of Jesus can share with adherents of Shinto that he or she will not find *ikigai* in economic or material gain, in art or cultural tradition, in clan or community relationships, or in academic achievement, but only in Jesus.

GLOSSARY

Bushido: The "way of the warrior"; the rigorous code of cultural loyalty and self-discipline associated with the medieval Japanese warriors, the *samurai. Bushido* was influenced by many religious and nonreligious forces, including the Shinto ideals of loyalty to the nation and ritual purity. Bushido still influences the cultural ethos of Japan.

Harai: The act of ritual purification or the state of ritual purity central to Shinto. *Harai* removes both inward and outward defilement and permits the *kami* to be present in helpful ways.

Hitogami: The class of *kami* (*gami*) associated with sacred persons like shamans, sages, or saints. In contrast to the *ujigami* system, the *hitogami* system is strongly individualistic.

Honji suijaku: The theory of "true nature, trace manifestation" used in the early medieval period, especially to unify Buddhist and Shinto deities. Either Shinto *kami* were seen as manifest traces of true Buddhist realities, or, conversely, the various buddhas and *bodhisattvas* (those who have attained buddhahood) were understood as manifest traces of the great Shinto gods.

Kagura: Traditional Shinto sacred dance and music used in classical Shinto ritual. Performed by young maidens, the *miko*, it derives from ancient shamanistic traditions used to call forth the *kami.*

Kami: Literally, anything that is above the ordinary, including the many sacred forces, human and natural, that dwell in the world and are manifested through especially sacred places, objects, or persons; more specifically, the gods of Shinto.

Kami no michi: Literally, the "way of the gods"; an alternative way of reading Shinto in Japanese.

Kokoro: The center or focus of feelings and refined sensitivity within a human person; used by Christians for heart, the very core of one's person.

Makoto: Truth, sincerity, or purity in intention. A central concept of Shinto, it describes the ideal human state as well as the essence of the *kami.*

Matsuri: Local Shinto festivals that celebrate a local *kami* and invoke its presence. Broadly, *matsuri* includes all Shinto ritual, including the ritualization of life itself.

Shintai: An object that "embodies" (*tai*) the *kami* (*shin*). The deity dwells in a *shintai* which could be a mirror, jewel, or sword. A shintai is located in the place of prominence in a Shinto shrine, but it is not itself the direct object of worship.

Ujigami: The class of *kami* (*gami*) associated with families, clans, or a related local region. In contrast to the *hitogami*, the *ujigami* are the *kami* that a Japanese person would venerate when participating, as part of family duty, in ancestor worship.

Witnessing Tool:
Shiakari Pass, by Ayako Miura. This is the powerful true story of a young Japanese man who discovers his own sinful nature as he tries to live a good life in his own power. Available in both book and video. Order through The Japan Network.

BIBLIOGRAPHY AND RESOURCES

Earhart, H. Byron. *Japanese Religion: Unity and Diversity,* 2nd ed. Encino, Calif.:Dickenson, 1974. Contains a good annotated bibliography of works in English on Japanese religion.

Earhart, H. Byron. *Religion in the Japanese Experience: Sources and Interpretations.* Encino, Calif.: Dickenson, 1974.

Earhart, H. Byron. *Religions of Japan: Many Traditions Within One Sacred Way.* San Francisco: Harper & Row, 1984.

Ellwood, Robert S. *The Eagle and the Rising Sun: Americans and the New Religions of Japan.* Philadelphia: Westminster, 1974.

Ellwood, Robert S. and Richard Pilgrim. *Japanese Religion: A Cultural Perspective.* Prentice-Hall Series in World Religions. Englewood Cliffs, N.J.: Prentice-Hall, 1985. Excellent work showing how religion and culture are intertwined in Japan.

Hearn, Lafcadio. *Japan's Religions: Shinto and Buddhism.* New Hyde Park, N.Y.: University Books, 1966.

Ichiro, Hori. *Folk Religion in Japan.* Chicago: University of Chicago Press, 1968.

Kato, Genichi. *A Historical Study of the Religious Development for Shinto.* Shoyu Hanayama (trans.). New York: Greenwood Press, 1988.

Kitagawa, Joseph M. *On Understanding Japanese Religion.* Princeton: Princeton University Press, 1987. Major work by leading University of Chicago scholar.

Kitagawa, Joseph M. *Religion in Japanese History.* New York: Columbia University Press, 1966.

Mason, J. W. T. *The Meaning of Shinto: The Primaeval Foundation of Creative Spirit in Modern Japan.* Port Washington, N.Y.: Kennikat Press, 1935.

Morioka, Kiyomi and William H. Newell, eds. *The Sociology of Japanese Religion.* Leiden, Netherlands: E. J. Brill, 1968.

Muraoka, Tsunetsugu. *Studies in Shinto Thought.* Delmer M. Brown and James T. Araki, trans. New York: Greenwood Press, 1988.

Reader, Ian, Esben Andreasen, and Finn Stefansson. *Japanese Religions: Past & Present.* Honolulu: University of Hawaii Press, 1993. An anthology of introductory essays and original readings.

Ross, Floyd Hiatt. *Shinto: The Way of Japan.* Boston: Beacon Press, 1965.

Schwade, Arcadio. *Shinto— Bibliography in Western Languages.* Leiden, Netherlands: E. J. Brill, 1986. Invaluable list of over 1,600 sources on Shinto.

Woodard, William P. *The Allied Occupation of Japan 1945–1952 and Japanese Religions.* Leiden, Netherlands: E. J. Brill, 1972.

Yamamoto, J. Isamu. *Beyond Buddhism: A Basic Introduction to the Buddhist Tradition.* Downers Grove, Ill.: InterVarsity, 1982. A book about Buddhism that shows how a person who understands the ethos of Japan reflects on his Christian faith.

ORGANIZATIONS

Japanese Evangelization Center
1605 Elizabeth St.
Pasadena, CA 91104
Phone: (626) 794-4400
Provides research and information on Japanese evangelism world-wide.

The Japan Network
7925 - 186th Street SW
Edmonds, WA 98026
Phone: (206) 672-1794
Helps American Christians reach Japanese for Christ; also provides materials.

Japanese Christian Fellowship Network
P.O. Box 260532
Highlands Ranch, CO
80126-0532
Phones:(303) 730-4226 (direct line for Japanese-speaking people)
(303) 730-4160 (ext. 126 or 224)
E-mail: SKuroda@aol.com
Has a nationwide network that helps locate Christian fellowships for Japanese.

Taoism

Kent Kedl
and Dean C. Halverson

INTRODUCTION

It is important to understand the concepts of Taoism because they lie at the heart of the Asian cultures—China, Korea, Japan, and Vietnam. One Chinese scholar wrote,

No one can hope to understand Chinese philosophy, religion, government, art, medicine—or even cooking—without a real appreciation of the profound philosophy taught in [the *Tao Te Ching*].... No other Chinese classic of such small size has exercised so much influence (Chan, 136, 137).

But what is Taoism all about? What are the principles that lie behind this religion/philosophy that was founded over 2,500 years ago and that has had such a grip on the thinking of the Asian world and now, increasingly, on the West?

THE HISTORY OF TAOISM

The Ritual-Music Culture. Harmony characterized the Chinese society during the first four centuries of the Chou dynasty (1111–249 B.C.; Chan, xv). The basis for the harmony was a

The Taoist yin-yang symbol has been widely adopted in the West.

set of principles called the Ritual-Music Culture (see also chapter on Confucianism).

The Ritual-Music Culture was based on the idea that there are certain "ways" of doing things that were mandated by heaven (the *Tao*). These "ways" were termed "rituals," or *li*, but the idea of "rituals" went beyond our limited understanding of that term. "Rituals" referred to the proper way of doing things, especially in regard to how to relate to people of higher or lower classes and to those within the family. It was the responsibility of the emperor to rule according to the *li*, and, as he did so, it was presumed he would promote the welfare of the people.

The term "music" in the Ritual-*Music* Culture referred to the sense in which the customs of society were to be like music in that they were to be "conducted with style like an artistic performance" (Graham, 11).

The idea, then, behind the Ritual-Music Culture was that social harmony would result when the rulers promoted a sense of civility, appropriateness, and virtue among the people.

The principles of the Ritual-Music Culture succeeded in producing harmony in China for four centuries. That harmony began to falter, however, when the feudal states within China started to fight against one another for land and power.

In an effort to restore the harmony, a number of itinerant scholars and political theorists traveled throughout the country attempting to influence the rulers with their theories and worldviews (Mair, 1994, xvii). Confucius (551–479 B.C.) was the most influential of those scholars and political theorists. He pushed for a return to the precepts of the Ritual-Music Culture. The innovation that Confucius brought to the situation was that *all the people,* not just the emperor, were to live according to the mandated pattern of heaven, or the *Tao* (Lau, 28).

In spite of Confucius's efforts, however, the social conditions in China continued to deteriorate. What was especially shocking to the Chinese was that the fighting was without restraint. Conflicts had arisen even during the Chou dynasty, but they were fought in accordance with established rules. The present wars, however, were being fought without regard for the proper ways of doing battle. For example, the victorious rulers would sometimes boil the bodies of the defeated and then drink the soup (Welch, 19).

Lao Tzu. Lao Tzu (pronounced "Lau-tz"), a contemporary with Confucius, considered Confucius and his Ritual-Music Culture to actually be responsible for China's state of chaos. He wrote in the *Tao Te Ching,* the scripture of Taoism: "When righteousness is lost, only then does the doctrine of propriety arise. Now, propriety is a superficial expression of loyalty and faithfulness, and the beginning of disorder" (chap. 38; Chan, 158). Lao Tzu was saying that the imposing of external laws reflects the breakdown of internal laws, and harmony will not result when laws are imposed on the people.

Legend has it that Confucius met with Lao Tzu in order to ask about the rituals. Lao Tzu responded to Confucius by saying: "Give up, sir, your proud airs, your many wishes, mannerisms, and extravagant claims. They won't do you any good, sir! That's all I have to tell you" (Blakney, 27). Lao Tzu was telling Confucius that he was going about creating harmony in the wrong way. He was accusing Confucius, rightly or wrongly, of imposing a morality on the people. He considered it a natural reaction of the people to rebel against the imposition of such a moral authoritarianism.

Lao Tzu, on the other hand, saw that the answer to the social chaos was to be found in the *Tao* (pronounced "dow") and in the principle of *wu-wei*, which is the principle of purposeful "inactivity." To realize harmony again, taught Lao Tzu, our only "action" should be to align ourselves with the natural flow

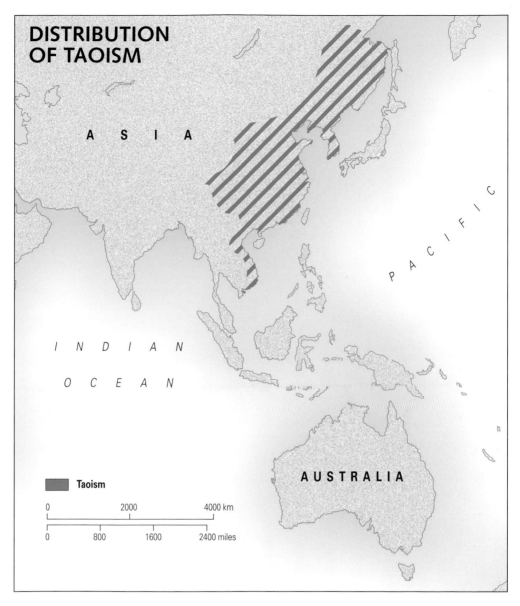

DISTRIBUTION OF TAOISM

A S I A

P A C I F I C

I N D I A N

O C E A N

AUSTRALIA

Taoism

| 0 | 2000 | 4000 km |
| 0 | 800 | 1600 | 2400 miles |

of the *Tao* and to let it work its natural course through us. The less the government is involved in this process, the better.

Chuang Tzu. Chuang Tzu, who lived sometime between 399 and 295 B.C., took the ideas in the *Tao Te Ching* as his starting point, developed them further, and emphasized the mystical nature of the *Tao.* Chuang Tzu's work is called the *Chuang Tzu.*

Chuang Tzu places more emphasis

than did Lao Tzu on the ability of the individual to transform himself or herself through the realization of the *Te* (pronounced as "duh"), which is the universal *Tao* manifested in the individual.

The Search for Immortality. The teachings of Lao Tzu, Chuang Tzu, and Lieh Tzu—another teacher who came after Chuang Tzu—comprise the foundations for *philosophical* Taoism. In the centuries that

Opposite: Taoist shrine, China.

followed, however, Taoism left its philosophical and metaphysical roots and turned to what has been called *religious* Taoism. This religious Taoism would more appropriately be called "magical" Taoism, for it concerned itself with the development of techniques to utilize the forces of the *Tao* in order to attain magical powers and immortality.

The change from philosophical Taoism to religious Taoism took place when the developers of religious Taoism interpreted passages from the three foundational teachers in a literal way. Such passages, however, were probably intended to be interpreted figuratively—goals to be aimed for only in a spiritual sense (Welch, 92).

Out of this literalistic movement flowed several streams of thought and practice (Welch, 92–97):

■ *Hygiene:* This stream of thought was not the idea that "cleanliness is next to godliness," but that one can use the *ch'i*—the breath, or vital energy, within—to purify oneself and to thereby attain immortality.
■ *Alchemy:* This stream in Taoism sought to change natural elements into an elixir of life that would make one immortal.
■ *P'eng-lai:* This name refers to a mythical island (or islands) that was actually being searched for at the time. The belief was that immortal beings and a drug that prevents death would be found on this island.

After a while, these three streams of thought and practice in Taoism merged together and were joined by other magical techniques for attaining immortality. Plus, religious Taoism incorporated a movement that created a host of gods.

Around the third century A.D., however, philosophical Taoism made a resurgence through a movement called "Pure Conversation." In "Pure Conversation" scholars again studied the primary scriptures of Taoism—the *Tao Te Ching* and the *Chuang Tzu.* This resurgence of philosophical Taoism has continued to this day.

ABOUT THE ORIGINS OF THE TAO TE CHING

Lao Tzu's life is clouded in legend. There is considerable doubt that a person named Lao Tzu actually existed. For one thing, Lao Tzu, which means "the old philosopher" or "the old master," is a term of respect rather than an actual name.

Not surprisingly, then, there is also disagreement among scholars concerning the origins of the *Tao Te Ching.* Some say it is the work of several authors whose verses were collected over the course of several centuries, and others say that it is the work of one man named Li Ehr, who was given the honorary title of Lao Tzu.

The controversy about one or many authors is beyond the scope of this chapter; and for the sake of simplicity, we will assume the "one man" theory.

THE BELIEFS OF TAOISM

1. The *Tao.*
The *Tao Te Ching,* in most translations, begins with the following two lines:

> The Tao (Way) that can be told of is not the eternal Tao;
> The name that can be named is not the eternal name (chap.1; Chan,139).

As these words imply, the *Tao* is a mysterious thing; it's beyond knowing, beyond description, and beyond identification. If we think we understand the *Tao,* it's because we have oversimplified it.

Nevertheless, even though the *Tao* is unknowable and indescribable, the *Tao Te Ching* does attempt to describe it, as in the following passage:

> There was something undifferentiated and yet complete,
> Which existed before heaven and earth.
> Soundless and formless, it depends on nothing and does not change.
> It operates everywhere and is free from danger.

It may be considered the mother of the universe.
I do not know its name; I call it Tao (chap. 25; Chan, 152).

In one sense, then, the *Tao* is the force of existence itself. In another sense, though, it is beyond even the force of existence, for the *Tao Te Ching* talks about nonexistence as being even more ultimate than existence: "All things in the world come from being. And being comes from nonbeing" (Chan, 160).

The *Tao Te Ching* goes on to clarify that there is an interplay between existence and nonexistence: "Being and nonbeing produce each other" (chap. 2; Chan, 140). This mutuality is seen in the following analogy: "Clay is molded to form a utensil ["being," or existence], but it is on its nonbeing that the utility of the utensil depends" (chap. 11; Chan, 145). In other words, a spoon is useful because of the "emptiness" (nonbeing) within the curve (being) of the spoon.

Also, out of nonbeing and being comes the rest of the world:

Tao produced the One.
The One produced the two.
The two produced the three.
And the three produced the ten thousand things (chap. 42; Chan, 160).

Therefore, from nonbeing has come being. And from being has come the "two," which is the *yin* and the *yang* (discussed later). And from the "two," has come the three, which is the *yin, yang, and ch'i* ("breath" or "vital energy"). And from the "three" has come the ten thousand things, or the world.

The *Tao* is not only the force of existence from which the world flows, but it is also the "Way" or "Pattern" within that world. The picture that the word *Tao* connotes is the "Way" in which a river flows naturally along its course (Lewis and Travis, 297). The idea is that the *Tao* is that underlying force that flows through nature and that guides and moves every object in

YIN	YANG
Female	Male
Cold	Hot
Passive	Active
Negative	Positive
Dark	Light
Death	Life
Good	Evil
Right	Left
Weak	Strong
Responsive	Aggressive
Contraction	Expansion

the way that is natural to it.

In addition, the way in which the *Tao* flows always leads toward harmony, health, and peace (Lewis and Travis, 297). By aligning ourselves with that underlying flow, we will experience such things in our lives.

2. The *Te*.

Te is that pattern within each object that makes it what it is; it is our individuality, our uniqueness. *Te*, moreover, is each individual's inner connection to the universal *Tao*. Therefore, as we are true to who we are in our own unique nature, we will then work in harmony with the natural flow of the universe.

Taoism says that we need to accept the *Te*—the unique pattern—for what it is, both in ourselves and in other things. We should resist, therefore, making everything conform to our limited idea of what's right. When such conformity is imposed on an object or a person, it will resist, and that resistance is the result of our having not taken into consideration the unique pattern within that person or object. For example, while we as humans would be uncomfortable sleeping in a damp place, a frog would feel right at home (chap. 2; Fung, 11). But which way of sleeping is right? Both, depending on whether we're talking about a frog or a

person. It would go against the *Te*, though, to impose either way of sleeping on the other.

The resistance that is elicited when one's *Te*, or unique pattern, is violated is why we should act toward others with a certain "inactivity," as discussed in the next section.

3. The Principle of Inactivity (*Wu-Wei*).

Lao Tzu observed the fighting that was going on between the feudal states, and he noticed that force was inevitably responded to with force. He also noticed that the initial force eventually brought about its own defeat (Welch, 20). Lao Tzu wrote, "Violent and fierce people do not die a natural death" (chap. 42; Chan, 161). He saw that this principle was true not only in the cases involving physical violence but also in the cases of one person imposing his or her will on someone else. It was because when someone imposed his or her will on an object or a person, the pattern—*Te*—within that object or person resisted.

The way, then, to achieve one's purpose, says Lao Tzu, is to work with the patterns—the *Te*—within things

rather than to impose one's will on them. This is, in essence, the principle of *wu-wei*, or "inactivity." *Wu-wei* is a purposeful "taking no unnatural action" (Chan, 791); it's a deliberate removing of one's hands from something and letting nature, or the *Tao*, take its course.

4. The *Yin/Yang* Duality.

The *Tao Te Ching* said that "The One produced the two." The "two" are the *yin* and the *yang*—the opposing but, at the same time, balancing and interacting forces within nature. The following are some examples:

Even though the two forces are opposites of each other, they also interact with each other, and by doing so life and nature are produced.

As we look at nature, we are to view it as a whole, as manifesting both the *yin* and the *yang*, for they are mutually dependent—we cannot know the one apart from the contrast of the other. For example, we cannot know the good without the evil to give us perspective. The symbol for *yin* and *yang*—a circle with black and white halves curling into each other—denotes this interactive and interdependent relationship.

Taoism and Christianity Contrasted

	TAOISM	CHRISTIANITY
THE ULTIMATE	The *Tao*: An impersonal force of existence that is beyond differentiation. We are to align ourselves with the *Tao*, but we cannot know it in an interpersonal way.	God: The personal Creator who is ontologically separate from His creation. He both knows us (Jeremiah 12:3) and can be known by us in a personal way (John 17:3).
THE MEANING OF GOODNESS	The ultimate form of the *Tao* is beyond moral distinctions. The *yin-yang* duality that flows from the *Tao* represents the balance and the interaction between good and evil. Thus, good and evil are coequal and mutually dependent.	The existence of good is prior to the existence of evil; and moral righteousness is based on the very character of God. Contrary to Taoism, evil is necessary neither to the existence of nor the knowledge of God's goodness.
NATURE	Nature has always existed; it is not created. Nature is moral in the sense that moral laws are like the laws of nature—impersonal principles that have inevitable cause-and-effect consequences.	A creation of God and an expression of the creativity of His being. Nature is morally neutral; persons are moral.
HUMANITY'S PRIMARY PROBLEM	Human life is in chaos because we do not align ourselves with the "Way" that flows through nature. Such non-alignment results in disorder and disharmony in society— and in one's self.	Human life is in chaos because we have rebelled against God, our Creator. This has caused us to be separated from Him, and it leads to spiritual emptiness.
THE SOLUTION	Reliance on our ability to become aware of the way in which the *Tao* operates in the world and to align ourselves with it. Transformation comes from our purposeful inactivity (*wu-wei*) and to "go with the flow" of the *Tao*.	Reliance on what God has accomplished on our behalf through Jesus Christ. Transformation comes as we repent of our sins (selfishness), trust in the forgiving and reconciling work of Jesus Christ, and allow the Holy Spirit to give us new life.
THE OUTCOME	The result of aligning ourselves with the *Tao* is to have order and harmony in society and peace within one's self. "To know harmony means to be in accord with the eternal" (chap. 55; Chan,166).	As we repent of our sins and trust in Christ, we will have peace with God and within our selves, meaning in life, and society will be more ordered.
THE AFTERLIFE	The person's individual consciousness ceases to exist, but his/her life force is "recycled." Through remembrance, the family keeps them "immortal."	The person's individual consciousness continues to exist, either in fellowship with God or separated from Him.

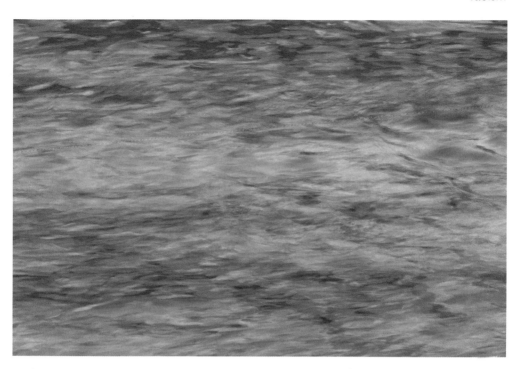

The *yin* and the *yang* were also used in the Taoist—in fact, in the Chinese—practice of divination. In Chinese religious life, the summer and winter solstices were the most important times of the year, when the forces of *yin* and *yang* reached their peaks and gave way to each other. The Spring Festival (also called Chinese New Year) is one of these times. To a people who believed that their lives were centered in the flow of the natural world, this was an important time for divining the future. Fortune tellers and mediums were sought for help in making big decisions, such as weddings, funerals, and large investments; and their advice was followed to the letter.

Even today and in the most modern of Chinese cities, spiritual advisors are regularly consulted for big decisions. What we in the West would call "superstition," the Chinese would call "going with the flow," and would, at all costs, avoid getting out of touch with the natural flow of nature. With respect to the *yin/yang* duality, one does not try to avoid one or the other; rather, it is important to live in harmony between them both, never having too much of either.

SUMMARY

Taoism is a compelling system of ideas, many of them paradoxical and contrary to the Western way of thinking, which is often more comfortable with distinct differences between things.

Taoism is decidedly naturalistic in that nature is the measure of all things. It is also "societistic" in the sense that human society is the arena wherein the "Way" plays out and is understood. While practical in every way, Taoism retains a sense of the mystical and unattainable in that the true "Way" can only be approached, it can never be fully understood or modeled. And yet, while the "Way" is beyond being fully understood, it is decidedly this-worldly in that it is not beyond but within humanity, expressing itself through daily life in the mundane world.

The *Tao*, moreover, is not personal and can neither know us nor be known by us in a personal way. In all

Lao Tzu wrote that the great rivers and seas are kings of all mountain streams because they skillfully stay below them.

the Taoist scriptures the sage talks about the *Tao*, never to the *Tao*.

SUGGESTIONS FOR EVANGELISM

1. Appreciate Taoism

A. *Appreciate the Relevance of Taoism.* The temptation might be to dismiss Lao Tzu and Chuang Tzu as outdated philosophers whose writings are no longer relevant. But such an attitude would be a mistake.

First, *Taoism lies at the heart of the Chinese and Asian cultures.* In order to understand the Asian peoples, one must understand the Naturalism of Taoism.

Second, these ancient Chinese teachers *wrestled with issues and circumstances that are similar to our situation today.* They lived in a time during which the culture was unraveling. The former foundation for harmony—the Ritual-Music Culture—was no longer working. Chinese teachers, like Lao Tzu and Chuang Tzu, were trying to find a belief system that would bring harmony back to a culture that had gone awry. We see the same issues facing us today.

Third, *these Chinese teachers struggled with questions that are always relevant* to humanity, questions that have to do with the ultimate issues of life: What is Ultimate Reality? What is the meaning of life? What happens after death?

B. *Appreciate the Wisdom of Taoism.* For one thing, we can agree with the principle in Taoism that says *when you impose your will or viewpoint or law on someone, he or she will inevitably resist.* As one considers the culture war that America is experiencing, one can see how such a principle is relevant. For example, when one side of the culture war blasts the other side, we should not be surprised when they respond with equal or greater vehemence. Neither should we be surprised that what results is polarization, not communication.

Moreover, the application of the principle of imposition is that the *"soft" approach works best.* Such a soft approach is similar to the wisdom of Jesus: "Love your enemies and pray for those who persecute you" (Matthew 5:44), and Paul: "If your enemy is hungry, feed him. . . . In doing this, you will heap burning coals on his head" (Romans 12:20).

We should appreciate as well the wisdom of Taoism in *its emphasis on how each individual and object is unique and how that uniqueness should be taken into consideration.*

Then, finally, we can appreciate the wisdom of Taoism when it talks about *the principles of leadership.* Lao Tzu wrote:

The great rivers and seas are kings of all mountain streams because they skillfully stay below them. That is why they can be their kings. Therefore, in order to be the superior of the people, one must, in the use of words, place himself below them (chap. 66; Chan, 170–171).

What a beautifully descriptive analogy of what it means to be a servant leader! Jesus taught and exemplified such leadership when He washed the feet of His disciples (John 13:12–15), and when He said, "the Son of Man did not come to be served, but to serve, and to give his life as a ransom for many" (Matthew 20:28).

2. Point to the Evidence for a God Who Is Personal.

One of the crucial issues that separates Christianity from Taoism is that of whether God is personal or impersonal. Christianity holds that God is personal, which means He has personal attributes such as an intellect, a will, emotions, creativity, an appreciation for beauty, and moral standards. Such characteristics cannot be attributed to the impersonal *Tao*.

The following, however, are evidences within Taoism that can be used to stimulate the thinking of the Taoist toward reconsidering the

impersonal nature of Ultimate Reality and considering the validity of believing in a God who is personal.

A. *The Foundation for Our Uniqueness and Our Complexity.* Uniqueness comes from complexity. If, for example, something has no complexity within it (it is internally undifferentiated), then there is nothing by which to distinguish it from something else. Only if an object has internal complexity can it be unique and different from other objects.

Taoism says that our uniqueness comes from *Te,* which is the personal and individual extension of the impersonal and universal *Tao.* But is *Te* sufficiently complex to produce uniqueness? Taoists describe our relationship to the *Tao* as being like streams that flow from a lake. But the water in the streams (the *Te*) is just as undifferentiated as the water in the lake (the *Tao*). There is insufficient complexity within the water to make it unique from other water.

An analogy that better illustrates why we are unique as persons is that we are like a painting that flows from a painter's brush. The painter provides the complexity in the painting that distinguishes it from other paintings.

In light of the above discussion, it is enlightening to read Chuang Tzu's thoughts on the matter of what is a sufficient cause for our complexity and uniqueness:

> If there is no other, there will be no I. If there is no I, there will be none to make distinctions. This seems to be true. But what causes these varieties? It might seem as if there would be a real Lord, but there is no indication of His existence. One may believe He exists, but we do not see His form. He may have reality, but no form (chap. 2; Fung, 46).

Chuang Tzu is struggling here with the clear and observable fact that complexities—or "varieties"—come from persons. If it takes persons to produce complexity, Chuang Tzu ponders, then it would seem that the complexity we see in the world around us would indicate the workings of a personal God. Chuang Tzu refrains, however, from coming to a firm conclusion on the matter.

Taoism teaches that we are like a painting that flows from a painter's brush.

As Christians, we would agree with Chuang Tzu's trend of thought in that it seems more reasonable to say that our complexity and uniqueness is the result of the amazing creativity of a personal and intelligent Designer, not of an undifferentiated oneness, such as the *Tao*.

B. *Humanity's Moral Sensitivities.* For Taoism, good and evil are like opposing but interacting natural forces, similar to that of hot and cold, light and dark. Thus, both sides of the moral spectrum—good and evil— must be accepted as coequal, neither side standing above the other. In addition, neither good nor evil can be known, or even exist, without the other, for, as Chuang Tzu writes, "'This' and 'that' are mutually dependent; right and wrong are also mutually dependent" (chap. 2:5; Mair, 1994, 15).

Christianity says, on the other hand, that the good is *prior* in its existence to evil, for God, who is absolutely holy (1 John 1:5) and good (Matthew 19:17), is the One who created all things and was therefore before all things. Rather than good and evil being mutually dependent, evil is instead a rebellion against and a denial of the good. The existence of evil is not necessary either for goodness to exist or to be known by us.

What does all this have to do with providing evidence for the existence of a personal, transcendent God? Plenty.

One ramification of saying that good and evil are mutually dependent is that then the distinctions between the two become not only blurred but arbitrary. One person's goodness could be another person's evil, and vice versa; and there would be no basis on which to say that either person's perspective is wrong, or right. The two perspectives would merely be different. That is because no one would have the moral authority to say what is good and what is evil. If someone claims to have such moral authority, they are claiming to stand above the good and

evil. But that is precisely the point!

In order to distinguish the difference between good and evil, we need a moral standard that stands above them. But the *Tao* cannot provide such a moral authority, for it is void of moral distinctions. Only a personal, transcendent, and holy God, as presented in the Bible, provides the moral authority for making such moral distinctions.

C. *"Deep Love."* Another line of evidence for God's existence as a personal Being is found in a statement that Chuang Tzu made: "When Heaven is to save a person, Heaven will protect him through deep love" (chap. 67; Chan, 171).

One can ask the Taoist:

■ What is meant by "deep love"?
■ Is the *Tao* capable of having such a "deep love"?

Why are these questions relevant? Because it takes a Being with personal attributes to have the capacity to love. The *Tao* is incapable of such love, however, because it's impersonal, an undifferentiated oneness—void of all personal attributes.

Chuang Tzu's statement gives the Christian an opportunity to point to the deep love of God that He demonstrated toward us through Jesus Christ: "Greater love has no one than this, that he lay down his life for his friends" (John 15:13; see also John 3:16; Romans 5:8; 1 John 4:8–10).

We have given at least three lines of evidence from Taoism that can be used to point to the personal nature of God. The issue of God being personal is important for at least two reasons. First, because the Taoist can then begin to understand that God cares for him or her. Second, because the personal nature of God provides a basis for the Taoist to come to a conviction about the seriousness of sin. Sin is serious because it is rebellion against God, and it causes our relationship with God to be broken, which means spiritual death.

According to the Tao Te Ching, growing weak and dying are evidences that people are failing to live in harmony with the Tao.

3. Raise the Issue of Sin.

Put in terms of Taoism, the result of sin is disharmony. If there is disharmony in society, in the family, or in our lives, it is because we are not living in alignment with the *Tao*. It is easy enough for a Christian to help a Taoist see that there is disharmony in his or her life.

The difficult issue, though, is helping the Taoist understand that he or she is incapable of remedying the problem of sin through his or her own effort, but that he or she needs a radical work of inner transformation. This is difficult because Taoists believe that as they "let go" (purposeful inactivity), transformation will happen naturally.

A. *Point to the Impossibility of Meeting the Standards of the Tao.* Taoism itself contains evidences that will help the Taoist see the hopelessness of depending on his or her own human effort to attain the standards set forth in even the *Tao Te Ching*. For example, the following words are repeated twice in the *Tao Te Ching:*

That things with age decline in strength,
You may well say, suits not the Way;
And not to suit the Way is early death
(chap. 30; Blakney, 108; also chap. 55).

Blakney, the translator, comments: "If he [the person] continues with the Way there will be no decline in his strength or virtue. If he departs from the Way, he is doomed" (Blakney, 108).

Such a standard is impossible to meet. After all, do not all people experience a decline in their strength as they grow old? Moreover, do not all people die? According to the *Tao Te Ching,* then, growing weak and dying are evidences that people are failing to live in harmony with the *Tao!* Where, then, is our hope?

Consider, too, other standards for living according to the *Tao:*

I treat those who are good with goodness, And I also treat those who are not good with goodness (chap. 49; Chan, 162).

Whether it is big or small, many or few, repay hatred with virtue (chap. 63; Chan, 169).

Such standards are commendable—even biblical. But if this is what it means to live according to the *Tao*, then we are all falling far short of such standards!

On the one hand, then, those who live in ways that do not "suit the Way" will meet an "early death." On the other hand, such standards are impossible to attain.

Reading the above quotes, one is reminded of the verses in the Bible that say, "For all have sinned and fall short of the glory of God" (Romans 3:23), and "The wages of sin is death" (Romans 6:23).

B. *Desiring to Do That Which Is Right but Not Being Able to Do It.* Not only is the standard for living according to the *Tao* impossible to meet, but, even if it were attainable, there is something in us that prevents us from living up to it.

That "something" could be termed "selfishness." The word "selfish" communicates more clearly to a Taoist than does "sin" for describing what is wrong with humanity. In our desire to serve ourselves, we turn against God and against other people (Isaiah 53:6). Such selfishness causes disharmony.

Lao Tzu made an interesting statement when he wrote, "All the world knows that the weak overcomes the strong and the soft overcomes the hard. *But none can practice it*" (chap. 78; Chan, 175, emphasis added). Lao Tzu is saying that we all know what to do, but none of us has the power to live consistently with such knowledge.

Romans 7:14–25 is a good place to begin with a friend from a Taoist background, especially verse 18: "I have the desire to do what is good, but I cannot carry it out." In this passage, the apostle Paul is saying that he knows that he should do the right thing; he even knows, basically, what the right thing to do is. But in his flesh (on his own human power) he cannot do it. Instead, he is bound to a "law of sin" (v. 23)—a power that turns him to seek his own will.

All people can identify with *desiring*

to do the right thing, but then actually *doing* the wrong thing. There comes a time when we need to cry out for help as Paul does, "Wretched man that I am! Who will rescue me from the body of this death?" (v. 24).

Where is our hope? It does not seem to be within us!

4. Forgiveness—the Foundation for Hope.

The *Tao Te Ching* gives a glimmer of the hope, but the full measure of that hope is not to be found in Taoism.

A. *The Reason the Tao Is to Be Treasured.* One glimmer of the hope comes when the *Tao Te Ching* answers the question, Why is the *Tao* to be most treasured? Surprisingly, that which is to be most treasured about the *Tao* is its *forgiveness*!

> Why did the ancients so treasure this DAO?
> Is it not because it has been said of it:
> "Whosoever asks will receive;
> Whosoever has sinned will be forgiven"?
> Therefore is DAO the most exquisite thing on earth.
> (chap. 62; Wilhelm, 55; see also Mair, 1990, 32; Blakney, 115)

But how can it be that forgiveness is to be the most treasured thing about the *Tao*? After all, forgiveness means that a moral standard has been broken. But the *Tao* is beyond such moral distinctions! Also, only persons are capable of forgiveness. But such forgiveness is beyond the capability of an impersonal force of being, such as the *Tao*.

So the *Tao Te Ching* speaks of the need for forgiveness, but the *Tao* is incapable of such forgiveness. Only the personal God of the Bible is capable of such forgiveness.

B. *The Means for Forgiveness.* The *Tao Te Ching* gives another glimmer for hope, and it is found in a passage that was mentioned earlier. This passage speaks of how no one consistently practices the way of the

Tao. Consider, though, how Lao Tzu completed that thought:

All the world knows that the weak overcomes the strong and the soft overcomes the hard.
But none can practice it.
Therefore the sage says:
He who suffers disgrace for his country
Is called the lord of the land.
He who takes upon himself the country's misfortunes
Becomes the king of the empire.
Straight words seem to be their opposite
(chap. 78; Chan, 175, emphasis added).

The way in which those words foreshadow the Gospel is uncanny, for they begin with the thought that there are none who live up to the law or principle that is known by all (see Romans 1–3). The passage goes on to speak, though, of one who will suffer "disgrace for his country" and take "upon himself the country's misfortunes" (see Isaiah 53:6, Romans 5:8; 2 Corinthians 5:21). Such a person, moreover, has the right to be called the "lord of the land" and the "king of the empire" (see Philippians 2:6–11; Revelation 17:14).

Again, where is the hope to be found for us who are not able to live up to whatever standard we face? Lao Tzu's words seem to foreshadow the need for one who would suffer in our place.

C. *The Forgiveness Found in Jesus.* Hope, then, is found in forgiveness. And where is forgiveness to be found? In one who would suffer in our stead. Jesus fulfills such a description. The Bible says,

Therefore, my brothers, I want you to know that through Jesus the forgiveness of sins is proclaimed to you. Through him everyone who believes is justified from everything you could not be justified from by the law of Moses (Acts 13:38–39; also 1 John 1:9).

That which we could not accomplish through our own human effort, no matter what moral law we're talking about, God has accomplished for us through Jesus Christ, who suffered and died on our behalf.

5. Appreciate the "Soft" Way of Jesus.

As Taoists know, the way of the *Tao* is "soft"; it accomplishes all that it needs to accomplish without forcing itself on anything. Lao Tzu wrote: "The softest things in the world overcome the hardest things in the world" (chap. 43; Chan, 161; see also chap. 78; Chan, 174).

Considering how Taoism values the "softness" of the Way (*Tao*), it is likely that the Taoist will be able to *empathize with and appreciate the "softness" of the way of Jesus,* for

■ when arrested, He did not resist (Matthew 26:50–56);
■ when put on trial, He did not speak in His own defense (Matthew 26:60–63; 27:12–14);
■ when spit upon and struck in the face, He did not retaliate (Matthew 26:67);
■ when stripped, mocked, and tortured with a crown of thorns, He did not defend himself (Matthew 27:28–30);
■ when nailed to the cross, He responded, "Father, forgive them, for they do not know what they are doing" (Luke 23:34).

As it says in Acts, "He was led like a sheep to the slaughter, and as a lamb before the shearer is silent, so he did not open his mouth" (8:32; quoting Isaiah 53:7–8).

And yet, even though He did not resist, even though He went with "the flow of things," He nevertheless accomplished everything on our behalf! Jesus took upon himself all that death and evil could spew out. They spent themselves entirely on Jesus. When the powers of death were finished with Him, however, then God raised Him to life. The good news is that as we place our faith in Jesus Christ, we, too, can receive

A Summary of the Suggestions of Evangelism

SUGGESTION POINTS OF DISCUSSION	EVIDENCES FROM TAOISM	THE POINTS TO BE MADE
1. Appreciate the wisdom and the relevance of Taoism.		
2. Point to the evidence for a God who is personal.		
A. The foundation for our uniqueness and complexity.	Chuang Tzu: If there is no I [no person], there will be none to make distinctions" (chap. 2).	A personal God is a better explanation for our uniqueness and complexity than is an undifferentiated oneness.
B. Humanity's moral sensitivities.	Chuang Tzu: "Right and wrong are mutually dependent" (chap. 2); you can't have one without the other.	With respect to existence, goodness is prior to evil. Without a transcendent standard of morality (as provided by a personal, holy God) there is no foundation by which to distinguish between good and evil, right and wrong.
C. "Deep Love"	Chuang Tzu: "When Heaven is to save a person, Heaven will protect him through deep love" (chap. 67)	Love is beyond the capacity of the impersonal *Tao*. The personal God of the Bible has demonstrated His "deep love," for, "Greater love has no one than this, that he lay down his life for his friends" John 15:13; see also Romans 5:8; 1 John 4:8–10).
3. Raise the issue of sin.		
A. Point to the impossibility of meeting the standards of the Tao.	Lao Tzu: "That things with age decline in strength, You may well say, suits not the Way" (chap. 30). Lao Tzu: "Repay hatred with virtue" (chap. 63).	The *Tao Te Ching* has established standards for living according to the *Tao* that are impossible to meet consistently, and yet not to meet them means death.
B. Desiring to do that which is right but not being able to do it.	Lao Tzu: "The soft overcomes the hard. But none can practice it" (chap. 78).	Paul: "I have the desire to do what is good, but I cannot carry it out" (Romans 7:18).

SUGGESTION POINTS OF DISCUSSION	EVIDENCES FROM TAOISM	THE POINTS TO BE MADE
4. Forgiveness— the foundation for hope.		
A. The Reason the Tao is to be treasured.	"Why did the ancients so treasure this DAO? Is it not because it has been said of it: 'Whosoever asks will receive; Whosoever has sinned will be forgiven'?" (chap. 62).	The *Tao*, being impersonal, is incapable of forgiving. Only a personal God is capable of forgiveness.
B. The means for forgiveness	"He who suffers disgrace for his country is called the lord of the land" (chap. 78).	"God made him who had no sin to be sin for us, so that in him we might become the righteousness of God" (2 Corinthians 5:21).
C. The forgiveness found in Jesus		"Through Jesus the forgiveness of sins is proclaimed to you" (Acts 13:38–39).
5. Appreciate the "soft" way of Jesus.	Lao Tzu: "The softest things in the world overcome the hardest things in the world" (chap 43).	"He was led like a sheep to the slaughter, and as a lamb before the shearer is silent, so he did not open his mouth" (Isaiah 8:32), but God raised Him from the dead, and, through faith in Him, we, too, can have life.

eternal life and righteousness: "When you were dead in your sins ... God made you alive with Christ. He forgave us all our sins" (Colossians 2:13).

Jesus' way is also *"soft" in the way He acts toward us,* for He does not force himself on us or coerce us into making a decision. Instead, His way is the way of love, which draws people to Him: "But I, when I am lifted up from the earth [upon the Cross], I will draw all men to myself" (John 12:32). Jesus does not demand that we come to Him, but He invites us with love and with the prospect of finding rest:

Come to me, all you who are weary and burdened, and I will give you rest. Take my yoke upon you and learn from me, for I am gentle and humble in heart, and you will find rest for your souls. For my yoke is easy and my burden is light (Matthew 11:28–30).

And the way that we can receive His rest is through the "soft" way of acknowledging our need for inner transformation and allowing God to do His work of transformation in our lives.

Then we can live in the "soft" way of allowing the Holy Spirit to empower us (Romans 8:9) and to give us life, for, as Jesus said, "the water I give him will become in him a spring of water welling up to eternal life" (John 4:15; cf., 7:38–39; Romans 8:11).

BIBLIOGRAPHY AND RESOURCES

Blakney, R. B. *The Way of Life: Lao Tzu.* New York: The New American Library, Inc., 1955.

Chan, Wing-Tsit. *A Source Book in Chinese Philosophy.* Princeton, N.J.: Princeton University Press, 1963.

Chang, Chung-yuan. *Tao: A New Way of Thinking.* New York: Harper & Row, 1975.

Dreher, Diane. *The Tao of Peace.* New York: Donald I. Fine Inc., 1990.

Fung, Yu-Lan. *Chuang-Tzu.* New York: Paragon Book Reprint Corp., 1964.

Graham, A. C. *Disputers of the Tao: Philosophical Argument in Ancient China.* La Salle, Ill.: Open Court, 1989.

Hoff, B. *The Tao of Pooh.* New York: Dutton, 1982.

Hoff, B. *The Te of Piglet.* New York: Dutton, 1992.

Lau, D. C. *Confucius: The Analects.* New York: Viking Penguin Inc., 1979.

Legge, J. *The Religions of China: Confucianism and Taoism Described and Compared with Christianity.* London: Hodder & Stoughton, 1880 and 1976.

Mair, Victor. *Tao Te Ching: The Classic Book of Integrity and the Way.* New York: Bantam Books, 1990.

Mair, Victor. *Wandering on the Way: Early Taoist Tales and Parables of Chuang Tzu.* New York: Bantam Books, 1994.

Mote, F. W. *Intellectual Foundations of China.* New York: McGraw Hill, 1989.

Overmyer, D. L. *Religions of China: The World as a Living System.* San Francisco: Harper & Row, 1986.

Welch, Holmes. *Taoism: The Parting of the Way.* Boston: Beacon Press, 1966.

Wilhelm, Richard (trans. into German). *Tao Te Ching.* H. G. Oswald (trans. into English). New York: Penguin Books, 1990.

Is Jesus the Only Way to God?

A defense of the exclusive claims of Jesus Christ

Rick Rood

INTRODUCTION

Many people stumble over Christianity's claim that Jesus Christ is the only way to a saving relationship with God. The belief that there are many ways to God is increasing in the culture of the United States.

The exclusiveness of Christ is difficult to accept not only for many Americans but also for those who come from other nations or families where Christianity was not embraced in their cultural tradition. Many of these people hold to the view that all religions are equally valid ways to God or to Ultimate Reality. Such a view is known as "religious pluralism."

Christians need to think seriously about how to respond to those who challenge the exclusivity of the Christian faith and who suggest that all religions are of equal value.

The best place to begin is with Scripture. We need to understand biblically why Christians consider Christ to be the only way of salvation. One of the most important reasons for such exclusivity has to do with what the Bible says is the problem that lies at the core of the human condition and the unique solution that such a problem requires.

Cross on the roof of a Greek church.

Majority of population:

- Christian
- Muslim
- Buddhist
- Hindu
- Buddhist, Confucian and Taoist
- Buddhist and Shintoist
- Jewish
- Sikh
- Animist

| 0 | 2000 | 4000 km |
| 0 | 800 | 1600 | 2400 miles |

HUMANITY'S PROBLEM AND THE BIBLE'S SOLUTION

What Does the Bible Say Is Wrong With Humanity? The Bible teaches that although we are created in God's image and are of unique and special value to Him, nevertheless we are deeply and permanently stained by sin. Sin is, at its root, an attitude of rebellion against and independence from God. The Bible says, moreover, that all have sinned (Romans 3:23).

The most severe consequence of our sin is that it separates us from God. The prophet Isaiah wrote, "But

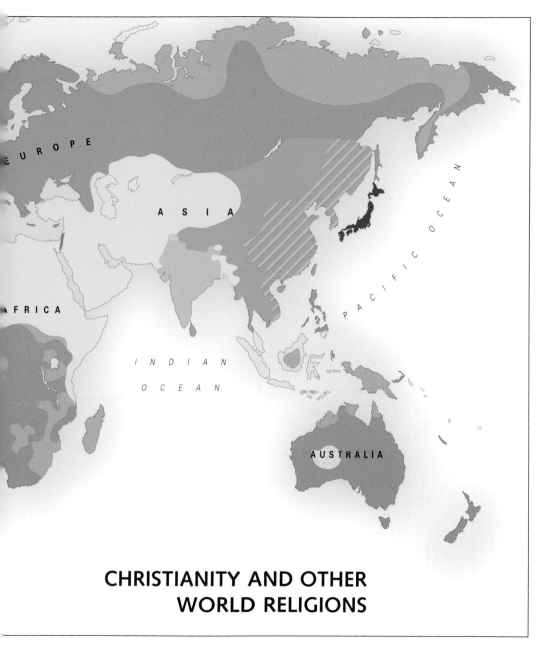

CHRISTIANITY AND OTHER WORLD RELIGIONS

your iniquities have separated you from your God; your sins have hidden his face from you" (59:2; see also Habakkuk 1:13).

Another consequence of our sin is that it causes our spiritual death. Just as physical death occurs when the spirit is separated from the body, so spiritual death results when we separate ourselves from God. Paul wrote, "You were dead in your transgressions and sins" (Ephesians 2:1). No other religion portrays humanity as being as bad off spiritually as does Christianity, for a person cannot be any worse off than being dead.

A believer experiences Christian baptism.

WHAT IS THE BIBLICAL SOLUTION FOR HUMANITY'S PROBLEM?

The Bible uses several terms to describe what is the solution to humanity's problem, and each term implies that there is only one way to resolve that problem.

Forgiveness: The Bible says we have offended a holy God and that we need to be forgiven of that offense before we can be in fellowship with God. There are not many ways to receive such forgiveness, because only the One who has been offended can forgive us of our offense (Mark 2:5–7). Jesus alone paid the penalty for our sin through His death on the cross (2 Corinthians 5:21). He thereby cleared the way both for God to remain true to His holy character and for Him to extend the offer of forgiveness to us. Thus, John could write, "If we confess our sins, [God] is *faithful and just and will forgive* us our sins" (1 John 1:9, emphasis added; see also Romans 3:22–26).

Reconciliation: The Bible says we have separated ourselves from God relationally because of our rebellion and sin: "We all, like sheep, have gone astray, each of us has turned to his own way" (Isaiah 53:6). The solution to our being separated from God is that we need our relationship with God to be restored. Our need for such reconciliation indicates, again, that there is only one way to resolve the problem of our having separated ourselves from God.

How many ways are there, after all, for me to restore a relationship that I am entirely responsible for having broken? Only one! Through the confession of my guilt, and the hope that the offended one will be gracious enough to forgive me.

Humanity is in the same kind of situation with God. If we are ever to have any hope of being in a relationship with God, we need to take steps to restore our relationship, which means to confess our guilt before God.

Regeneration: The Bible says we are spiritually dead. Such a concept, again, implies exclusiveness with respect to the solution to humanity's problem. That is because dead people cannot help themselves, and the only one who has the power to give life is God. Our need is to be made spiritually alive, or regenerated. To be made spiritually alive is the meaning of such biblical phrases as to be "born again" (John 3:3–6) and to be "born of God" (John 1:12). God provided Jesus Christ as the One through whom that life would come: "God, who is rich in mercy, made us alive with Christ even when we were dead in transgressions" (Ephesians 2:4–5). Jesus said, "I am the resurrection and the life. He who believes in me will live, even though he dies" (John 11:25). He demonstrated the truth of those words by rising from the dead. No other founder of a religion can make such an astounding claim.

GOD'S FORMS OF REVELATION

Another reason Christians talk about the exclusivity of the Gospel is because several passages in the Bible emphasize the necessity of "hearing" the good news about Jesus as a necessary precursor to coming to salvation. Paul, in Romans 10:17, says, "Faith comes from hearing the message, and the message is heard through the word of Christ" (see also Galatians 3:2; Ephesians 1:13; 2 Timothy 3:15; James 1:18; 1 Peter 1:23–25).

It is important to distinguish between what can be known about God through what we normally call "general revelation" and what can be known about Him only through His "special revelation." General revelation is called that because it is truth about God that can be known to all people in general. The following are biblical passages that speak of general revelation:

The heavens declare the glory of God; the skies proclaim the work of his hands (Psalm 19:1).

For since the creation of the world God's invisible qualities—his eternal power and divine nature—have been clearly seen, being understood from what has been made, so that men are without excuse (Romans 1:20; see also Acts 14:17).

General Revelation Contrasted With Special Revelation

GENERAL REVELATION	SPECIAL REVELATION
THE METHOD	
Creation, the heavens (Psalm 19:1–2; Acts 14:17; Romans 1:19–20).	Divine intervention in history (e.g., the parting of the Red Sea).
God's moral law written on our hearts, and our conscience (Romans 2:15). The law written on our hearts tells us there is a transcendent moral standard, and the conscience tells us we are guilty of falling short of that standard.	God's word spoken to humanity (directly—Genesis 12:1; through dreams—Genesis 20:6; visions—Daniel 8:1; angels—Acts 10:3).
	God's Word written by men through the inspiration of the Holy Spirit (1 Timothy 3:16; 2 Peter 1:21).
	God the Son incarnated as a man (John 1:14; Hebrews 1:1–2)
THE RECIPIENTS	
Available to all people, at all times and places.	Available to those who witness such events, or who hear or read such words.
THE CONTENTS	
Truth about God: His existence, power, goodness, and moral nature (Romans 1:20).	Truth about our being spiritually dead and separated from God (Romans 6:23; Ephesians 2:1).
Truth about our failure before the law written on our hearts (Romans 2:15, "Their thoughts now accusing, now even defending them").	Truth about God's plan and provision of salvation (John 14:6; Acts 4:12; Romans 10:13–17).

The fish has been a Christian symbol since early times.

Such verses tell us that through the creation we can perceive that there is a personal Creator God who is both powerful and good. Through Romans 2:15—"the requirements of the law are written on their hearts"—Paul further tells us that through our conscience and the law of God written on our hearts, we can know there is a Lawgiver.

It is possible to know much about God through His "general revelation," but there is no indication in Scripture that the way to be reconciled with God can be known through any other means than the "special revelation" of the good news about Jesus Christ. Paul wrote,

> Everyone who calls on the name of the Lord will be saved. How, then, can they call on the one they have not believed in? And how can they believe in the one of whom they have not heard? And how can they hear without someone preaching to them? (Romans 10:13–14).

CHRISTIANITY AND THE OTHER RELIGIONS

What is the biblical attitude toward other religions? At least four things can be said in response to this question.

First, it is certainly possible that other religions contain truths obtained through either general or even special revelation. Several religions teach many truths of both a theological and ethical nature that coincide with Christian teaching. For example, Orthodox Judaism and Islam affirm theism. Of course, a handful of religions contain truths available through special revelation by virtue of having had contact with the Jewish and Christian Scriptures. Islam, for example, affirms teachings such as Jesus' virgin birth.

Second, being sinful, humanity's tendency is to corrupt the truth about God. The Bible speaks of humanity "suppressing the truth" of God as revealed through creation (Romans 1:18). Paul wrote, "For although they knew God, they neither glorified him as God nor gave thanks to him" (Romans 1:21). Such suppression is the source of our religious inclinations.

Third, there is no indication in Scripture that any other religious message besides the Gospel of Jesus Christ is capable of restoring us to a relationship with God. Jesus himself said, "I am the way and the truth and the life. No one comes to the Father except through me" (John 14:6; see also Peter's words in Acts 4:12).

We know that on the human level,

the only way for two people who have been estranged to be reconciled is for the issues that separated them to be resolved. This is no less true in our relationship with God than in our relationship with one another. Only by agreeing that our sin is the source of our alienation from God, and only by accepting His solution for the problem—the atonement of Jesus Christ—can we be reconciled to Him.

Finally, the Bible teaches that there is a spiritual dimension in the origin of religions, and that the intention of the spirits is to deceive humanity and to deflect us from the truth (see John 8:44; 2 Corinthians 11:13–14). Paul wrote that people will "follow deceiving spirits and things taught by demons" (1 Timothy 4:1). From the beginning, Satan has distorted the truths of God (Genesis 3:1–5), and his purpose all along has been to "blind the minds of the unbelieving" (2 Corinthians 4:4).

One of Satan's lies, and one of the ways in which he blinds people to the truth, is through religions that deflect us from recognizing the full extent of our sinful condition and from accepting God's provision of grace through Jesus Christ. For example, the non-Christian religions have either denied, diminished, or disregarded the absolute holiness of God (see World Religions Overview). As God's holiness is distorted, we become vulnerable to being deceived into thinking that perhaps the goal of salvation is achievable through our own human effort, thus blinding us to our need for a Savior.

COMMON OBJECTIONS TO THE EXCLUSIVE CLAIMS OF CHRIST

1. "Isn't it arrogant and intolerant to claim that Christianity is the only true religion?"

It certainly is possible to adopt an arrogant and intolerant attitude in claiming to possess the truth about anything, and this is no less possible for Christians. Of course, such attitudes are wrong.

It is important to clarify, however, that to claim that something is true to the exclusion of competing claims is not necessarily arrogant or intolerant. Everyone makes statements that they believe are exclusively true. We must point out also that the exclusive claims of the Christian message are really claims made by Jesus Christ

The cross, the universal symbol of Christianity.

One way of witnessing to the Christian faith.

evaluated as being false or inferior to any other religious belief. All beliefs should be granted equal status as a claim to truth.

Without question, Christians—and everyone else—should practice both legal and social tolerance. But "uncritical" tolerance demands a price too high for Christians—or most other people—to pay. It requires that we accept as equally valid all truth-claims, even though they contradict one another. Truth, then, loses all value whatsoever.

2. "Hasn't the idea that Christianity is the only true religion led to wars of persecution against other religions?"
Yes, there have been wars of persecution waged by Christians (or at least those who professed to be Christians) against followers of other religions. The fact that professing Christians did such things, however, does not mean that what they did was right or that the message of the Bible was wrong. Jesus Christ claimed to be the exclusive way to God, but He would never condone such kinds of acts in His name. Neither does their profession of the Christian faith require us to believe that they were indeed true Christians.

We should not forget, moreover, that Christians have been the object of persecution throughout history as well.

about himself and not by Christians about themselves.

In regard to tolerance, we must distinguish among three kinds (adapted from Dr. Erwin Lutzer's *Christ Among Other Gods,* 29):

- ■ *"Legal" tolerance:* The recognition that each person has the legal right to believe whatever he or she determines is true or best.
- ■ *"Social" tolerance:* The recognition that people ought to be treated with dignity and respect regardless of their religious beliefs.
- ■ *"Uncritical" tolerance:* The notion that no religious belief should be

Theories of "Truth"

PRAGMATIC THEORY	"Truth is what works."
EMPIRICIST THEORY	"Truth is what we can experience or observe."
RATIONALIST THEORY	"Truth is what can be proved by reason."
COHERENCE THEORY	"Truth is harmony among a set of ideas."
EMOTIVIST THEORY	"Truth is what I feel."

(Adapted from The *Handbook of Christian Apologetics,* by Kreeft & Tacelli)

The Differences Between the Religions

	HINDUISM	BUDDHISM	ISLAM	CHRISTIANITY
ULTIMATE REALITY	Impersonal essence; or many gods	No god; or impersonal "Buddha essence"	A Creator who is unknowable	A Creator who is personal and who has made himself known
THE NATURE OF HUMANITY	Divine in our essence	No personal essence	Created by God, but nothing is at all like Him	Created by God and in His image
HUMANITY'S PROBLEM	Trapped in reincarnation in an illusory world, due to ignorance and karma	Trapped in reincarnation in a world of suffering, due to desire and karma	Under the judgment of Allah, due to failure to keep the Law	Under God's judgment, due to sinful rebellion
SALVATION	Deliverance from the world through knowledge, works, or devotion	Deliverance from the world of suffering through the cessation of desire (by own works, or "divine" help)	Deliverance from judgment through obedience to the Law	Deliverance from judgment by faith in God's gracious provision of salvation through Jesus Christ
FINAL STATE	Merging with ultimate reality, or heavenly bliss in the presence of gods	Extinction of suffering, desire, and individuality (*nirvana*)	Paradise or hell	Heaven or hell

3. "I think all religions are equally true."

This is a very popular and commonly held idea today, probably because it appears to promote an attitude of mutual respect among followers of different religions. Such a perspective, however, is a false foundation for respect because it refuses to acknowledge the very real and irreconcilable differences that exist among the various religions. It instead dismisses such differences as unimportant. How, though, does one respond to such a belief?

Not a rational belief: First of all, the idea that all religious beliefs are true cannot be held rationally. For if such an idea were true, then the opposite idea—that all religious beliefs are not true—would also have to be true, since it, too, is a religious belief in that it addresses the ultimate issues. Such a statement, however, would cancel out the former one!

Definition of truth: Second, it is impossible to hold that all religions are true unless we change our definition of the word "true" from its normally accepted meaning. Generally, when we say that a statement is "true," we mean that it corresponds to a reality that does in fact exist independently of our beliefs. This is called the "correspondence" theory of truth.

What most "religious pluralists" in fact do is change their definition of "truth" to one of the other definitions listed in the chart entitled

"Theories of 'Truth.'" Although truth is indeed consistent with experience and reason, and it is coherent, it is more than that. Such definitions are deficient because they do not ground truth in an objective reality. Truth is best defined as that which corresponds with reality—the way things really are. Moreover, such definitions of truth are insufficient because they are not comprehensive; they approach reality from a partial or incomplete perspective.

Irreconcilable differences: Finally, though it is possible to find many similarities among the world's religions, a closer look will reveal irreconcilable differences among their most basic teachings. Many people believe that the religions differ on the surface, but on a deeper level they are the same. In fact, the opposite is true: the religions are similar on the surface level, but on the deeper level—the level of their fundamental beliefs and teachings—they are very different.

It is evident that if what we mean by the word "true" is "that which corresponds with reality," then not all of these religions can be true, for they are contradictory in their fundamental beliefs, and to both affirm and deny the same thing in the same respect is to make a statement without meaning. Salvation, for example, is either a wage to be earned (Hinduism, Buddhism, Islam) or a gift to be received (Christianity); it cannot be both. Also, God is either impersonal or personal, not both, for the two concepts of God have mutually exclusive characteristics.

It is true that all the religions in the chart could be false, but it is not true that they could all be true!

4. "I think all religious truth-claims are relative."

When a person makes such a statement, he or she usually means one of three things. First, he or she might mean that since none of us can claim to know the whole truth about anything, what appear to be mutually contradictory statements could both be partially true descriptions of a greater whole. Such a view is called *"pure" relativism*.

Second, he or she might mean that we cannot know anything at all to be true (or at least anything about religion). This is known as *skepticism*.

Third, he or she might mean that all truth (or at least all religious truth) is simply a matter of subjective opinion and feeling. This is *subjectivism*, which holds that "what is true for you may not be true for me, and vice-versa."

"Pure" relativism. In responding to "pure" relativism, keep the following thoughts in mind. First, even though it is true that none of us can know the whole truth about anything (particularly about God), this does not imply that we cannot know anything at all, nor does it imply that what we can know is inaccurate. God may not reveal everything to us about himself, but what He has revealed can be truly known!

Second, though it is possible that two parties may possess complementary truths (partial truths that complete each other) about a matter, if they are contradictory (denying and affirming the same thing) they cannot both be true.

Furthermore, it is impossible for a relativist to live out his or her philosophy in the real world. In real life we must decide whether it is true that a car is racing toward us or not and act accordingly. We cannot live with the conclusion that the car both is and is *not* racing toward us!

Skepticism. In responding to skepticism, to say that it is impossible to know the truth about anything at all is self-refuting. The person who makes such a statement is at least claiming to know that the statement—"truth cannot be known"—is true.

Some people acknowledge that truth can be known about "ordinary" things, but it cannot be known about God. Christian apologists (defenders of the faith) Peter Kreeft and Ronald Tacelli respond,

Now if the religious skeptic is right, we can know nothing about God. And if we can know nothing about God, how can we know God so well that we can know that he cannot be known? How can we know that God cannot and did not reveal himself—perhaps even through human reason? (Kreeft and Tacelli, 371).

What Kreeft and Tacelli are saying is that there is a *hidden presumption of knowledge* behind the skeptic's *apparent denial of knowledge*. In other words, be aware of the certainty of knowledge that lies under the ostensible uncertainty. Consider the following:

1. They are saying that they know what God would be like, they know how He would reveal himself, and they know that He hasn't revealed himself in those ways.

But what if, as Kreeft and Tacelli suggest, our human reason is a form of God revealing who He is? What about our moral sensibilities as revealing God's holiness? What if,

through our need for love, God is revealing how He loves us and how much we need Him? What if our creative abilities are a way by which God has revealed that we are made in His image, which is creative?

2. The skeptic questions our ability to know God because of the assumed certainty that there is no compelling reason for us to postulate His existence. As Carl Sagan summarized the conclusion of Stephen Hawking's *A Brief History of Time,* there is "nothing for a Creator to do" (Hawking, x). The skeptic has complete faith in the sufficiency of the scientific theories and methods (i.e., the theory of evolution, etc.), which are based on Naturalism, to explain everything—if not now, then at some time in the future.

Often, though, such naturalistic assumptions contain inherent contradictions. A statement by Francis Crick will serve as an example of such a contradiction. Crick, the biochemist who is the co-discoverer of the structure of the DNA, wrote in his

If the religious skeptic is right, we can know nothing about God.

book *The Astonishing Hypothesis* that our minds are nothing more than matter.

> The Astonishing Hypothesis is that *you*, your joys and your sorrows, your memories and your ambitions, your sense of personal identity and free will, are in fact no more than the behavior of a vast assembly of nerve cells and their associated molecules (quoted in Johnson, 63).

But as Philip Johnson, the UC Berkeley law professor who has taken those who hold to the theory of evolution to task, comments, "The plausibility of materialistic determinism [which is what Crick's hypothesis leads to] requires that an implicit exception be made for the theorist" (Johnson, 64). In other words, for Crick to make the kind of statement that he does—matter alone produces mind—requires that he exempt himself from the truth of that statement. For if Crick's materialistic hypothesis is true, then we have no way of knowing or trusting whether or not the nerves and molecules in Crick's brain—or in our brains, for that matter—are conveying anything that resembles reality. The skeptic "knows" the "truth" of materialistic determinism only because to question it would make room for something other than what their materialistic assumption allows—the supernatural hypothesis, which is apparently, to the skeptic, an even more astonishing hypothesis.

Again, such assumptions of Naturalism and the sufficiency of the scientific method are presumptive certainties that lie beneath the skeptic's ostensible uncertainty.

Challenge the skeptic to be skeptical of the certainty of his or her underlying assumptions, for a skepticism that is skeptical only about the existence of God is a selective skepticism indeed.

Another approach to the skeptic is to point out the overextended claims of the skeptical assertion. Consider, for example, that the assertion of skepticism—that we can know absolutely nothing about God—can be true for only one of two reasons: (1) because He does not exist, or (2) because, if He does exist, He has not made himself known to humanity in any discernible fashion. For a skeptic to make the claim, however, that either reason is true, which the skeptical assertion implicitly does, the skeptic must say that he or she has investigated all knowledge and all history, for God might have revealed himself in ways outside his or her limited experience. Obviously, then, by making such a statement about ultimate truth, the skeptic is going far beyond his or her limited knowledge, for such an assertion claims more than can be known by any one person or even group of people (see *Handbook of Christian Apologetics*, by Kreeft & Tacelli, chap. 15).

Subjectivism. The "subjectivist" says that truth (or at least religious truth) is not something objective, but resides within the individual. We each create our own spiritual values (truths). But what the subjectivist fails to see is that his or her belief that all religious truths are subjective is based on an objective truth claim—that religious truth is subjective. Subjectivism refutes itself.

5. "I don't think reason or evidence apply to religion; I think it's totally a matter of one's subjective experience."

Sometimes people, especially those affected by Eastern thought (for example, Hinduism), will reject any use of reason or objective evidence in spiritual matters and insist that religion is entirely a matter of experience. There are really two issues here.

Persons who claim that reason and evidence are irrelevant to religion must be asked why they believe this is true. If they respond by appealing to any kind of reason or evidence to support their belief, they are refuting it in the process.

In the second instance, if we base our religious beliefs solely on personal experience, we still need an objective framework by which to interpret and evaluate our experience. Any experience can be described, but without an objective framework we cannot interpret or evaluate that experience. For example, when we have a fever, we can describe how we are feeling. But it takes a thermometer and other diagnostic tools to interpret and evaluate our fever.

The same is true with religious experience. The true nature and meaning of an experience is not necessarily self-evident to the one having it. A person might *feel* that he or she has just experienced God, but it could have been a deceiving spirit.

In order to obtain an accurate understanding of the source and significance of the experience, the person must have true knowledge of the contextual framework—the spiritual reality—in which the experience occurred. The person can describe what happened, but that does not qualify him or her to answer questions such as, "Who or what was the source of this experience?" or, "What should I conclude about reality as a result of having this experience?" Such questions can only be answered by one who has knowledge of the objective framework in which the experience occurred.

God would certainly be a source of such knowledge, because He is the ultimate context and He is by definition infinite in knowledge. But how can we gain access to His knowledge by which to interpret our experience? If it can be shown that the Bible is an authentic revelation from God, then this is the "objective framework" of truth, the source of true information by which I can interpret my experience.

The reason we can believe the Bible's claim to be that revelation from God is because of the overwhelming evidence that supports its claim to be the Word of God (see the chapter on "How Can We Know the Bible Is the Word of God?").

The subjectivist might accuse us of our own kind of subjectivism in that we have chosen the Bible as our "objective framework." Such an accusation will not stick, however, because we are subjecting our commitment to the Bible to the tests of reason and evidence.

Bethlehem, birthplace of Jesus. Christianity is based in history.

Sikh holy men in Delhi, India. If faith in Christ is necessary for salvation, what about those who have never heard of Christ?

Opposite: "Ecce Homo," a painting by Richard Westall depicting Jesus in captivity before his crucifixion.

6. "I believe religions should be evaluated on their practical effects rather than on their objective truth-claims."

In a day of widespread pragmatism, this is not an uncommon idea. Consider the following, however.

Simply because an idea yields some practical benefits in the life of the one holding it does not mean it is true. A person could believe falsely that all people are divine and that they should therefore be loved and respected. The love and respect he or she shows to people may be good, but it does not make the idea that they are divine true.

Moreover, evaluating religions on the basis of their practical benefits is not as easy as one might think. For one thing, not everyone can agree on what constitutes a good result in people's lives. What may be a good result in the mind of one might not be so good in the mind of another. For example, is it a virtue to accept all forms of sexual behavior, or are there limits to such behavior? Such opposing beliefs are both based on religious perspectives.

Furthermore, if true goodness involves not only outward actions but also inward attitudes and motives, then goodness is indeed a very difficult thing for people to measure.

7. "If, then, faith in Christ is necessary for salvation, what about those who have never heard of Christ?"

This is one of the most frequently raised objections to Christian faith. We must respond with care, for in the mind of the person making the objection this issue raises questions about the fairness and justice of God. Not all Christians will respond the same way to this question, but that which we present here represents a biblical response.

Some Christians believe that God will accept the sincere efforts of the "unevangelized" in lieu of personal faith in Christ. If an individual responds appropriately to whatever truth he or she does possess (whether through creation, conscience, or another religion), and if he or she has no opportunity to hear about Christ, this is enough for God. However, though it is hypothetically possible that God could respond in this way, there is simply no clear biblical evidence that He does! Also, this position assumes the innocence of the person who has not heard. The Bible, however, teaches that "all have sinned and fall short of the glory of God" (Romans 3:23).

We believe that the more biblical response to the issue of those who have not heard but who respond to the truth they possess about God (through creation, conscience, or the elements of truth in another religion) is that God will see that they receive the Gospel so as to come to faith in Christ. According to Scripture, God's normal way of communicating the Gospel is through another human messenger ("How shall they hear without a preacher?" Romans 10:14).

This viewpoint appears to be supported by a statement of Jesus in Luke 8:18, "To him who has shall more be given." That is, to the person

who welcomes that which God has already revealed to him or her, God will reveal more. To the person who genuinely receives God's "general" revelation, God will reveal His "special" revelation about salvation through Jesus Christ. The experience of Cornelius provides a case in point (Acts 10).

8. "What has happened to my ancestors to whom God evidently did not send the Gospel?"

It may be tempting to offer a word of assurance that one's ancestors are with the Lord, but this is something we simply are not capable of doing. And, we should offer no false hope when there is no basis for it.

On the other hand, we do not know for certain that they are not with the Lord. God has ways of communicating with people beyond the normal means, and it is not impossible that even at the point of death (before actually departing this world) God did exactly that. In any case, we must leave this question with the God who judges with justice and with love!

It is possible that even at the point of death God communicated beyond the normal means with ancestors who did not hear the Gospel.

THE CRITERIA FOR EVALUATING RELIGIOUS TRUTH-CLAIMS

In the previous section we gave attention to a number of approaches to the question of truth-claims that we rejected (relativism, skepticism, etc.). But what criteria should we use in determining the truthfulness of religious truth-claims? Here are what we believe to be the most important criteria.

1. Religious belief must be rationally consistent.

This is the test of "logical consistency." A claim is worthy of our belief if it is free from internal contradictions. Since it is impossible to even discuss religious truth-claims without using reason, such truth-claims must themselves be consistent with the laws of logic, in particular the law of noncontradiction. In other words, a religion cannot both affirm and deny the same thing and in the same respect, and then still hope to make any sense.

To put religions under the scrutiny of reason is not to say, however, that all religious beliefs can be fully explained by reason. The Christian doctrine of the Trinity is an example. Some would say the doctrine of the Trinity contradicts itself by saying God is both three and one. Even though the doctrine of the Trinity—God is one in Essence and three in Person—is beyond our finite understanding, it is not a contradiction, for it does not deny and affirm the same thing in the same respect. Essence and Person are not the same things. Reason might not be capable of explaining how this is so, but it is not irrational to believe that it is so.

2. Religious belief must be consistent with known facts.

This is the "empirical" test. The God of truth would not ask us to believe that which is contradicted by facts that are known through ordinary means. The Bible, for example, is best interpreted in many passages as an

historical document claiming to describe actual historical events. Archaeologists have consistently confirmed the historical accuracy of such biblical narratives. *The Book of Mormon*, on the other hand, claims to give an historical account about the native peoples who populated North America during ancient times. Its accounts, however, do not conform with archaeological findings, thereby throwing doubt on its veracity (Martin, 161–163; Gowan, 48–51).

3. Religious beliefs must be able to explain why reality is the way it is.

This is the test of "comprehensiveness." It is not reasonable to embrace a system of belief that cannot offer an acceptable explanation for why things are the way they are.

For instance, if the ultimate ground of our being is an impersonal force that is without differentiation (the belief held in common by the New Age, Hindu, and evolutionary belief systems), then there is no sufficient foundation for why we should value ourselves as persons above anything else (since personhood would then be a regression from the impersonal ultimate). Such a belief, then, does not sufficiently explain why we do value ourselves as persons above other things.

The Garden of Gethsemane, Jerusalem, Israel.

4. Religious beliefs should enable us to live in the everyday world.

This is the test of "viability." Can we live consistently with such a belief-system, or does it force us into a situation that causes us to live in a way that is inconsistent with some of the belief-system's fundamental precepts?

If, for example, there are no ultimate moral absolutes—as pantheists and relativists hold—how then can they justify making moral judgments about the actions of people and of nations, as they inevitably do? Such moral judgments go beyond the cultural relativism to which they hold.

APPROACHING THOSE WHO OBJECT TO CHRIST'S EXCLUSIVE CLAIMS

Our ultimate aim in this chapter is not merely to refute false intellectual ideas, but to gain a hearing for the truth that can lead one to an eternal relationship with God. Here are a few things to keep in mind.

Be careful to express understanding concerning your friend's hesitancy to accept the exclusive claims of Christ. The claims that Jesus made are indeed awesome in nature. You should not expect, therefore, that such claims will be accepted apart from careful scrutiny. Point out, though, that Jesus Christ welcomes our scrutiny.

Encourage a thorough examination of the claims of Christ. You should challenge your friend to read the New Testament and to document the precise nature of the claims Jesus made. Be prepared to guide your friend in a study of these claims from the Gospels. Note particularly these passages: John 8:58; 10:30; 20:28. Go on to show why it is that you believe these claims are true. Point to some of the prophecies fulfilled by Christ (see chapter on Judaism) and to the astronomical odds against their being fulfilled "by coincidence." Point to His perfect life (confirmed by His closest companions—1 Peter 2:22, and unimpeached even by His enemies—Matthew 26:59–60) and His many miracles (again, acknowledged even by those who opposed Him—John 11:47–48). Focus especially on His resurrection from the dead and on the overwhelming evidence for it. Use Morison's book as a tool (see Bibliography and Resources).

Without bringing undue pressure to bear on your friend to trust in Christ before he or she is truly convinced of His identity, do not hesitate to emphasize the importance of examining the evidence and coming to a decision about Christ. If there is even a possibility that what Jesus said about the importance of believing in Him is true, then there could be no more significant issue in our lifetime!

Be prepared to help your friend deal with lingering doubts about the Gospel of Jesus Christ. Many times a person may acknowledge that there is a good deal of evidence in favor of trusting in Jesus, but lingering doubts and the specter of counting the cost of following Christ hold the person back from faith. Encourage your friend to honestly confront his or her doubts.

Point out as well, however, that there comes a time when the evidence is so weighty in support of faith that lingering doubts must not stand in the way of reaching a verdict. In a court of law a verdict must be reached when *no reasonable doubts* remain. This does not mean that there may be *no conceivable doubt*, but it should not keep us from reaching a decision.

Expose them to Christians from their own religious background, or who have themselves successfully dealt with the issues that may be troubling them. God uses many people in leading someone to the Savior.

BIBLIOGRAPHY AND RESOURCES

Anderson, Sir Norman. *Christianity Among the World's Religions.* Downers Grove, Ill.: InterVarsity Press, 1984.

Clarke, Andrew D. and Bruce W. Winter, eds. *One God, One Lord.* Grand Rapids, Mich.: Baker, 1992.

Corduan, Winfried. *Reasonable Faith.* Nashville: Broadman & Holman Publishers, 1993.

Cowan, Marvin. *Mormon Claims Answered.* Salt Lake City: Marvin Cowan, 1975

Crockett, William and James Sigountos, eds. *Through No Fault of Their Own?: The Fate of Those Who Have Never Heard.* Grand Rapids, Mich.: Baker, 1991.

Harbin, Michael A. *To Serve Other Gods.* Lahman, Md.: University Press of America, 1994.

Hawking, Stephen. *A Brief History of Time.* New York: Bantam Books, 1988

Kreeft, Peter and Ronald K. Tacelli. *Handbook of Christian Apologetics.* Downers Grove, Ill.: InterVarsity Press, 1994.

Lutzer, Erwin W. *Christ Among Other Gods.* Chicago: Moody Press, 1994.

Martin, Walter. *The Kingdom of the Cults.* Minneapolis: Bethany House Publishers, Revised, 1985.

Morison, Frank. *Who Moved the Stone?* Grand Rapids, Mich.: Zondervan, 1958.

Nash, Ronald H. *Is Jesus the Only Savior?* Grand Rapids, Mich.: Zondervan, 1994.

Netland, Harold A. *Dissonant Voices.* Grand Rapids, Mich.: Eerdmans Publishing Co., 1991.

Nichols, Bruce, ed. *The Unique Christ in Our Pluralistic World.* Grand Rapids, Mich.: Baker, 1994.

Richard, Ramesh. *The Population of Heaven.* Chicago: Moody Press, 1994.

How Can We Know the Bible Is the Word of God?

Norman L. Geisler

THE QUESTION POSED

Christians claim the Bible is God's Word. That means they believe the Bible is a verbal revelation from God that makes it unique from every other book. But how can such a claim be verified?

First, we would expect certain things to be true about a book from God. Such characteristics would include the following:

■ It would claim to be God's Word.
■ It would be historically accurate when it speaks on historical matters.
■ The authors would be trustworthy.
■ The book would be thematically unified and without contradictions.
■ We would have received accurate copies of the original manuscripts.

The characteristics listed above might also be true about humanly authored books, but we would expect that, at the very least, they would be true about God's book.

Second, because God is unique, His book would bear characteristics that could be true of it alone. These characteristics would include the following:

■ It would make statements that would reveal knowledge about the way things work beyond the knowledge of its day.
■ It would make predictions about the future that could not be known

through natural means.
■ The message would be unique.
■ The messengers would be confirmed by miracles.
■ The words would have a transforming power.

The above characteristics would distinguish God's book from all other books in such a way that it could not be counterfeited.

Now let's look at the characteristics listed to see if they are indeed true about the Bible.

CHARACTERISTICS THAT MUST BE TRUE OF GOD'S WORD, BUT COULD ALSO BE TRUE OF A HUMANLY ORIGINATED BOOK

1. The Bible Claims to Be God's Word.

A. The Authors Claimed to Speak God's Words. Much of the Bible was written by prophets of God. The prophet was someone who was to say exactly what God told him to say, no more and no less. Jeremiah was commanded:

> This is what the Lord says: Stand in the courtyard of the Lord's house and speak to all the people. . . . Tell them everything I command you; do not omit a word (Jeremiah 26:2).

The prophet was to speak "everything the Lord had said" (Exodus 4:30). Throughout the Scriptures, moreover, the authors, whether they were called a prophet or not, claimed to be under the direction of the Holy Spirit: "Prophecy never had its origin in the will of man, but men spoke from God as they were carried along by the Holy Spirit" (2 Peter 1:21; see also 2 Samuel 23:2; Matthew 22:43).

B. The Bible Claims to Be "Breathed Out" by God. Writing about the entire Old Testament, the apostle Paul declared: "All Scripture is *God-breathed*" (2 Timothy 3:16; emphasis added). Jesus described the Scriptures as the very "word that *comes from the mouth of God*" (Matthew 4:4; emphasis added).

C. The New Testament Was Seen As Being Revealed Scripture As Well. When the New Testament authors used the word "Scripture" they usually had only the Old Testament in mind, since the New Testament was still in the process of being written. Nevertheless, they were also well aware something would happen in their midst, because Jesus had told the apostles that the Holy Spirit would continue the process of inspiring new Scripture (John 14:26; 16:13). Paul, for example, understood his own writings to be "words taught by the Spirit" (1 Corinthians 2:13; see also Galatians 1:11–12; 1 Thessalonians 2:13; 2 Peter 3:15–16), and he taught that God was continuing the process of revelation in others as well (Ephesians 3:4–5).

D. What the Bible Says, God Says, and Vice Versa. Another way the Bible claims to be the Word of God is expressed in the formula, "What God says, the Bible says." This is manifested in the fact that often an Old Testament passage will claim God said it, yet when this same text is cited in the New Testament it asserts that "the Scriptures" said it. The reverse is true as well. What the Bible says, God says. The following chart cites only two of many examples.

E. The Biblical Writers Claim, "Thus Said the Lord." Phrases like "says the LORD" (Isaiah 1:11, 18; Jeremiah 2:3,

Christians claim the Bible is God's Word.

What God Says

"The LORD said to Abram, 'All peoples on earth will be blessed through you'" (Genesis 12:1, 3).

"Then the LORD said to Moses, 'Get up early in the morning, confront Pharaoh and say to him ... I have raised you up for this very purpose, that I might show you my power and that my name might he proclaimed in all the earth'" (Exodus 9:13, 16).

The Bible Says

"The Scripture foresaw that God would justify the Gentiles by faith, and announced the gospel in advance to Abraham: 'All nations will be blessed through you'" (Galatians 3:8).

"For the Scripture says to Pharaoh: 'I raised you up for this very purpose, that I might display my power in you and that my name might be proclaimed in all the earth'" (Romans 9:17).

What the Bible Says

"For this reason a man will leave his father and mother and be united to his wife, and they will become one flesh" (Genesis 2:24) [said by the author of Genesis].

"Why do the nations conspire and the peoples plot in vain?" (Psalm 2:1) [written by David].

God Says

"'Haven't you read,' [Jesus] replied, 'that at the beginning the Creator made them male and female,' and said, 'For this reason a man will leave his father and mother and be united to his wife, and the two will become one flesh'?" (Matthew 19:4–5).

"You spoke by the Holy Spirit through the mouth of your servant, our father David: 'Why do the nations rage and the peoples plot in vain?'" (Acts 4:25).

5; etc.), "God said" (Genesis 1:3, 6; etc.), "the word of the LORD came to me" (Jeremiah 34:1; Ezekiel 30:1; etc.) and other similar phrases occur hundreds of times in the Old Testament. Their significance is that the writer is claiming to be giving the very Word of God.

The Bible is also spoken of as being *"the word of God."* For example, Jesus told the Jews of His day, "Thus you nullify the *word of God* for the sake of your tradition" (Matthew 15:6, emphasis added). Paul speaks of the Jews as having "been entrusted with *the very words of God"* (Romans 3:2, emphasis added; see also Hebrews 4:12).

F. The Bible Claims to Have Divine Authority in All Its Parts. The Bible claims to be divinely authoritative with respect to all that is written within it (2 Timothy 3:16). That includes its very words (Matthew 22:43; 1 Corinthians 2:13; Galatians 3:16), the tenses of the verbs (Matthew 22:32; Jesus draws significance from the present tense of "I am"), and even to the smallest parts of the words (Matthew 5:17–18). Even though the Bible was not verbally dictated by God to the authors, nevertheless, the result is just as perfect as if it had been. For the biblical authors claimed that God is the source of the very words of Scripture, since He supernaturally superintended the process by which they wrote but still used their own vocabulary and style: "But men spoke from God as they were carried along by the Holy Spirit" (2 Peter 1:21).

G. Christ Testified That the Bible Is From God.

Jesus had an extremely high view of Scripture. For example,

■ He said, "Man does not live on bread alone, but on every word that comes from the mouth of God" (Matthew 4:4).
■ He said that the Bible is imperishable (Matthew 5:17–18).
■ He asserted that the Bible cannot be broken, or fail in its purpose (John 10:35).
■ He affirmed the ultimate supremacy of the authority of the Bible over human tradition (Matthew 15:3, 6).
■ He considered the Bible to be without error (Matthew 22:29; John 17:17).
■ He considered the Bible to be historically reliable (Matthew 12:40; 24:37–38).

2. The Bible Is Historically Accurate.

The Bible is not merely a book containing theological teachings that are unrelated to history. Instead, the theological statements of Scripture are integrally linked to historical events. For example, Paul maintained that if Christ's bodily resurrection from the dead was not a historical fact, then our faith is futile (1 Corinthians 15:17). Such a statement indicates that the people, like Paul, whom God inspired to write the Scripture were not a group of gullible and ignorant religious folks who were ready to believe anything that came along. They were those who considered the facts, and it was the facts that led them to belief.

The history given in the Bible has been confirmed by archaeology to a remarkable degree. Noted archaeologist, Nelson Glueck, states,

> It may be stated categorically that *no archaeological discovery has ever controverted a biblical reference.* Scores of archaeological findings have been made which confirm in clear outline or exact detail historical statements in the Bible (Glueck, 31, emphasis added).

Archaeologist Millar Burrows notes that "more than one archaeologist has found his *respect for the Bible increased by the experience of excavation in Palestine"* (Burrows,

The site of the Temple of Artemis (Diana) Ephesus, which Paul saw on his visit.

269

1, emphasis added).

William Ramsay is one such example of an archaeologist who went from believing that the Bible contained fabricated myths to believing that the Bible was not only accurate historically but that it was the Word of God.

Earlier in his life, Ramsay had been influenced by a liberal theology that taught that the writers of the Bible were more interested in promoting a biased theological perspective than in recording history accurately. In the course of his studies, however, Ramsay was surprised to find extensive archaeological evidence for the accuracy of the biblical narratives. One thing that impressed Ramsay about Luke, the writer of Acts, was his accuracy with respect to ostensibly insignificant details. For example, Luke accurately names the rulers of Thessalonica "politarchs," Gallio the "Proconsul of Achaea," the official in Ephesus a "temple warden," the governor of Cyprus a "proconsul" and the chief official in Malta "the first man of the island." Such titles have since been confirmed in numerous Greek and Latin inscriptions.

What Ramsay began to realize was that the Bible was not mythical, but that it was a document that recorded history with extreme accuracy. He wrote, "Luke is an historian of the first rank" (Wilson, 114). And if the Bible was accurate in its historical details, then Ramsay considered there to be a good chance that the biblical authors could be trusted to accurately relate the spiritual significance of the historical events as well.

3. The Trustworthiness of the Biblical Authors.

As we saw in point one—"The Bible Claims to be God's Word"—the biblical authors claimed to be receiving their messages from God. Now, if the biblical writers were known perjurers, there would be no reason to accept their claim. But they were men of integrity, which lends support to the credibility of their claim of having been inspired by God. Their integrity is evident by the following:

First, they taught the highest standard of ethics, including the obligation to always tell the truth: "Therefore each of you must put off falsehood and speak truthfully to his neighbor" (Ephesians 4:25; see also Exodus 20:16; Psalm 15:2; Revelation 22:15).

Second, the writers of the Bible paid a high price for their truthfulness. For example, Peter and the eleven apostles (Acts 5), as well as Paul (Acts 28), were all imprisoned. Most were eventually martyred for their witness for Christ (2 Timothy 4:6–8; 2 Peter 1:14). Indeed, being "faithful, even to the point of death" was an earmark of early Christian conviction (Revelation 2:10).

People sometimes die for what they believe to be true and isn't. But few are willing to die for what they know to be false. Yet the biblical witnesses died for the truth they proclaimed, believing that their message had come from God. While not being proof, such evidence is an indication that the Bible is what the biblical writers claimed it to be—the Word of God.

4. The Testimony of the Amazing Unity of the Bible.

The Bible is amazing in its unity amid its vast diversity. Even though the Bible was composed by many persons of diverse backgrounds and in different time periods, nevertheless it manifests a unity that would indicate there was one Mind behind its writing.

Consider the diversity of the Bible:

■ It was written over a period of some fifteen hundred years or more (from at least 1400 B.C. to nearly A.D. 100).
■ It is composed of 66 different books.
■ It was written by some 40 different authors.
■ It was composed in three languages—Hebrew, Greek, and some Aramaic.
■ It contains discussions on hundreds of different topics.
■ It was written in a variety of

different literary styles, including historical, poetic, didactic, parabolic, allegorical, apocalyptic, and epic.

■ It was composed by authors of many different occupations.

Yet in spite of all this vast diversity, the Bible reveals an amazing unity. First, it is one continuous unfolding drama of redemption from Genesis to Revelation; from paradise lost to paradise regained; from the creation of all things to the consummation of all things (Sauer, *Dawn and Triumph*).

Second, the Bible has one central theme—the Person of Jesus Christ (Luke 24:27). In the Old Testament, Christ is seen by way of anticipation; in the New Testament by way of realization. In the Old Testament He is predicted, and in the New Testament He is present (Matthew 5:17–18). The Old Testament expectation of Christ came to a historical realization in the New Testament.

Third, from beginning to end the Bible has one unified message: humanity's problem is sin (Genesis 6:5; Romans 3:23), and the solution is salvation through Christ (Luke 19:10; Mark 10:45).

Such incredible unity amidst such great diversity is best accounted for by a God who stands outside time and history and who was therefore able to direct the writing of the Bible. The very same Mind that the writers of Scripture claimed to have inspired them also appears to have superintended them, weaving each of their pieces into one overall mosaic of truth.

To highlight the incredible unity of the Bible by way of contrast, suppose that a book containing family medical advice was composed by 40 doctors over 1,500 years, in different languages, on hundreds of different medical topics, etc. What kind of unity would it have, even if all the succeeding authors knew what the preceding ones had written? One chapter would say all disease is caused by demons that need to be exorcised. Another would claim that disease is in the blood, which needs to

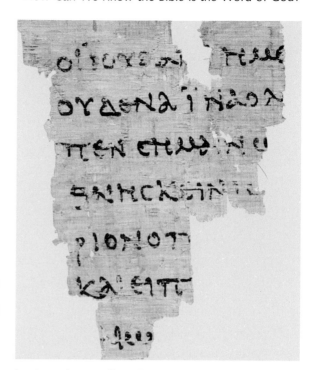

Very early fragment of John's Gospel.

be drained out. Still another would claim disease is psychosomatic—mind over matter. Such a book would lack unity, continuity, and no one would seriously consider it to be a definitive source to answer what is the cause and cure of disease.

Yet the Bible, with even greater diversity in the topics addressed, is the world's perennial best-seller and is sought by multiplied millions as the solution to humanity's spiritual problems. It alone, of all books known to humankind, needs the Deity to account for its amazing unity in the midst of such diversity.

5. The Documents We Possess Are Accurate Copies of the Originals.

In 1948, Bedouin shepherds discovered Old Testament manuscripts in the Qumran caves near the Dead Sea. These manuscripts had been hidden for 2,000 years. They now serve as a control by which to gauge the accuracy of the manuscripts that had been copied during the time the Dead Sea Scrolls were hidden in the caves.

What did the scholars find when

Reliability of the New Testament Documents

AUTHOR/BOOK	TIME GAP BETWEEN THE ORIGINAL AND THE COPY	NUMBER OF COPIES
Herodotus, *History*	ca. 1,350 yrs.	8
Thucydides, *History*	ca. 1,300 yrs.	8
Plato	ca. 1,300 yrs.	7
Demosthenes	ca. 1,400 yrs.	200
Caesar, *Gallic Wars*	ca. 1,000 yrs.	10
Livy, *History of Rome*	ca. 400 yrs. ca. 1,000 yrs.	1 partial 19 copies
Tacitus, *Annals*	ca. 1,000 yrs.	20
Pliny Secundus, *Natural History*	ca. 750 yrs.	7
New Testament	fragment of a book: ± 50 yrs. books of the NT: 100 yrs. most of the NT: 150 yrs. complete NT: 225 yrs.	5,366

(based on Geisler and Nix, 408)

they compared the Qumran manuscripts with the present-day copies? Millar Burrows, who wrote a book on the Dead Sea Scrolls, said, "It is a matter of wonder that through something like a thousand years the text underwent so little alteration" (Geisler, 1986, 366–367).

Old Testament scholar Gleason Archer wrote concerning the two copies of the book of Isaiah found in the caves,

> [They] proved to be word for word identical with our standard Hebrew Bible in more than 95% of the text. The 5% variation consisted chiefly of obvious slips of the pen and variations in spelling (Geisler, 1986, 367).

Thus, we can say with assurance that those who copied the text of the books of the Old Testament did so with great care.

What about the textual accuracy of the New Testament? The degree of accuracy of the New Testament exceeds 99%, which is greater than that of any other book from the ancient world (see Geisler, 1986, chap. 22). The reasons for this amazing accuracy are that, with respect to the Bible, the number of New Testament manuscripts that we have is greater than for other books from the ancient world, and the biblical manuscripts are much closer in time to the originals than those of other works from ancient times. Consider the chart above.

It must be clarified that Christians claim that God inspired, or "breathed out," the text of the *original* manuscripts, not everything in the copies. The copies are without error only insofar as they were copied correctly. It is nevertheless true that the copies were copied with great care and with a very high degree of accuracy. Christians believe that God in His providence preserved the copies from all substantial error.

There are, however, some minor copyist variants in the biblical manuscripts. It is important to note that:

■ such variants are relatively rare in the copied manuscripts;
■ in most cases we know which one is wrong from the context or the parallel passages;
■ in no case do the variants affect any doctrine of Scripture;
■ the variants actually vouch for the accuracy of the copying process, since the scribes who copied them knew there were variants in the manuscripts, still they were duty-bound to copy what the text said;
■ the variants do not affect the message of the Bible.

In fact, one must make a distinction between the text and its message, for one can receive a text with variants and still receive 100% of the message. For example, suppose you receive a message from Western Union as follows:

#ou have won seven million dollars

No doubt you would gladly pick up your money. And if the telegram read this way, then you would have no doubt at all about its message:

Y#u have won seven million dollars.

Yo# have won seven million dollars.

You #ave won seven million dollars.

Why are we more sure of the message when there are more variants? Because each variant is in a different place, and with each new line we get another confirmation of every other letter in the original message.

Three things are important to note:

1. Even with one line—variant and all—100% of the message comes through.

2. The more lines, the more variants. But the more variants, the more sure we are of what the intended message really was.

3. There are hundreds of times more biblical manuscripts than there are lines in the above example. And there is a greater percentage of variants in this telegram than in all the biblical manuscripts combined.

In caves in these cliffs at Qumran, near the Dead Sea, Israel, the Dead Sea Scrolls were discovered.

CHARACTERISTICS THAT COULD BE TRUE ONLY OF GOD'S WORD

1. Scientific Knowledge Before Its Time.

One of the amazing things about the Bible is that it makes scientifically accurate statements about the body, the earth, and the heavens that predate their discoveries by usually 2,000–3,000 years. Moreover, such scientific statements were made in the midst of cultures that were largely superstitious and not at all scientific in their approach.

A. The Body.

In the 1840s, there was a one in six rate of a pregnant woman dying from "childbirth fever" after entering a particular hospital in Vienna, Austria. Ignaz Semmelweis, one of the doctors, noticed that their deaths were not random, but that the patients had been examined by doctors who had just autopsied victims of "childbirth fever." So Dr. Semmelweis implemented a policy that all doctors must wash their hands after doing autopsies. As a result, the mortality rate among pregnant women dropped dramatically to one in eighty-four. But instead of Dr. Semmelweis receiving accolades, the other doctors failed to see the connection and considered the constant washing of hands to be a bother. Dr. Semmelweis was ostracized and eventually left Vienna to practice medicine in Budapest, where the same story repeated itself (Cairney, "Prescience 2," 137–142).

What is significant about Dr. Semmelweis's story is that the cleanliness laws set down by God through Moses predated by 3,500 years the principles of washing to prevent the spread of disease. Moses wrote:

> For the unclean person [someone who has touched a dead person or animal], put some ashes from the burned purification offering into a jar and pour fresh water over them. . . . The person

being cleansed must wash his clothes and bathe with water, and that evening he will be clean (Numbers 19:17, 19).

Such a statement assumes a knowledge about how that which is unseen to the naked eye—germs and bacteria—is responsible for spreading disease. But such knowledge was not discovered until the 1800s! Moreover, washing was not a common practice in the surrounding cultures at the time of Moses (Cairney, "Prescience 2," 129).

B. The Earth.

The following are physical phenomena mentioned in the Bible that not only went against the wisdom of the surrounding cultures at the time but that also predate the earliest scientific discoveries of such phenomena by 2,000–3,000 years:

- The ocean floor contains deep valleys (2 Samuel 22:16; Job 38:16; Psalm 18:15) and towering mountains (Jonah 2:6). The people of ancient times thought the ocean floor was "flat, sandy, and bowl-like" (Barfield, 170).
- The ocean contains underwater springs (see Genesis 7:11; Job 38:16; Proverbs 8:28). The other civilizations believed the ocean was fed only by rain and rivers (Barfield, 171).
- Moses wrote, "For six years you are to sow your fields and harvest the crops, but during the seventh year let the land lie unplowed and unused" (Exodus 23:10–11). Allowing the ground to lie fallow every seventh year was not a custom in the non-biblical cultures. It is a practice, however, that scientists have since discovered was way ahead of its time (Cairney, "Prescience 1," 134).

C. The Heavens.

One of the amazing things about the Bible, when it comes to statements about the heavens, is the errors that the biblical writers *did not* make, even though such errors were common beliefs in the surrounding cultures. The biblical writers

Church of the Nativity, Bethlehem. The Bible predicted that the Messiah would be born in the city of Bethlehem.

■ did not consider the stars to be near us and fixed in their positions. Genesis 1:8, 14–17 speaks of the heavens as an "expanse," which literally means "spreading out." Jeremiah implies that the heavens cannot be measured (31:37; Barfield, 102).

■ did not consider the heavens to have existed from eternity, but taught that they had a beginning (Genesis 1:1), a fact that was discovered by astronomers only during the first part of the twentieth century and with much reluctance (Overbye, 39; Jastrow, 112–113).

The biblical statements about the heavens are common assumptions today, but they were anything but common in the days when the books of the Bible were penned.

2. The Supernatural Predictions of the Biblical Prophets.

Unlike any other book in the world, the Bible is the only one to offer specific predictions hundreds of years in advance that were literally fulfilled. In some cases very different prophecies were made—and then fulfilled—about cities that were relatively close to each other. The following is only one of several possible examples.

A. Memphis and Thebes:
The prophet Ezekiel wrote in the sixth century B.C.:

> This is what the Sovereign Lord says: "I will destroy the idols and put an end to the images in Memphis.... I will ... inflict punishment on Thebes. I will ... cut off the hordes of Thebes" (Ezekiel 30:13–15).

Both Memphis and Thebes were destroyed hundreds of years after Ezekiel's prophecy. What is most significant, though, is that the idols were removed entirely from Memphis, but they were not removed from Thebes, just as Ezekiel had predicted (Bloom, 179–181).

B. The First Coming of Christ.
Many of the Bible's predictions center around the first coming of Christ. Consider the following predictions, made centuries in advance, that said the Messiah would

275

■ be from the seed of Abraham (Genesis 12:1–3; 22:18; cf., Matthew 1:1; Galatians 3:16),

■ be of the tribe of Judah (Genesis 49:10; cf., Luke 3:33; Hebrews 7:14),

■ be of the house of David (2 Samuel 7:12ff; cf., Matthew 1:1),

■ be born of a virgin (Isaiah 7:14; cf., Matthew 1:21f),

■ be born in the city of Bethlehem (Micah 5:2; cf., Matthew 2:1 and Luke 2:4–7),

■ be anointed by the Holy Spirit (Isaiah 11:2; cf., Matthew 3:16–17),

■ perform miracles (Isaiah 35:5–6; cf., Matthew 9:35),

■ be rejected by the Jews (Psalm 118:22; cf., 1 Peter 2:7),

■ die a humiliating death (Psalm 22; Isaiah 53:3; cf., Luke 9:22) at about A.D. 33 (Daniel 9:24ff),

■ be rejected by His own people (Isaiah 53:3; cf., John 1:10–11; 7:5, 48),

■ be silenced before His accusers (Isaiah 53:7; cf., Matthew 27:12–19),

■ be mocked (Psalm 22:7–8; cf., Matthew 27:31),

■ be pierced in His hands and feet (Psalm 22:16; cf., John 20:25),

■ be put to death with thieves (Isaiah 53:12; cf., Luke 23:33),

■ pray for His persecutors (Isaiah 53:12; cf., Luke 23:34),

■ be pierced in His side (Zechariah 12:10; cf., John 19:34),

■ be buried in a rich man's tomb (Isaiah 53:9; cf., Matthew 27:57–60),

■ have people casting lots for His garments (Psalm 22:18; cf., John 19:23–24),

■ rise from the dead (Psalm 16:10; cf., Acts 2:31; Mark 16:6).

Note several unique features about the biblical prophecies, in contrast to all other examples of attempted predictions today. First, unlike many psychic predictions, many of these prophecies were very specific. For example, they gave the very name of the tribe, city, and time of Christ's coming.

Second, unlike the forecasting found in the tabloids at the check-out counter, none of these predictions failed.

Third, since these prophecies were written hundreds of years before Christ was born, no one could have been reading the trends of the times or simply made intelligent guesses.

Fourth, many of these predictions were beyond human ability to force a fulfillment. For example, as a mere human being, Christ had no control over when, where, or how He would be born, how He would die (considering others were responsible for His death), or whether He would rise from the dead.

The best explanation for the fulfillment of such predictions made hundreds of years earlier is the existence of a transcendent God who knows all things, including "the end from the beginning" (Isaiah 46:10).

Skeptics sometimes claim equal authority for predictions from psychics. But there is a quantum leap between the fallible human prognosticators and the unerring prophets of Scripture. Indeed, one of the tests of the false prophets was whether their predictions came to pass (Deuteronomy 18:22). Those whose predictions failed were killed by stoning (v. 20)—a practice that no doubt caused serious pause in any who were not absolutely sure their messages were from God! Amid hundreds of prophecies, biblical prophets are not known to have made a single error.

By comparison, a study made of top psychics revealed that they were wrong 92% of the time (Kole, 69–70)! Jean Dixon, for example, predicted that Jacqueline Kennedy would not remarry, but she married Aristotle Onassis the next day (Kole, 70)!

3. The Uniqueness of the Biblical Message.

Romans 6:23 encapsulates the uniqueness of the biblical message: "For the wages of sin is death, but the gift of God is eternal life in Christ Jesus our Lord."

Garden tomb, Jerusalem. Jesus Christ is the only founder of a religion who has risen bodily from the dead.

A. Spiritual Death.

The Christian Gospel begins with the message that the spiritual condition of humanity is hopeless in that humanity is spiritually dead (Ephesians 2:1). In this, Christianity is unique.

Other religions acknowledge that there is something spiritually wrong with humanity, but they also hold out the hope that we are somehow fixable through some form of human effort. According to the Bible, however, we are not fixable through our own effort. Just as physically dead people can't give life to themselves, so there is no way we who are spiritually dead can give life to ourselves (Ephesians 2:8–9).

Moreover, our being spiritually dead is related to God's being absolutely holy. God will not allow sin in His presence: "With you the wicked cannot dwell" (Psalms 5:4). The problem is that "all have sinned" (Romans 3:23).

B. Eternal Life.

Even though the news about humanity's spiritual condition is terribly bad, God has given us tremendously good news. That good news is that we can have the assurance of eternal life. Such eternal life is not merely some continued existence after death on a spiritual plane, but it is fellowship with God himself (John 17:3). No other religion promises to draw us as close to God as does the Gospel of Christ (Hebrews 4:16). Such fellowship with God, moreover, can begin now.

Plus, no other religion can confirm the hope of eternal life like Christianity, because Jesus Christ is the only founder of a religion who has risen bodily from the dead.

C. A Gift.

The Christian Gospel is also unique because the gift of eternal life is entirely free. A gift is not a gift if it is earned; it can only be received. The means by which to receive God's gift is, first, to acknowledge our need for life, since our sin has caused our spiritual death; and, second, to trust in the finished work of Jesus Christ, who paid the penalty of sin—death— on our behalf (2 Corinthians 5:21).

The offer of the gift of eternal life through Jesus Christ is the core message of the Bible, and it sets the

The Sea of Galilee, where Jesus walked on water. Miracles were a mark of Jesus' ministry.

Bible apart from all other books in all of history.

4. The Miraculous Confirmation of the Biblical Witnesses.

The biblical prophets claimed to receive their message from God. Of course, as even the Bible admits, there are false prophets (Matthew 7:15; 1 John 4:1). One of the sure ways a true prophet can be distinguished from a false one is by miracles (Acts 2:22; Hebrews 2:3–4). A miracle is an act of God, and God would not supernaturally confirm a false prophet to be a true one.

Miracles are a divine confirmation of a prophet's claim to be speaking for God. But of all the world's religious leaders, only the Judeo-Christian prophets and apostles were supernaturally confirmed by genuine miracles of nature that could not possibly have been psychosomatic or trickery. When Moses was called of God, for example, he was given miracles to prove that he spoke for God (Exodus 4:1f). Likewise, Elijah on Mount Carmel was confirmed by fire from heaven to be a true prophet of God (1 Kings 18). Paul wrote that "signs, wonders and miracles" were "the things that mark an apostle" (2 Corinthians 12:12). The apostles

spoke in tongues they had never known (Acts 2:4). Peter healed a man who had been crippled from birth (Acts 3:1–10). Paul raised a man from the dead (Acts 20:10). Luke writes that the "apostles performed many miraculous signs and wonders among the people" (Acts 5:12; see also Hebrews 2:3–4).

Moreover, miracles were an earmark of Jesus' ministry. When asked by John the Baptist if he was the Messiah, Jesus cited his miracles, such as making the blind to see, the lame to walk, the lepers to be healed, the deaf to hear, and the dead raised to life (Luke 7:20–22). Nicodemus acknowledged to Jesus, "Rabbi, we know you are a teacher who has come from God. For no one could perform the miraculous signs you are doing if God were not with him" (John 3:2). Jesus, for example, turned water into wine (John 2), instantaneously cured organic sickness in people (John 5), multiplied the number of loaves of bread for a huge crowd (John 6), walked on water (John 6), immediately cured one who had been born blind (John 9), and raised the dead (John 11). Peter said, "Jesus of Nazareth was a man accredited by God to you by miracles, wonders, and signs" (Acts 2:22).

Significantly, even though Muhammad acknowledged how the prophets before him were confirmed by miraculous signs (*Surahs* 3:184; 17:103; 23:45), he refused to perform similar miracles when challenged by unbelievers (*Surahs* 2:118; 4:153; 6:8, 9, 37).

Only the Bible has been supernaturally confirmed to be the Word of God by special acts of God (see Geisler, 1994, chaps. 8–9).

5. The Testimony of the Transforming Power of the Bible.

The writer of the book of Hebrews declared,

> For the word of God is living and active. Sharper than any double-edged sword, it penetrates even to dividing soul and spirit, joints and marrow; it judges the thoughts and attitudes of the heart (Hebrews 4:12).

There is indeed something "living and active" and "penetrating" about the Bible that is different from any other book. The Bible rings with the chords of truth, and it speaks to the hearts of men and women. It has changed the lives of millions of people.

Of course, the Bible speaking to one's heart is a personal matter—not empirically verifiable by others—but that does not make it any less significant. Our challenge to you is, if you have not read the Bible, try it. A good place to begin is with the book of John, which is in the New Testament portion of the Bible. The book of John was written "that you may believe that Jesus is the Christ . . . and that by believing you may have life in his name" (John 20:31).

CONCLUSION

We have seen that the Bible has met the criteria that support its claim for being the Word of God. With respect to the criteria that could also be said about a humanly authored book, the Bible claims to be the Word of God, it is historically accurate, its authors were trustworthy, it is unified amidst an amazing diversity, and accurate copies of the original manuscripts have been passed down to us.

With respect to the criteria that could be said only of God's Book, the Bible contains scientific statements that predate their discoveries by 2,000–3,000 years, it made accurate predictions that were fulfilled hundreds of years later, its message is unique, its messengers were confirmed by miracles, and the words have a transforming power.

There is no other book like the Bible!

BIBLIOGRAPHY AND RESOURCES

Archer, Gleason L., Jr. *Encyclopedia of Bible Difficulties*. Grand Rapids, Mich.: Zondervan, 1982.

Barfield, Kenny. *Why the Bible Is Number One*. Grand Rapids, Mich.: Baker, 1988.

Bloom, John. "Truth Via Prophecy." *Evidence for Faith*. John W. Montgomery, ed. Dallas: Word, 1991.

Burrows, Millar. *What Mean These Stones?* New Haven, Conn.: American Schools of Oriental Research, 1941.

Cairney, William. "Biomedical Prescience 1: Hebrew Dietary Laws." *Evidence for Faith*. John W. Montgomery, ed. Dallas: Word, 1991.

Cairney, William. "Biomedical Prescience 2: Pride & Prejudice in Science." *Evidence for Faith*. John W. Montgomery, ed. Dallas: Word, 1991.

Earle, Ralph. *How We Got Our Bible*. Kansas City, Mo.: Beacon Hill Press, 1992.

Geisler, Norman L. *Answering Islam: The Crescent in the Light of the Cross*. Grand Rapids, Mich.: Baker Book House, 1994.

Geisler, Norman L. and William E. Nix. *General Introduction to the Bible: Revised and Expanded*. Chicago: Moody Press, 1986.

Geisler, Norman L., ed. *Inerrancy*. Grand Rapids, Mich.: Zondervan, 1980.

Glueck, Nelson. *Rivers in the Desert: A History of the Negev*. New York: Farrar, Strauss & Cudahy, 1959.

Jastrow, Robert. *God and the Astronomers*. New York: W. W. Norton & Co., Inc., 1978.

Kole, Andre. *Miracle and Magic*. Eugene, Ore.: Harvest House, 1984.

McMillen, S. I. *None of These Diseases*. Old Tappan, N.J.: Revell, 1961.

Overbye, Dennis. *Lonely Hearts of the Cosmos*. New York: HarperCollins Publishers, 1991.

Ramsay, W. M. *St. Paul the Traveler and the Roman Citizen,* 3rd ed. Grand Rapids, Mich.: Baker Book House, 1949.

Sauer, Erich. *The Dawn of World Redemption*. G. H. Land, trans. London: Paternoster, 1951.

Sauer, Erich. *The Triumph of the Crucified*. G. H. Land, trans. London: Paternoster, 1951.

Sherwin-White, A. N. *Roman Society and Roman Law in the New Testament*. Oxford: Clarendon, 1963.

Warfield, Benjamin B. *The Inspiration and Authority of the Bible*. Philadelphia: Presbyterian & Reformed, 1948.

Warfield, Benjamin B. *Limited Inspiration*. Philadelphia: Presbyterian & Reformed Publishing Co., 1961; originally published in 1864, Baker reprint, n.d.

Wilson, Clifford. *Rocks, Relics, and Biblical Reliability*. Grand Rapids, Mich.: Zondervan, 1977.

Index

Page numbers in *italics* denote pages with illustrations